Le Cordon Bleu

COMPLETE

Cooking Techniques

The Indispensable Reference Demonstrates
Over 700 Illustrated Techniques
with 2,000 photos and 200 Recipes

Jeni Wright & Eric Treuille

William Morrow and Company, Inc.
New York

A CARROLL & BROWN BOOK
Created and produced by
Carroll & Brown Limited
5 Lonsdale Road
London NW6 6RA

Publishing Director Denis Kennedy
Art Director Chrissie Lloyd

Project Editor Laura Price
Editor Jo-Anne Cox

Designers Vicki James,
Adelle Morris, Karen Sawyer

Production Manager Wendy Rogers
Assistant Kate Disney
Production Consultant Lorraine Baird

Photographer David Murray

Library of Congress Cataloging-in-Publication Data

Wright, Jeni
    Le Cordon Bleu complete cooking techniques : the indispensable reference
demonstrates over 700 illustrated techniques with 2000 photos and 200 recipes.
    p.   cm.
    "Jeni Wright and chef Eric Treuillé ... describe and demonstrate the
techniques" – Introd.
    Includes index.
    ISBN 0-688-15206-6
    1. Cookery, French.   I. Treuille, Eric.   II. Title.
TX719.W75 1997
641.5944–DC21   97–7952
                                                        CIP

Printed in Italy

First U.S. Edition

    4 5 6 7 8 9 10

INTRODUCTION

For over a century, Le Cordon Bleu has been at the heart of French gastronomy: explorer of new trends, yet ambassador for the traditional disciplines of classical French cuisine and pâtisserie. Today with schools on all continents it teaches the widest range of students the skills necessary to recreate dishes of all kinds.

WITH MORE THAN one hundred years' worth of culinary expertise behind it, *Le Cordon Bleu Complete Cooking Techniques* is the repository of more skills and know-how than many people could learn in a lifetime. Created by master chefs, but with the home cook in mind, the book is a unique and indispensable reference work that is destined to become one of the world's great culinary classics. In its clear, close-up, color photographs, readers will be able to see how to select the best ingredients, how to prepare them most effectively, how to cook them successfully in a multitude of ways and, finally, how to present them at the table with mouthwatering finesse.

EVERYTHING YOU WANTED TO KNOW ABOUT INGREDIENTS ... The variety of ingredients that can be found on sale today can be as bewildering as it is exciting yet, as every great chef knows, careful selection of the raw ingredients is the first step towards a successful dish.

In *Le Cordon Bleu Complete Cooking Techniques*, readers can see what characterizes the freshest foodstuffs, how to look beyond the ordinary, and how to choose from among the many culinary products now available with confidence and pleasure. Here, too, they will be able to familiarize themselves with the many new and unusual vegetables, fruits and flavorings that are appearing so regularly on supermarket shelves. Much of this information is essential to the enjoyment of preparing and eating dishes from the various ethnic cuisines so popular today.

PREPARING THE FOUNDATIONS ... Even the most splendid and perceptively chosen ingredients need to be prepared to be cooked in ways that at once preserve their nutrients, enhance their flavors, and show them off at their best – techniques in which the chefs at Le Cordon Bleu excel.

Throughout the fifteen chapters, and in hundreds of individual steps, the skills that will enable cooks to prepare an enormous range of ingredients for cooking are shown in specially taken photographs.

Here readers will discover how to best store and clean shellfish of every description; scale, trim and fillet fish; bone and truss poultry; and create doughs of many kinds, including yeast breads and pasta. Meat preparations of all sorts are detailed, while step-by-step directions will help you to master the skills needed to chop, shred and slice vegetables; peel, stone and skin fruit; melt and temper chocolate; beat cream; concoct soups and sauces and incorporate batters – to highlight just a few.

OUT OF THE FRYING PAN ... Once correctly prepared, ingredients offer themselves to be cooked in myriad ways and served up with stunning results.

For everything that needs doing there are, of course, good methods, and better methods! Throughout *Le Cordon Bleu Complete Cooking Techniques* readers will discover the correct ways of roasting, braising, pan-frying, poaching, steaming, stir-frying, baking, broiling, grilling and barbecuing, and the best ones to choose for each foodstuff.

A WORLD OF FLAVORS ... Take a culinary tour with *Le Cordon Bleu Complete Cooking Techniques* and discover how sushi, saté, Chinese dumplings, tempura, Oriental duck and dashi are made. Learn to assemble a croquembouche, poach a ballotine, fry fish Cajun-style, steam tamales and simmer a tagine. Unveil the mystery of icing éclairs, curling chocolate, creating decorations, swirling coulis and piping sorbet – *Le Cordon Bleu Complete Cooking Techniques* shows them all.

RECIPES, EQUIPMENT AND MUCH, MUCH MORE ... While designed to help readers achieve success with any recipe – no matter what the source – *Le Cordon Bleu Complete Cooking Techniques* also contains more than 200 classic and contemporary recipes. Master chefs from the schools have contributed their favorite recipes, from well-known cooking staples such as French Onion Soup, Coq au Vin, Braised Lamb and Austrian Cheesecake to crowd pleasing standouts such as Szechuan Fish, Snail-Stuffed Ravioli, Stuffed Quail, and Gâteau des Deux Pierre, with exciting garnishing ideas for each main chapter.

Nor is this all. Dotted throughout are informative charts with details on portion control, cooking times, equivalencies and substitutions and a detailed glossary, covering the well-known and the more arcane cooking terms, rounds off the book. The batterie de cuisine listing selects everything necessary for the well-equipped kitchen, though specialist tools are showcased throughout. Herbs, spices and flavorings – both Eastern and Western are set out along the way, and sprinkled among the pages are tricks of the trade, details of the types and variety of foods available and fascinating historical information on dishes and ingredients.

THE NEW KITCHEN BIBLE ... For all these reasons and more, this is the book that all keen cooks will want in their kitchens. Whether readers are just beginning their culinary adventures or perfecting preexisting skills, *Le Cordon Bleu Complete Cooking Techniques* will empower them to create the dishes of their dreams as well as everyday fare. Fashions change and chef-inspired, ingredient-led or occasion-oriented cookbooks may wax and wane, but *Le Cordon Bleu Complete Cooking Techniques* will never go out of style. The clear, concise text, plethora of pictures and visual excitement of the material, will both instruct and inspire all who read it.

LE CORDON BLEU IN HISTORY ... In the sixteenth century, King Henry III of France created *L'ordre du Saint-Esprit* (the Order of the Holy Spirit) whose members became almost as renowned for their sumptuous banquets and feasts as for the broad blue ribbons they wore. Ever since, the name Cordon Bleu (Blue Ribbon) has been synonymous with culinary excellence.

Over 300 years later, the launch of culinary magazine *La Cuisinière Cordon Bleu* in 1895 by Marthe Distel heralded the start of the Paris Academy, with the first demonstration of cooking held the following year. This past century, Le Cordon Bleu has perfected a complete regime of culinary training, as more than thirty full time master chefs pass on their standards of excellence and culinary brilliance.

LE CORDON BLEU TODAY ... Incorporating influences from all over the world, with schools in London, Paris, Tokyo, Sydney and North America, Le Cordon Bleu is at the cutting edge of culinary art. The unique step-by-step teaching method of its master chefs, valued by students the world over, has been captured in *Le Cordon Bleu Complete Cooking Techniques*.

THE MANTLE OF EXCELLENCE ... *Le Cordon Bleu Complete Cooking Techniques* was made possible through the invaluable advice and expertise of Le Cordon Bleu chefs, all enthusiastically supported by their president, André Cointreau. Jeni Wright and Chef Eric Treuillé, both of whom worked previously with Le Cordon Bleu on the *Le Cordon Bleu Classic French Cookbook* ably describe and demonstrate the techniques. Carroll & Brown Limited developed the original concept and their impressive organisation provided invaluable help with the creative work in terms of design, editorial and photography. Le Cordon Bleu is very proud to have collaborated with Amy Carroll and Denise Brown who are among the top cookbook producers in the world.

HOW TO USE THIS BOOK

Le Cordon Bleu Complete Cooking Techniques opens the doors of Le Cordon Bleu to the home cook.

Its extremely accessible format leads you through 15 chapters, each focusing on a different food or food category – from Stocks and Soups to Cakes and Biscuits.

Each begins with essential information about choosing the best ingredients; the following pages demonstrate favored preparation methods and cooking techniques. These pages are bursting with information boxes on everything from equipment to serving ideas and many chapters have a special section on finishing touches, with a step-by-step guide to the more elaborate finishes.

In each chapter you will also find a Chef's Special – every one a signature dish of Le Cordon Bleu's master chefs. These demonstrate what the home cook can achieve in terms of a stunning presentation.

The book opens with a batterie de cuisine – listing all the essential equipment a cook will need, while the final chapter delves into the mysteries of flavors, herbs and spices from the East and the West, finishing with a series of quick-reference equivalency charts, a glossary of cooking terms, and a comprehensive index.

Reader, enquire within... and, whatever your cooking question, it will be answered.

Contents

BATTERIE DE CUISINE

Along with the best ingredients, the right tools for preparing and cooking foods are essential for successful results. Although some cooks are able to make do with a few, multi-purpose utensils, specialist equipment can make many techniques easier to master, and may be required for an authentic presentation of ethnic dishes.

MEASURING EQUIPMENT

The first necessity for culinary success is to ensure that the correct amounts of ingredients are used. When using dry foodstuffs, the measure must be leveled off – unless the recipe calls for heaped teaspoons or tablespoons – and liquids should be viewed from eye level to ensure they reach the required depth.

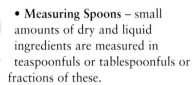

• **Measuring Spoons** – small amounts of dry and liquid ingredients are measured in teaspoonfuls or tablespoonfuls or fractions of these.
• **Measuring Cups** – for measuring the volume of ingredients. The volume of both dry and liquid ingredients can be measured in cups and fractions – ¼, ⅓ and ½ – of a cup. Usually sold in nesting sets.
• **Liquid Measuring Cups** – for measuring a larger volume of ingredients, especially liquids. These cups usually have markings for fluid ounces, cups and pints.
• **Scales** – essential when recipes call for ingredients by weight. There are many varieties from balance scales to digital display types; the best show metric as well as pounds and ounces.

GENERAL

This catch-all category takes account of the basic utensils required for preparing and handling both raw and cooked ingredients. Among their many uses are lifting, draining, shaping, pitting, grating and mashing.

• **Timers** – ranging from simple sand-in-glass vial devices to battery-operated bell ringers, these help keep track of important preparation and cooking stages.
• **Thermometers** – there are three different types: deep-fat, meat and sugar. They are essential to the cooking process as they ensure that the safe and desired internal temperatures of meat and poultry are achieved and that fat and sugar reach their required temperatures.
• **Kitchen Scissors** – choose sturdy all-purpose scissors with a comfortable grip. They should be made of stainless steel for easy cleaning. Poultry shears (see page 93) are designed to cut poultry bones easily.

• **Vegetable Peelers** – several varieties are available: those with swivel blades are especially good; some have a bean slicer in the handle and a pointed tip for coring.
• **Chopping Boards** – use either wood or polypropylene; these do not blunt sharp knives. Keep different boards for different purposes, those for raw meats and strong-smelling items, such as garlic, should be kept separate from general purpose boards. Clean boards thoroughly after use.
• **Tongs** – a "V"-shaped piece of stainless steel that comes together when squeezed. Used for picking up and transferring delicate foods.
• **Ladles** – come with various capacity bowls attached to a long handle. Used for serving liquids, some ladles have a lip on one side to make pouring more accurate.
• **Slotted Spoons** – wide flat spoons with holes pierced through the surface and with slightly pointed tips. Used for lifting and draining foods out of hot liquid or oil; also for skimming.
• **Pitter** – use to remove cherry and olive pits. Made of stainless steel or aluminum, it consists of two arms hinged together in the center. One has a holder for the fruit, the other a prong that pushes out the pit.
• **Canelle Knife** – has a short rounded stainless steel head with a small "V"-shaped blade running horizontally across it. Use to peel fine strips of zest from citrus fruits or vegetables, such as cucumber. When sliced, the fruit or vegetable has an attractive ridged edge.
• **Zester** – the stainless steel rectangular head has five holes along the top edge, designed to remove fine shavings of citrus zest, leaving behind the bitter white pith.
• **Graters** – the most common type is a hollow box with various cutting perforations on each side. Rotary graters with different blades are also available, and specialist single-sided graters for citrus zest and Parmesan cheese. For nutmeg, there is a concave version with a compartment for the whole spice.
• **Mouli or Food Mill** – a stainless steel or plastic food mill that clamps over a bowl and is used for puréeing soft fruits and vegetables. It comes with a selection of fine and coarse discs. A crank is used to turn the chosen disc and push the food through the mill into the bowl.

• **Skimming Spoon** – large flat round head with a series of very fine holes or mesh in the center. Used for removing scum and fat from the surface of hot liquids, such as stock.

• **Pancake Turner** – a large square or rectangular blade that will slide easily under delicate flat foods, such as fish fillets. It has holes to let fat or liquid drain through and is available in metal or plastic; it can have a non-stick coating.

• **Narrow Spatula** – available in various sizes. The blade is thin, flat and flexible with a rounded end. Use for turning and transferring flat items such as fish fillets or cookies and for spreading decorative icings.

• **Offset Spatula** – sometimes called a cookie spatula, the long flexible rectangular blade is angled to help lift food from edged pans and dishes.

• **Bulb Baster** – A giant syringe-like object, used to suck up fat from meat juices and gravy.

• **Tweezers** – Small pincers, usually about 3 in. long, useful for removing fish bones and placing delicate garnishes and decorations in position.

• **Scrubbing Brush** – rectangular brush with hard bristles. Designed for scrubbing seafood shells and vegetables.

• **Wooden Toothpicks** – for holding small pieces of food and for securing cut openings.

• **Apple Corer** – a cylindrical blade that fits neatly around the core of an apple, on the end of a shaft long enough to go through the fruit and remove the core in one piece.

• **Melon Baller** – two bowl-shaped blades, one slightly larger than the other, fixed either side of a central handle. Make the balls by rotating the blade.

• **Ice Cream Scoop** – comprised of a hollow handle through which body heat is conducted and a large bowl-shaped scoop at one end, usually made of stainless steel or aluminum. The conducted body heat warms the bowl and makes scooping and releasing the ice cream easier. Trigger scoops are also available – the ice cream is released from the scoop by activating a lever which pushes it cleanly out.

• **Lemon Squeezers** – most popular type is made of glass or plastic and has a ridged, pointed cone in the center for squeezing the juice from halved citrus fruit. The wooden variety, called a reamer, has a similarly shaped cone attached to a handle; the juice is extracted by holding the cut fruit over a bowl and inserting the squeezer.

• **Potato Masher** – a perforated disc attached to two prongs which are shaped and connected to a handle. Used to pulp down cooked potato and other root vegetables, such as carrots and parsnips.

• **Potato Ricer** – two hinged arms, one has a basket with a fine mesh base that holds the food, the other has a flat disc that pushes the food through the holes. Produces very finely mashed, almost puréed results.

• **Cake Knife** – a flat triangular metal blade, shaped to a rounded point to fit easily under a wedge of cake or pie.

KNIVES

Vital for a large number of tasks, the accomplished cook should have on hand a range of both general-purpose and task-specific knives. These should be kept sharp, and stored in wooden blocks to prevent dulling.

• **Cleaver (Western)** – the weight of the large flat rectangular blade is heavy enough for cutting through bone and meat.

• **Chef's Knife** – also known as a cook's knife, this has a long triangular-shaped blade ranging in length from 6–12 in. The slightly curved edge enables you to rock the knife for easy chopping.

• **Slicing Knife** – has a long flexible blade measuring about 8 in. in length. Ideal for raw fish, fruits and vegetables.

• **Boning Knife** – has a long rigid blade (3½–6 in.) curved to a fine sharp tip to make boning meat and poultry easier.

• **Serrated Knife** – a small 5 in. long knife cuts cleanly through fruits and vegetables. A larger knife is good for slicing bread and cakes neatly and evenly.

• **Small Paring Knife** – shaped like a chef's knife but with a blade only 2–3 in. long, this is one of the most useful knives. Because of its size, it has excellent control for cutting fruits, vegetables, meat and cheese, etc.

• **Mezzaluna** – Italian for "half moon," a curved steel chopping blade (also called a crescent cutter) with a vertical wooden handle at each end. Used with a rocking motion.

• **Carving Knife and Fork** – a knife with a long narrow blade is suitable for slicing hot cooked meats; a fluted one with a rounded tip is for slicing cold meats. A carving fork has two long prongs to secure meat during carving. It should have a good grip and may be fitted with a guard to protect your hand.

• **Sharpening Steel** – a long rod of coarse-textured steel. To sharpen, run the edge of the knife blade along the steel at an angle of approximately 45°.

STOVETOP

For top-of-the stove use, cookware should have long, fireproof handles, be of sufficient weight to rest securely on a burner but not be too heavy to lift, and should distribute heat evenly.

• **Frying Pans and Skillets** – these wide, shallow, flat-bottomed pans come in a variety of sizes. Generally used for cooking thin, flat pieces of food quickly in fat, so pans of heavy gauge, good heat-conducting metals are best. Long, straight handles make them easy to maneuver.

• **Non-stick Frying Pans and Skillets** – special coatings line these pans, precluding the use of fats. Special care must be taken to prevent the lining from becoming scratched.

• **Saucepans** – the workhorses of the kitchen, these are found in many different sizes and shapes.

Some are short and squat, others tall and deep. Generally differentiated by capacity – either liters or quarts or both – they are normally sold complete with lids. Heavy-gauge stainless steel pans are good conductors of heat.

• **Double Boiler** – a two-saucepan set with a large bottom pan and a thin small pan that fits inside or on top. Use as a *bain marie* for cooking delicate foods over boiling water to buffer direct heat.

• **Stockpot** – also useful for cooking pasta, this should be taller than it is wide and of a large capacity.

• **Steamer** – a perforated container that fits into a saucepan and permits vegetables to be cooked without them touching the water. Special stacking steamer pans are also available.

• **Griddle** – A heavy (usually cast iron), flat cooking utensil, sometimes with non-stick coating, with excellent heat-transferring abilities. Use to cook drop scones and pancakes. Ridged cast-iron types are good for cooking fish, meat and vegetables to give a "chargrilled" effect.

• **Crêpe Pan** – traditionally made of cast iron, this shallow-sided pan is ideal for producing perfect crêpes. It should be "proved" or seasoned before use and wiped clean rather than washed.

ASIAN EQUIPMENT

Designed for preparing food for traditional fast cooking over a high heat, these tools are usually sold alongside specialist ingredients in Asian shops.

• **Chinese Cleaver** – has a large flat blade with short wooden handle. Suitable for all sorts of chopping and slicing, it is an excellent all-in-one knife. The wide blade makes a useful scoop.

• **Chopsticks** – use long wooden ones for handling and arranging delicate food and for stirring; use the shorter more elegant variety (avoid slippery finishes) for eating.

• **Wok and Shovel** – a bowl-shaped iron pan that comes with one handle (best for stir-frying) or two handles (for greater stability when deep-frying, braising or steaming). For family use, a 14-in. wok is ideal; some have domed lids, which are useful for steaming and braising. The metal shovel or wok spatula, has a long handle with a flat head. It is curved along the outer edge to fit neatly into the shape of the wok and has a lip around the back to catch the food as it is turned about during stir-frying.

• **Bamboo Mat** – made of flexible woven bamboo, place inside cooking pots or woks to prevent meat from sticking to the base during long, slow cooking, or use to roll sushi. Wash after use and dry thoroughly before storing.

• **Wooden Saté Skewers** – come in a variety of lengths, the long ones are mainly used for skewering meat and vegetables ready for broiling or barbecuing. Soak in water for 30 minutes before using to prevent the wood from charring.

• **Japanese Omelette Pan** – a square-shaped shallow pan made of cast iron or aluminum with a sturdy wooden handle. The pan is used to make thin symmetrical omelettes. To clean, wipe with oil then a damp cloth.

• **Large Oriental Straining Spoon** – has a long bamboo handle with a flat wire head, used for lifting and straining food from hot oil or liquid.

• **Bamboo Steamer** – consists of three parts: two round 2 in-deep baskets with lattice bases which allow the steam to circulate, and a woven lid. Ideal for steaming a selection of foods in a wok or over a large pan of water. Different ingredients can be cooked in layers at the same time.

• **Small Thin Rolling Pin** – usually about 24 in. long, and can be even in width or tapered at the ends. Ideal for rolling out very thin pieces of pastry or bread dough. Wipe with a damp cloth after use – do not soak or the wood may crack or warp.

• **Omelette Pan** – Heavier and larger than a crêpe pan, this special frying pan should have a thick base to distribute heat evenly, and curved, gently sloping sides that permit the cooked omelette to easily slide out onto the serving plate. An angled handle makes maneuvering easier. Omelette pans should be seasoned before use and wiped rather than washed.

• **Fish Kettle** – a long narrow pan, as deep as it is wide, this contains a perforated rack on which to lift the fish in and out of its poaching liquid.

• **Deep Fryer** – a heavy, lidded saucepan and wire basket set, the latter's handle should enable it to be lowered into fat and supported for draining.

• **Pressure Cooker** – deep, heavy, lidded saucepan incorporating pressure gauge and safety valve, this uses internal steam to cook food in about half the normal time.

OVENWARE

Baking dishes, pans and pots made to withstand high temperatures or to conduct heat are available to suit specific tasks. Many are sufficiently decorative to be used at the table.

• **Casseroles** – cast iron, earthenware and china are popular materials for deep, lidded, single or double-handled cooking pots. Some are flameproof – for use on top of the stove as well.

• **Terrines** – generally of earthenware, usually oval and lidded with air vents in the top, these straight-sided containers are designed for cooking ground and chopped meat mixtures.

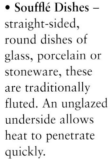

• **Soufflé Dishes** – straight-sided, round dishes of glass, porcelain or stoneware, these are traditionally fluted. An unglazed underside allows heat to penetrate quickly.

• **Ramekins** – individual-sized soufflé dishes that are also useful for baking custards and cold or hot desserts.

• **Gratin Dishes** – wide and shallow with straight or sloping sides and handles. Usually flameproof so they can be used under the broiler and in the oven to produce dishes with crusty tops.

• **Roasting Pans** – rectangular or oval, flat-based metal pans with straight or slightly sloping sides, used for cooking meat and baked dishes. Deep pans usually have integral racks.

• **Racks** – primarily used to allow fat and juices to run free from roasting poultry and meat into the pan below, these footed grills can be cradle-shaped or rectangular.

• **Metal Skewers** – long and thin with a sharp pointed end to cut through chunks of meat and vegetables; for making kebabs, piercing baking potatoes and testing for doneness.

BAKEWARE

The home baker requires a wide variety of specialist items to turn out perfect breads, pies, tarts, cakes and cookies.

• **Cake Pans** – metal, square, round or rectangular pans for making single and multi-layered cakes, which can be deep or shallow. Decorative shapes are also sold. Some pans have loose bases, which enable the cake to be removed easily.

• **Ring Mold** – when baking heavy batters, the central hole ensures that heat reaches the center of the cake. With light and airy mixtures, the ring supports the cake on rising.

• **Springform Cake Pan** – has removable base and a spring-clipped side that make extraction easier.

• **Jelly Roll Pan** – shallow, rectangular metal pan designed specifically for cooking sheet of whisked sponge.

• **Baking Sheets** – thin, metal, rectangular sheets, sometimes with lipped edges. Good quality heavy sheets are essential for even conduction of heat and to prevent buckling.

• **Loaf Pans** – plain, rectangular pans with deep sides for baking breads and pâtés. Long, narrow baguette pans for French bread are usually made of tinned or blued steel.

• **Pie Pans** – shallow, slope-sided round pans may be made of glass or metal, or porcelain for serving at the table.

• **Flan Pans** – round and shallow, often fluted with removable bases. Can be made of tinned steel, black steel or ceramic; used for tarts, flans and quiches.

• **Flan Rings** – plain or scalloped metal hoops used with a baking sheet for tarts, flans and quiches; can also be used for layering cakes.

• **Baking Beans** – ceramic or metal beans help to weight down pastry in its pan when baking blind without a filling.

• **Tartlet Molds** – small, decoratively shaped metal molds often with fluted sides are ideal for petits fours and small pastries. Eclairs, madeleines, cup cakes, muffins and other small buns can be baked in pans that contain multiple molds.

• **Cake Racks** – round or rectangular, these footed open metal grids enable air to circulate beneath food during cooling.

• **Decorative Molds** – can be used for making breads, steamed or baked desserts, jellies, mousses, ice creams and bombes etc.

• **Cookie and Pastry Cutters** – sold individually or in sets, these thin, metal straight-sided cutters come in geometric and naturalistic shapes and in varying sizes.

• **Pastry Wheel** – wooden-handled cutter with fluted wheel, used to trim edges of pies decoratively.

SIEVES, STRAINERS AND SIFTERS

Designed to separate parts of, drain water from or incorporate air into ingredients, there are a number of essential tools.

• **Sieves** – metal, plastic or wooden frames with different-sized mesh. Conical ones, called *chinois*, are ideal for straining liquid ingredients into jugs and jars; bowl and drum sieves fit over bowls and are best for dry ingredients.

• **Colander** – perforated basin for draining water from cooked vegetables and pasta or washing fruits and vegetables. Comes in various sizes, with either single or double handles.

• **Sifters** – ideal for incorporating air into flour or sprinkling sugar in decorative patterns, these can be simple shakers with wide openings or mesh-bottomed cups with integral triggers.

• **Salad Shaker** – plain wire basket or plastic spinner that removes excess water from salad leaves without bruising.

• **Egg Separator** – a round spoon with holes or slots. Allows the egg white to drain through while trapping the yolk.

MACHINES

Though every task in the kitchen can be accomplished by hand, electric tools can help save time and labor.

• **Food Processor** – multi-purpose machine, ideal for chopping, grinding, and puréeing a wide variety of ingredients. Most are sold with slicing and shredding discs and blades for making and kneading dough.

• **Mixer** – hand-held and table models exist for mixing doughs and batters, whipping cream, whisking egg whites and creaming cake mixtures. Heavy-duty tabletop versions have a variety of attachments.

• **Blender** – ideal for making purées, pâtés and dips, soups, sauces and drinks. Also useful for chopping dry ingredients.

• **Ice Cream Maker** – small model churns the mixture in the freezer; large free-standing model, called a *sorbetière*, which produces a smooth professional result, has an integral stirring and cooling mechanism.

• **Grinder** – small-scale machine useful for grinding coffee beans, nuts and spices.

• **Deep-fat Fryer** – free-standing electric models with built in fryer baskets are the safest. They have their own thermostats to regulate temperature of oil.

MIXING, ROLLING AND DECORATING

Preparing foods – whether by stirring, beating or shaping – and decorating the finished item require a number of different, but important tools.

• **Mixing Bowls** – come in a large number of sizes. Stainless steel bowls are durable and good conductors of heat and cold; glass and ceramic bowls are sufficiently heavy to sit firmly on a counter while ingredients are beaten.

• **Wooden Spoons** – ideal for stirring, mixing, beating, and creaming, they are strong and inflexible and poor conductors of heat. Wood absorbs flavors, so always wash, dry and air spoons thoroughly after use.

• **Rubber Spatula** – useful for folding in whisked egg whites, as well as removing all traces of batter from mixing bowls, this flexible scraper is essential for non-stick pans.

• **Pastry Brushes** – for applying glazes to many different foods before or after baking, they may be round or flat and contain natural or plastic bristles.

• **Pestle and Mortar** – the mortar is a small bowl usually made of stone or marble, that has a rough inner surface. The pestle has a round unglazed end shaped to fit the contours of the bowl. Use for grinding spices and seeds and making pesto.

• **Rolling Pin** – plain, smooth, heavy hardwood roller may be handleless or have integral handles. Some rolling pin handles are fixed to a central rod in the roller.

• **Pasta Machine** – purpose made for both rolling and cutting out pasta, it is sold with a variety of cutters to make ribbons and noodles of varying widths.

• **Whisks** – hand-held balloon ones with wire loops and coiled metal handles are preferred by chefs for light and airy whisked egg whites, to blend sauces and to create lump-free batters. They are sold in various sizes to suit different tasks.

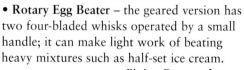

• **Rotary Egg Beater** – the geared version has two four-bladed whisks operated by a small handle; it can make light work of beating heavy mixtures such as half-set ice cream.

• **Piping Bags and Nozzles** – essential for creating piped decorations, differently sized bags accommodate small metal or plastic nozzles (also called tubes) with variously shaped openings.

STOCKS & SOUPS

BASIC STOCKS

SPECIAL STOCKS

CLEAR SOUPS

PUREED SOUPS

SPECIAL SOUPS

SPECIAL STOCKS

Different ingredients and techniques give these stocks unique textures and flavors, completing the culinary repertoire of stocks that are most frequently used. For basic stocks, see pages 16–17.

VEGETABLE STOCK

Light and mild, this stock can be used as a vegetarian substitute for chicken or meat stock (see page 16). Use about 1 lb. mixed vegetables, such as the carrots, onions, leek and celery shown here, a bouquet garni and 2 quarts water to make about 1.5 quarts stock. After cooling, refrigerate up to 3 days, or freeze up to 1 month.

1 Put chopped vegetables, bouquet garni and water in a pan. Bring to the boil and simmer for up to 1 hour.

2 Ladle into a fine sieve held over a bowl. Press the solids with the ladle to extract all of the liquid.

SEAWEED STOCK

Called dashi *in Japanese, this clear seaweed stock has a delicate fishy flavor. It is very quick and easy to prepare, and will keep refrigerated up to 3 days. Kombu (dried seaweed) and* bonito (dried fish) *flakes are generally available from large supermarkets and Japanese stores. For the recipe, see box, left.*

1 Add *kombu* seaweed to *bonito* flakes in pan of water and bring to the boil.

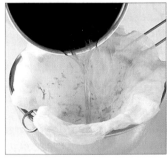

2 Slowly strain the liquid through a muslin-lined sieve set over a bowl.

DASHI

I quart water
I oz. bonito flakes
I oz. kombu seaweed

Pour the water into a pan and add the *bonito* flakes and *kombu* seaweed. Bring the water to the boil, then remove the pan from the heat and let the *bonito* flakes settle. Slowly strain the liquid through a muslin-lined sieve into a clean pan and simmer for 10 minutes. To concentrate the flavor, return the *bonito* flakes and *kombu* seaweed to the stock and repeat as above. Makes about I quart.

GAME STOCK

The carcasses of mature game birds make flavorful stock, especially if they are browned in butter first. To make about 2 quarts stock, use 2 lbs. chopped carcasses, about 2 cups chopped vegetables, such as onions, carrots and celery, and 2 quarts water.

1 Brown carcass pieces in butter to heighten the color and flavor of stock.

2 Add vegetables and water and bring to the boil. Simmer for 1–2 hours, skimming frequently. Strain, then cool and refrigerate for up to 3 days.

CONSOMME

A clear stock-based soup, consommé is prepared from chicken, beef or veal stock (see page 16), which is clarified by the addition of egg whites and vegetables. The vegetables also enhance flavor and color.

MAKING CONSOMME

This easy method of clarifying stock uses a mixture of egg whites, a mirepoix *of vegetables (see page 166) and an acid in the form of lemon juice. Chicken consommé is made here, but the same technique applies to making beef or veal consommé.*

1 Whisk 3–4 egg whites with a fork until frothy. Add 2 tbsp. lemon juice and about 2 cups *mirepoix*.

2 Add the egg mixture to 2 quarts warm stock; bring to the boil. Whisk until a crust forms, 4–6 minutes.

3 Make a hole in the crust for the liquid to simmer through. Simmer gently for about 1 hour – do not stir.

4 Line a sieve with damp muslin and hold it over a large bowl. Break the crust and ladle the consommé through the muslin. Reheat in a clean pan and garnish just before serving with a black truffle *julienne* and leaves of fresh chervil, as shown here. Or sprinkle with a vegetable *brunoise* (see page 166), the traditional garnish.

MAKING ASPIC

Add gelatin to consommé to make aspic that is firm enough to cut decoratively into shapes as a garnish. Liquid aspic is often used to set savory molds, mousses and terrines, and for glazing fish, meat and poultry (see page 225).

Soak gelatin for 2–3 minutes in a little of the measured amount of cold consommé (allow one ¼ oz. envelope or 4 leaves gelatine for every 2 cups liquid). Warm the remaining consommé, then add the gelatin and its soaking liquid. Stir over a gentle heat until the gelatin has melted. Test by chilling 1 tbsp. on a saucer.

CLEAR SOUPS

These are based on a stock or broth combined with other ingredients. They can be light and delicate – finely sliced vegetables, seafood or shredded meats in a flavorsome liquid such as *dashi* – or more substantial – like Scotch broth and minestrone, in which hearty ingredients have been simmered for a long time. The quality of these soups depends on using a good homemade stock (see pages 16–17).

see pages 16–17

VARIATIONS

Clear soups are enlivened by the addition of tasty ingredients. Here are some suggestions:

- A *julienne* of mixed vegetables.
- Thinly sliced mushrooms.
- Chopped scallions,
- Chopped or shredded cooked chicken.
- Small cooked shrimp or sliced scallops.
- Croûtons.
- Shavings of Parmesan or Gruyère.
- Grated citrus zest.

SIMPLE ADDITIONS TO STOCK

By adding just a few ingredients to homemade stock you can have a delicious soup in minutes. Some additions give extra taste, while starchy items like pasta, rice or dumplings give body to the soup. For other ideas, see box, left. Here two quick-and-easy Italian soups are illustrated, both using 1 quart chicken or fish stock. Both will be sufficient for four first-course servings.

PASTA IN BRODO
Bring stock to the boil, then reduce to a simmer. Add ½ lb. uncooked tortellini; cook for about 7 minutes.

STRACCIATELLA
Beat 2 eggs and whisk into simmering stock. Remove from the heat so that the hot stock cooks the eggs.

FRENCH ONION SOUP

3 cups thinly sliced onions (1 lb.)
6 tbsp. butter
1½ quarts brown stock (see page 16), made with beef bones
¾ cup dry white wine
1 bouquet garni
Salt and freshly ground pepper

Sweat the onions in the butter in a heavy-based pan for about 20 minutes or until tender and caramelized. Add the stock, wine, bouquet garni and salt and pepper to taste and bring to the boil, stirring. Lower the heat, cover and simmer for 30 minutes. Remove the bouquet garni and check seasoning. Serves 4–6.

MAKING A FRENCH ONION SOUP

This classic broth-based soup is made by first cooking the onions in butter, then simmering them slowly in beef stock. The essential technique is to caramelize the onions in the first stage. This ensures that the finished soup is deep brown in color and rich in flavor.

1 Sweat the onions over a moderate heat stirring frequently until caramelized, about 20 minutes.

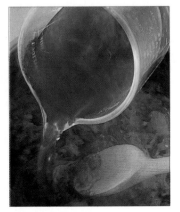

2 Add the stock and wine when the onions are a rich brown. Bring the liquid to the boil, stirring.

3 For a gratin topping, ladle the soup into heatproof bowls and sprinkle with grated Gruyère (see page 44).

MAKING A CHINESE-STYLE SOUP

This type of soup can be made in moments by adding Oriental ingredients and flavorings to simmering fish or chicken stock. Here sliced fresh shiitake mushrooms, dried oyster mushrooms that have been reconstituted and shredded, and strips of chicken breast are used as the main ingredients; for flavorings and other ideas, see box, right.

1 Add oyster mushrooms to shiitake mushrooms in simmering stock in wok. Cook for 1 minute.

2 Add strips of chicken breast and simmer, stirring frequently, for 3–5 minutes or until opaque.

3 Pour a beaten egg into soup off the heat and stir with chopsticks so the egg forms long threads.

A TASTE OF THE EAST

The following ingredients will give an instant Chinese flavor to clear stock. You can add just one or two, or several:

- Light or dark soy sauce.
- Rice wine or dry sherry.
- Peeled and thinly sliced or shredded fresh ginger.
- Cubes of tofu (bean curd).
- Cellophane noodles.
- Canned sliced bamboo shoots or water chestnuts.
- Shredded Chinese cabbage or *bok choi*.
- Bean sprouts.
- Dried shrimp.
- Fresh cilantro leaves.
- Sliced scallions.
- Sesame oil.

JAPANESE SOUPS

Dashi (see page 18) is the classic Japanese stock, used as a base for many Japanese soups. Each soup takes its character from the individual ingredients that are added to the stock. These can be a few delicately prepared items, such as those shown here, or a more substantial mixture of noodles, vegetables, meat and seafood.

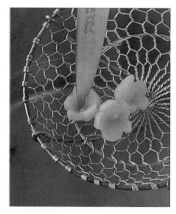

CARROT-FLOWER SOUP
Make honeysuckle blossoms from 2 medium carrots (see page 104). Bring 1 quart *dashi* to the boil, then lower the heat to a simmer. Add the carrots and simmer for 2 minutes. Ladle into warmed bowls and garnish with bean sprouts and cilantro leaves.

SHRIMP SOUP
Peel and devein 6 oz. cooked shrimp, leaving the tail shells intact. Bring 1 quart *dashi* to the boil, then lower the heat to a simmer. Add the shrimp and heat through for about 2 minutes. Serve in warmed bowls, with cilantro leaves.

Creole Bouillabaisse

Here the classic Provençal seafood stew is given a West Indian flavor by the addition of hot chili, peppers and rum. Use a mixture of fish, such as monkfish, cod, haddock, sea bass, bonito and sole – the best and most fresh you can buy.

SERVES 6

*5–6 lbs. mixed fish
(gutted and cleaned weight,
including bone)*

*12 fresh oysters
in shell*

½ cup olive oil

*1 onion,
finely chopped*

*1 celery stick,
finely chopped*

*1 red pepper,
deseeded and diced*

*½ green pepper,
deseeded and diced*

*2–3 garlic cloves,
finely chopped*

¼–½ tsp. dried chili flakes

Pinch of saffron threads

2 tbsp. chopped fresh parsley

1½ tsp. fresh thyme leaves

1 bay leaf

*1½ cup ripe tomatoes,
skinned, deseeded and
chopped*

1 quart fish stock

*Salt and freshly
ground pepper*

*1 lb. raw king or tiger prawns
in shell, peeled and deveined*

1–2 tbsp. dark rum

TO SERVE

Chopped fresh thyme

Rouille (see box)

Croûtes (see page 246)

Remove any scales from the fish and, if necessary, remove the heads and tails. Whether you fillet the fish or leave it on the bone, cut them into large, uniform pieces. The bones will add flavor to the stew. Open the oysters carefully, and reserve both the oysters and the liquor from their shells.

Heat the oil in a large flameproof casserole and add the onion, celery, peppers, garlic and the chili flakes. Crumble the saffron threads between your fingers and add to the vegetables. Cook gently for about 5 minutes, stirring occasionally, until all of the vegetables are softened and lightly browned.

Add the herbs, tomatoes, fish stock and seasonings, stir to mix, and bring to the boil. Lower the heat and simmer for about 30 minutes, stirring from time to time.

Bring the liquid back to the boil, then add the pieces of firm-fleshed fish, putting rich, oily fish in first and white fish on top. Boil rapidly for about 8 minutes, stirring gently once or twice. Add pieces of soft-fleshed fish and continue cooking for 6 minutes, adding the prawns after 2 minutes and the oysters and their liquor for the last minute or two. Remove the casserole from the heat and discard the bay leaf. Stir in the dark rum to taste, and taste and adjust the seasonings.

Serve the bouillabaisse hot, sprinkled with chopped fresh thyme, in a warmed large soup tureen. Hand the rouille separately. This can be added to the soup to taste or spread on to croûtes.

Making Rouille

Rouille is a thick sauce from Provence in the south of France. It is a fiery mayonnaise-like sauce, so named because of its color: rouille means rust.

Put 1 roasted, deseeded red pepper in a food processor with flesh of 1 baked potato, 1 tbsp. tomato purée, 1 egg yolk, 1 garlic clove and ¼ tsp. each salt and cayenne.

Work the ingredients in the machine to a purée, then add ½ cup extra-virgin olive oil while the machine is running and work until smooth and thick. Taste for seasoning.

PUREED SOUPS

Puréeing ingredients that have been cooked in stock, water or milk and then enriching the purée with cream or eggs or both is a simple method of making soup. It can be applied to almost any combination of ingredients, even fruit, and is a useful way of using up leftover vegetables.

FRUIT SOUPS

The puréeing method is ideal for fruit soups. Replace the stock with wine or fruit juices. Pair complementary fruits enhanced with fresh herbs or spices to make refreshing summer soups to serve chilled. Try the following:

- Morello cherry and nectarine.
- Raspberry, strawberry, cinnamon and nectarine.
- Strawberry and rhubarb.
- Melon, mango and basil.
- Apple, pear and cinnamon.
- White peach, apricot and cardamom.
- Papaya, peach and mint.

MAKING PUREED VEGETABLE SOUPS

These are made with one vegetable, such as the carrots here, or with several. Leeks or onions are usually added for flavor. The technique is to cook the vegetables until very soft for easy puréeing. For enriching after puréeing, see opposite page.

1 Sweat diced vegetables in butter over a moderate heat, stirring frequently, for 3–4 minutes until they soften.

2 Add stock or water to cover, and seasonings to taste. Simmer until very soft, about 20 minutes.

3 Purée in a blender, then reheat in a clean pan. Check both the seasonings and the consistency.

ALTERNATIVE METHODS OF PUREEING

Vegetable mixtures can be puréed in a number of ways depending on the ingredients they contain. Stringy vegetables, such as green beans and celery, and those with coarse skins like peppers and lima beans, need to be blended and sieved after cooking but before adding stock.

FOOD PROCESSOR
Can be used as an alternative to a blender, but softened vegetables must be puréed without liquid in order to prevent splashing.

HAND BLENDER
For blending small amounts of soup quickly. For hot soups, blend in the pan; for cold soups, decant into a large bowl.

FOOD MILL
Good for coarse-textured vegetables because the fibers are left behind in the mill. Drain vegetables from cooking liquid before milling.

FINE SIEVE
Essential for vegetables with skins such as the roasted yellow peppers shown here. Rub flesh through sieve, then discard skins from sieve.

MAKING A PUREED FISH SOUP

There are many types of puréed fish soup, the most famous of which is the classic French soupe de poissons *from Marseilles, made with a variety of Mediterranean fish. Another French classic is the* bisque, *a velvety smooth purée of shellfish, traditionally lobster. The techniques for making these soups are similar; here a puréed crab soup is shown.*

1 Soften chopped carrot, onion, potato and celery in butter in a heavy-based pan. Add about 12 small crabs and stir over a moderate heat until deep brown.

2 Flambé a few spoonfuls of brandy and pour over the crab, then sprinkle in 2 tbsp. plain flour and stir for 1–2 minutes until the flour has mixed completely with the liquid.

3 Add 2 quarts fish stock, ¾ cup dry white wine, 2 tbsp. tomato purée, 1 bouquet garni and seasonings to taste. Cover and simmer for 45 minutes.

4 Discard the bouquet garni and work the mixture in a food processor.

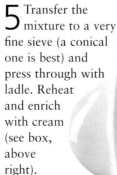

5 Transfer the mixture to a very fine sieve (a conical one is best) and press through with ladle. Reheat and enrich with cream (see box, above right).

FINISHING TOUCHES

Add colorful visual appeal to soups just before serving with a stylish garnish – even the most simple topping helps transform a plain soup into a special dish. Use tweezers or a small spoon to position small and delicate pieces of ingredients with precision.

KEEP IT SIMPLE

Your choice of garnish for a soup does not have to duplicate an ingredient in the soup, but it should complement all the flavors, and often the simplest of ingredients is the best. This is why many chefs favor using fresh herbs.

Clear and cream soups are most suitable for the more elaborate garnishes, while chunky soups are better finished with simple touches, such as finely chopped herbs or freshly grated cheese. Here are some more ideas for simple garnishes:

- A single sprig of herbs.
- A *chiffonade* of spinach or sorrel.
- Fennel fronds.
- Small celery leaves.
- Heart-shaped croûtons dipped in finely chopped fresh parsley.
- A light sprinkling of ground spices tapped off the end of a pastry brush.
- Coarsely crushed peppercorns or coriander seeds.
- Lightly toasted sesame or pumpkin seeds.
- Finely grated hard cheese, such as Parmesan or Romano.
- Blanched, julienned strips of citrus zest.
- Grated citrus zest.
- Flaked white crab meat.
- A single shrimp in the shell.
- A few peeled cooked shrimp.
- Petals from an edible flower, such as pansy, rose or violet, strewn over a chilled fruit soup.

RING OF HERBS
Arrange fresh herbs, such as these tiny dill and sage leaves, decoratively in the center or around edge of soup.

TOMATO AND HERBS
Accent a pale chilled soup with a *concassée* of tomatoes (see page 178) arranged with delicate herb leaves.

CLASSIC CHIVES
Chives are a classic garnish. Arrange them criss-cross fashion, as here, or finely snip over surface of soup.

TOASTED NUTS
Add extra texture and color to cream soups with lightly toasted golden almonds (see page 203) or other nuts.

OLIVE PETALS
Cut pitted black olives into slivers. Arrange as a flower with a small parsley sprig in the center.

DECORATIVE JULIENNE
Echo vegetable flavors in a soup with delicate sticks (see page 166), such as these cut from celeriac and carrot.

RIBBON CURLS
Use a vegetable peeler to pare thin ribbons (see page 167) from long vegetables, such as carrots and zucchini.

VEGETABLE MELANGE
Liven up the looks of clear and pale soups with finely diced carrot, zucchini and celeriac.

CHEESE AND CAVIAR
For a luxurious presentation, shape full-fat soft cheese into quenelles and arrange with caviar or lumpfish roe.

PEPPER PIECES
Use tiny aspic cutters to make unusual shapes from different colored peppers. Blanch the pieces before using.

ASPIC ACCENTS
Float tiny aspic shapes on top of chilled consommé. Cut the shapes from a layer of aspic chilled in a pan.

CARROT FLOWERS
Use a canelle knife to cut long grooves in a carrot, then slice crosswise. Float in clear broths.

MINI MUSHROOMS
Garnish mushroom-flavored soups with thin mushroom slices that have been lightly sautéed in butter or olive oil.

CRISPY CROUTONS
Sprinkle hot soups with deep-fried or toasted croûtons for a traditional garnish that adds texture.

DECORATING WITH CREAM

For a dramatic presentation of a brightly colored cream soup, spoon or swirl cream in the center, or use it to make these pretty patterns. The key to success is to make sure the consistency of the cream is similar to that of the soup – in most cases, the cream should be lightly whipped first. Make the pattern just before serving.

CATHERINE WHEEL
Stir a little pesto into lightly whipped cream. Place 1 tbsp. in the center of each serving. Draw the tip of a knife away from the center to make a swirl.

ROMANTIC RIM
Drip cream onto the soup in a circle. Draw the tip of a knife through each drop to form connecting hearts.

SPECIAL SOUPS

Some soups have such unique cooking methods and diverse ingredients that they create a category all of their own. Gumbo is one such example. Spicy and aromatic, this New Orleans specialty has a thick consistency and sultry flavor. Clam chowder is another regional American soup made thick and chunky with diced potato and onion.

MAKING GUMBO

There are two essential techniques for making a good, full-flavored gumbo. The first is to cook the roux for at least 15 minutes to give the finished soup a nut-brown color and rich depth of flavor. The second is to thicken it to the right consistency with filé powder, a special seasoning made from ground dried sassafras leaves.

1 Stir the roux constantly over a low heat for at least 15 minutes until rich brown. Watch the roux carefully, or it may burn.

2 Add the okra toward the end of cooking so they retain their shape and firm texture; if cooked too long, they will become slimy.

3 Add just enough filé powder to thicken the gumbo slightly. It must be added off the heat or it will become stringy.

MAKING A CHOWDER

Two of the world's most famous chowders are from Manhattan and New England. Both have a base of diced potatoes and onion, but Manhattan chowder is fresh and piquant with tomatoes and herbs, while New England chowder is pale and rich with milk and cream. Clams are the classic addition to both chowders.

MANHATTAN
Sweat diced potatoes and onions in butter until softened. Add stock, chopped tomatoes, thyme and salt and pepper to taste and simmer for 20 minutes. Add canned clams and their juice and heat through.

NEW ENGLAND
Sweat diced potatoes and onions in butter until softened. Add milk and salt and pepper to taste and simmer for 20 minutes. Add canned clams and their juice, heat through, then enrich with heavy cream.

EGGS, CHEESE & CREAMS

CHOOSING & USING EGGS

Eggs are one of our most valued and useful ingredients in the kitchen – many recipes simply wouldn't be possible without their aerating, thickening and emulsifying capabilities.

FREE-RANGE

Around 85% of eggs in the US are produced using the battery method. For eggs to be called free-range, the birds must be provided with access to runs and a variety of vegetation, such as grass and corn. Although they have more freedom, these hens are more affected by weather conditions and predators and, as a result, their eggs are a little more expensive.

SHELL COLORS

The color of an egg shell is determined by the breed of hen and its diet. The color can range from speckled (quail's egg) to blue (duck's egg). Hen's eggs, either white or brown, are most commonly used – they taste the same, the difference in color having no effect on flavor.

HOW TO TEST FOR FRESHNESS

First check the packing date (see Safety First box, opposite page). If there is no date, test the freshness by immersing the egg in water as shown here. As the egg gets older it loses water through the shell, making the air pocket larger – so the older the egg the lighter it will be.

A fresh egg is heavy due to its high water content. It will settle horizontally on the bottom of the glass.

With a less fresh egg the air pockets will expand and make the egg float vertically, tip down, in the water.

An old, stale egg contains too much air and will float to the surface of the water. Do not use the egg.

Clockwise, from bottom left: duck egg (off-white); duck egg (blue); hen's egg (white); pullet's egg (small brown); hen's egg (brown); quail's egg (small and speckled).

SEPARATING YOLK FROM WHITE

It is easiest to separate eggs when they are cold – the yolk is firm, and there is less chance that it will run into the white. Whites will not whisk properly if there is any yolk in them.

HAND METHOD
Crack egg into a bowl, then lift it up and cup it in your hand to let all the white drip through your fingers.

SHELL METHOD
Crack egg shell in half. Pass the yolk backwards and forwards between the halves until the white is in the bowl.

SAFETY FIRST

- Fresh eggs can be refrigerated for up to five weeks after the packing date (a number stamped on the carton from 1 to 365, with 1 representing Jan 1 and 365 representing Dec 31.
- Salmonella bacteria can enter eggs through cracks in the shell, so only buy eggs with clean, undamaged shells.
- Wash your hands before and after handling egg shells.
- The elderly, people who are suffering an illness, pregnant women, babies and children are vulnerable to the risk of salmonella. All should avoid eating raw eggs and foods containing them.
- It is important to cook all egg dishes thoroughly – heat destroys salmonella.

TRICK OF THE TRADE

BLENDING ALBUMEN STRANDS

Egg yolk is anchored in the white by thick albumen strands. The strands should be sieved or blended into the whites so that they help to stabilize the foam.

SIEVING
Work the egg white through a fine sieve held over a bowl with a spoon to break up the albumen strands.

BLENDING
Put the egg whites in a bowl and use chopsticks or a fork to lift the whites and break up the albumen strands.

WHISKING EGG WHITES

To achieve greater volume and stability before whisking egg whites, let them stand at room temperature for about 1 hour in a covered bowl. Whether whisking by hand or machine, make sure all utensils are free of grease and that the bowl is deep enough to hold the volume of whisked whites.

BY HAND

Put whites in a stainless steel or glass bowl. Whisk them from the bottom of the bowl upwards in a circular motion. For greatest volume, use a large balloon whisk.

BY MACHINE

With the whisk attachment of a tabletop electric mixer, start whisking slowly, to break up the whites, then increase the speed as they thicken. A little salt relaxes the albumen and makes whisking easier.

MAKING EGG WASH

A mixture of egg yolk and water is brushed over bread or pastry before baking to give a rich, golden color and a glossy glaze.

Mix 1 egg yolk with 1 tbsp. water and a pinch of salt. Whisk with a fork until combined. Brush the egg wash over bread or pastry with a pastry brush just before baking.

STORING EGGS

- Refrigerate eggs as soon as possible after buying them.
- Store eggs in their carton, away from strong-smelling foods.
- Store eggs pointed-end down to keep the yolks centered.
- Separated whites and yolks or shelled whole eggs should be refrigerated in airtight containers. Whites will keep for 1 week, yolks and whole eggs up to 2 days.
- Use food containing raw eggs within 2 days.
- Hard-boiled eggs in their shells will keep for up to 1 week.

NUTRITIONAL VALUE OF EGGS

Eggs are a valuable source of protein (one large egg contains 12–15% of the recommended daily allowance for an adult), supplying all essential amino acids needed by the body.

They also contain the minerals iron, iodine and calcium and vitamins A, B, D, E and K. Indeed, vitamin C is the only vitamin that is not present in an egg.

Eggs are also low in calories, supplying about 75 calories each. In the past, a limit on the number of eggs consumed per person per week was advised because of the cholesterol content, but more recent research shows that the dietary intake of saturated fat is the main cause of increased blood cholesterol levels. So, despite the fact that an egg contains 213 mg of cholesterol, all of which is within the yolk, the level of saturated fat is very low.

Although egg intake is restricted in some special diets, the current UK dietary guideline for egg consumption for an adult is 2–3 eggs per week.

COOKING EGGS

The art of cooking a perfect egg is simple – once you know how.
The techniques shown here may seem very basic, but they are an
essential part of every good cook's repertoire.

BOILING

Some cooks put eggs in cold water to start, others in hot. The hot-water method shown here is best for accurate timing. Always use fresh eggs at room temperature – the shells of eggs taken straight from the refrigerator are more likely to crack.

1 Put the eggs in a pan of gently bubbling water and add a pinch of salt. Start timing from the moment the water returns to the boil.

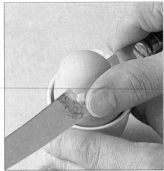

2 For soft-boiled eggs, simmer gently for 3–4 minutes. Remove with a slotted spoon and cut off the tops with a knife.

3 Remove the top part of the shell and any small pieces that have fallen into the egg. The white should be just set, the yolk runny.

HARD-BOILED
Simmer for 6–10 minutes. Plunge immediately into cold water, to prevent graying around the yolk, then peel.

TRICK OF THE TRADE

CAVIAR EGGS
For an elegant breakfast or brunch, serve soft-boiled eggs Russian-style.

Soft-boil the eggs and cut off the tops following the directions above, then spoon in a little caviar, or red lumpfish roe as shown here.

POACHING

Very fresh eggs and a wide, shallow pan are essential for successful poaching. For accurate timing, cook no more than four eggs at a time.

Add 1 tbsp. wine vinegar and a tarragon sprig to boiling water. Do not add salt. Turn off the heat, crack in the eggs and cover. Let stand until the whites are opaque, 3 minutes.

BAKING

It's tricky to get the whites set and the yolks runny at the same time when baking eggs. Here are two methods, the classic French oeufs en cocotte and the more unusual Mexican huevos rancheros. Stand the dishes on paper towels when baking in a bain marie, to prevent overcooking and cracking the china.

OEUFS EN COCOTTE
Put eggs in buttered ramekins and add 2 tbsp. cream and seasonings to each one. Cover and bake in a *bain marie* at 350°F for 6–8 minutes.

HUEVOS RANCHEROS
Put cooked sliced peppers and onions in individual gratin dishes. Top each with an egg. Cover and bake at 350°F for 8–12 minutes. Top with *salsa*.

SCRAMBLING

The secret of making perfect, creamy-textured scrambled eggs is to cook them over a low heat and patiently stir them all the time. Never attempt to rush scrambled eggs or they will be stiff and rubbery. For two servings, allow 4 eggs, 2 tbsp. cream or milk and seasonings to taste.

1 Put the eggs in a bowl with the cream or milk and salt and pepper to taste. Whisk with a fork for 1 minute. The seasoning prevents streaking.

2 Heat enough butter to coat the bottom of a frying pan. When the butter is foaming, pour in the egg mixture.

3 Stir constantly with a wooden spoon over a low heat for 5–8 minutes, then stir for 1–2 minutes off the heat. Serve immediately.

SHALLOW-FRYING

For most people, the perfect fried egg has a runny yolk and a set white. There are two ways of achieving this – by keeping the egg yolk "sunny-side up" during frying and basting it with hot fat, or by turning it "over easy" halfway through. This second method is less popular because the yolk can easily be broken during turning, and it loses its bright yellow color.

SUNNY-SIDE UP
Heat a shallow layer of oil or butter in a frying pan until hot but not smoking. Add the eggs and fry over a moderate heat, basting constantly with the hot fat, for 3–4 minutes. Baste the white only to keep the yolk runny, or the white and the yolk, as you like.

NEATLY SHAPED EGGS
Coat the bottom of a frying pan with oil, then place a metal pastry cutter (stainless steel is preferable) in the pan and heat until hot. Slide the egg into the cutter and fry as for sunny-side up eggs (see left). Remove cutter carefully before removing the egg.

DEEP-FRYING

This French technique is often used for eggs that are to be served on croûtes. Olive oil gives a delicious flavor, but other oils can be used. Butter is not suitable – it will burn.

Heat about 1 in. oil in a deep frying pan until it is very hot but not smoking. Add 1 egg, spoon the hot oil over it and fold the white over the yolk to enclose it. Cook for 1 minute. Remove the egg with a slotted spoon and drain on paper towels. Repeat with more eggs.

ADDITIONS TO SCRAMBLED EGGS

Many ingredients can be whisked into eggs before they are scrambled or while cooking to add texture and flavor.

- In the Basque dish *pipérade*, onions, peppers and mushrooms are fried, then the eggs are stirred in. Alternatives include chopped ham or pesto.
- One famous dish, Hangtown Fry, originated during the 1849 gold rush in California. It combines deep-fried breaded oysters with scrambled eggs.
- The Chinese make a dish called "red, green and yellow" – cubes of tomato and cucumber mixed with scrambled eggs.

DEEP-FRIED EGGS ESCOFFIER STYLE

4 tomatoes, halved
Salt and freshly ground pepper
4 tbsp. fresh white bread crumbs
1 tbsp. chopped fresh parsley
1 shallot, finely chopped
4 eggs

Place tomatoes, cut-side up, in a baking dish and season well. Mix together the bread crumbs, parsley and shallot and spoon over the tomatoes. Bake at 350°F for 10 minutes. Deep-fry the eggs (see left) and serve on warmed plates the tomato halves alongside. Serves 4.

OMELETTES

In classic French cuisine, an omelette is a folded, fluffy creation, simply made by whisking eggs and cooking them quickly in a traditional pan. In other parts of the world, however, an omelette is quite a different thing.

FLAVORINGS FOR OMELETTES

Add flavorings to the egg mixture before cooking or spoon fillings into the center of the omelette and fold over to enclose. The following combinations are delicious.

- Grated cheese and finely diced tomatoes.
- Snipped bacon sautéed in walnut oil until crisp with fresh spinach leaves.
- Sliced or diced peppers and shallots sautéed in butter with sliced mushrooms.
- Smoked salmon shavings and a little fresh dill.
- Chunks of cooked sausage and caramelized onion slices.
- Strips of smoked ham and blanched asparagus tips.

MAKING A FOLDED OMELETTE

This is the classic French omelette which is traditionally cooked in a well-seasoned cast-iron pan, although here a non-stick frying pan serves the same purpose. For best results, allow 1 tbsp. butter and 3 eggs per omelette in an 8 in. pan.

1 Immediately before cooking, lightly beat the eggs and seasonings with a fork. Do not overbeat the mixture or the finished omelette will be stiff.

2 Heat the butter over a high heat until foaming. Pour in the eggs. Mix with a fork for even distribution.

3 Cook quickly, drawing in the edges with a fork to allow the uncooked egg to run underneath.

4 Tilt the pan and fold the omelette over toward one side of the pan, pushing it with the fork to help it roll.

MAKING A JAPANESE OMELETTE

Japanese omelettes offer a symmetrical shape and light texture. They are traditionally made in an 8 in. square pan, and they are rolled as they are fried. If you do not have a pan of this shape, use a round pan and trim the sides of the omelette once cooked. Allow 1 egg and 2 tbsp. water for each omelette; the addition of water thins the batter to create light texture. Serve cut into slices or shreds (see opposite page).

1 Brush the pan with a little oil and heat. Pour in half the egg mixture. Tilt the pan to make an even layer. As surface bubbles appear, loosen the edges with a spatula.

2 Roll omelette toward you with chopsticks. Cook until set, about 1 minute. Make another omelette with remaining mixture.

MAKING OMELETTE SHREDS

In Asian cooking, shreds made from very thin omelettes are used as toppings and garnishes. For a dish to serve four, use 1 egg beaten with a pinch of salt. Cook the omelette in a wok.

1 Heat 1 tbsp. oil. Swirl in egg. Cook over moderate heat for 1–2 minutes.

2 Slide the omelette out of the wok, roll up and let cool. Shred crosswise.

MAKING A SOUFFLE OMELETTE

This type of omelette is made by separating eggs, beating the whites until stiff, then folding them into the yolks. As its name suggests, the finished omelette is therefore lighter and fluffier than a conventional omelette. In classic French cuisine, soufflé omelettes are often sweet, and the yolks are beaten to the ribbon stage with sugar before the whites are folded in.

Whisk 3 egg whites until stiff. Fold into 3 seasoned and whisked yolks. Cook as for a folded omelette (see opposite page), without mixing with a fork in step 2.

MAKING AN EGGAH

A traditional Persian dish, an eggah is a kind of thick, firm omelette baked in the oven and served sliced or cut into wedges, hot or cold. Eggahs can be made plain, with a touch of spice, but adding other ingredients is more traditional. Chopped spinach is used here, but fresh herbs, onion, garlic, peppers or other vegetables may be used.

1 Mix 6 beaten eggs with chosen flavorings. Pour into an oiled baking dish.

2 Bake at 325°F until firm, 15–20 minutes. Cut into wedges to serve.

SPANISH TORTILLAS

This omelette is similar to an Italian *frittata*, except for the cooking technique and some of the flavorings used. Onions and potatoes are fried in a generous amount of olive oil, then beaten eggs are added. Unlike *frittata*, which is finished by browning under the broiler, a *tortilla* is always flipped over in the pan to brown and set both sides.

MAKING A FRITTATA

A thick, flat Italian omelette, a frittata is partially cooked on top of the stove in a heavy-based pan, then broiled until brown and set. For a 12-in. frittata, use 1–2 tbsp. olive oil, 7–10 eggs and flavorings of your choice. The chopped peppers illustrated here are traditional, so too are asparagus, artichokes, sliced green beans, mixed chopped herbs, grated Parmesan, tomatoes, chopped onions and garlic.

Whisk eggs with flavorings and pour into hot olive oil. Cook for 15 minutes over a low heat, then brown under the broiler for 1–2 minutes.

Cheese Soufflés

These light-as-air cheese puffs are rightly called soufflés, despite their unconventional sabayon-type base. They are served floating on a rich cheese cream, called a fondue *after the French word for melt.*

....

SERVES 4

4 eggs, separated

½ cup dry white wine

Salt and freshly ground pepper

4 oz. Parmesan cheese, freshly grated

FOR THE FONDUE

¾ cup heavy cream

4 oz. Gruyère or other easy-melting cheese, grated

TO SERVE

Snipped chives

Freshly grated Parmesan cheese

Put the egg yolks and wine in a large heatproof bowl set over a pan of gently simmering water (*bain marie*) and whisk them together until they reach the ribbon stage. Remove the bowl from the *bain marie* and whisk until the mixture is cool.

In another bowl, whisk the egg whites until stiff. Fold the whites gently but thoroughly into the egg yolk mixture and add salt and pepper to taste.

Bring the cream to the boil in a pan and stir in the Gruyère until melted and smooth. Pour into four shallow ovenproof dishes.

Using two spoons, shape the egg mixture into quenelles (see page 76) and float on the fondue. Sprinkle each quenelle with one-quarter of the grated Parmesan. Bake at 350°F for 10 minutes or until the soufflés are puffed up and golden brown. Serve at once, sprinkled with snipped chives, with grated Parmesan cheese handed separately.

ALTERNATIVE FLAVORINGS

....

- Replace the Gruyère with blue cheese.
- Add a little rouille (see page 22) to the fondue.
- Add freshly chopped herbs to the fondue.

Making a Soufflé

Soufflés have a light, fluffy texture due to the incorporation of air. Here, a standard whisk is used over a bain marie; for even greater volume, use a large balloon whisk or a hand-held electric mixer. The bowl for the egg whites must be spotlessly clean or they will not whisk.

Whisk the egg yolks with the wine until the mixture is pale and thick enough to leave a ribbon trail when lifted.

Whisk the egg whites at a steady pace to a white foam that will hold a stiff peak.

Fold together using a scooping and cutting action to ensure you lose as little of the whisked-in air as possible.

BATTERS

Many cooks lack confidence when it comes to making crêpes, pancakes and Yorkshire puddings, and yet there is no mystique about them. Follow the techniques shown here for smooth batters and successful results every time.

CREPE BATTER

1 cup all-purpose flour
½ tsp. salt
2 eggs, beaten
1⅓ cup milk or milk and water

Sift the flour and salt into a bowl, make a well in the center and add the eggs. Gradually beat in the flour from the sides and slowly pour in the liquid to make a smooth batter. Sieve if necessary (see opposite page). Cover and let rest for 30 minutes or overnight. Beat thoroughly before using. Makes about 12 crêpes.

CREPE AND BLINI PANS

Crêpe and blini pans are made of cast iron, which conducts heat well and cooks food evenly. The only difference is the size – crêpe pans are usually 8½ in. in diameter, blini pans 5 in. Once the pan is "proved" or seasoned, it is practically non-stick. To prove, heat the pan and rub with salt. Wipe clean and repeat with oil. Do not wash the pan after use, just wipe it clean.

MAKING CREPES

French chefs use a special well-seasoned pan (see box, left) to make wafer-thin crêpes, but you can use a non-stick frying pan. Don't worry if the first few crêpes tear or stick. There are many elements to get right: the temperature of the pan, the temperature and amount of butter, and the consistency and amount of batter.

1 Put a knob of butter in the pan and heat over a moderate heat until foaming. Pour off the excess melted butter into a bowl, then pour in a small ladleful of batter, starting in the center of the pan.

2 Tilt the pan to swirl the batter over the base and reach the edges, adding more batter if necessary.

3 Cook for about 1 minute until golden underneath and bubbles appear. Loosen and turn with a spatula.

4 Cook the second side for 30 seconds–1 minute, then turn the crêpe out, first side facing down.

CIGARETTES

PANNEQUETS

FANS

MAKING YORKSHIRE PUDDINGS

For well-risen, crisp and light puddings, use very hot fat, otherwise the puddings will not rise.

Put about ¹/₂ tsp. vegetable shortening or oil in each cup of a Yorkshire pudding pan and heat at 425°F until very hot, almost smoking. Pour in the batter and bake for 20–25 minutes.

MAKING GRIDDLE PANCAKES

Traditional American pancakes are about 4 in. in diameter. Also popular are the fun-sized "silver dollars" shown here, so-called because of their shape. They are about 2 in. in diameter. Make them on a griddle, or in a heavy-based frying pan. Test the temperature of the pan by sprinkling over a little water; it should sizzle and evaporate. Grease lightly before spooning on the batter.

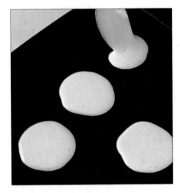

1 Make the batter (see box right). Place tablespoons of batter on the hot griddle, spacing them well apart.

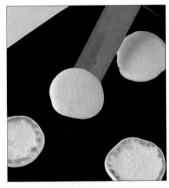

2 Cook until the edges are brown and the tops bubbling. Turn with a spatula; cook until golden.

TRICK OF THE TRADE

MAKING A SMOOTH BATTER

If making batter by hand, blend the flour and eggs with a balloon whisk for best results, and add the liquid gradually. If lumps occur, pour the batter through a sieve. For a foolproof method, work all the ingredients together in an electric blender; there should be no need to sieve.

After making batter by hand, pass it through a fine-meshed sieve to ensure smoothness.

For an ultra-smooth batter, work the ingredients in an electric blender for 1 minute until smooth.

VARIATIONS ON A THEME

You can make different batters by adapting the basic crêpe batter recipe (see box, opposite page). It is important that any batter you make is left to rest for at least 30 minutes before cooking, to allow time for the starch grains to absorb the liquid.

YORKSHIRE PUDDING BATTER
Substitute bread flour for the all-purpose flour in the original recipe – the extra gluten creates a more elastic batter, giving a better and more stable rise. Use a mixture of equal parts milk and water rather than all milk. The addition of the water will help to lighten the batter.

GRIDDLE PANCAKE BATTER
A thick batter is used for griddle pancakes because they need to hold their own shape as they cook unsupported on the griddle. Use 1⅔ cup all-purpose flour (significantly more than the amount given in the crêpe batter recipe) to each 1⅓ cup liquid and add 1–2 tbsp. melted butter and 1–2 tsp. baking powder. The butter will enrich the batter; the baking powder will aerate it.

SHAPES FOR CREPES

For rolled or folded crêpes as shown on the opposite page, spread filling in center, then proceed as follows:

• For cigarettes, fold in two opposite sides, then roll up from one of the other sides.
• For pannequets, fold in two opposite sides, then fold in the other sides and turn over.
• For fans, fold in half, then fold in half again.

CHOOSING CHEESE

It pays to use a reliable supplier; a shop that has a wide stock and a fast turnover is more likely to sell cheese of the required degree of ripeness. The vast differences in taste and texture discernible in individual cheeses are a result of the type of milk used, the manufacturing process and the length of aging. As a general rule, the longer a cheese has been aged, the stronger the flavor, the drier the texture and the longer it will keep.

SOFT CHEESE RIND should be evenly colored and slightly moist with a "bloomy" look. Avoid cheese with rind that has an orange tinge

HARD CHEESE RIND should not be too dry or cracked, nor look moist or "sweaty." When matured in cheesecloth, it should cling to the paste

HARD CHEESE should have a clean, firm or crumbly texture with no discoloration

SOFT CHEESES

Containing a high percentage of fat and moisture, these have been briefly ripened, have a creamy texture and are easy to spread. When fully ripe, some soft cheeses, such as Brie and Camembert, ooze gently. These have a characteristic "bloomy" rind, while others, such as Pont l'Evêque and Livarot have a "washed" rind and sharper, richer taste. Soft cheeses should be springy to the touch, and smell nutty, sweet and aromatic. Avoid any with a chalky white center or a strong smell of ammonia. **SEMI-HARD CHEESES** such as Reblochon and Port Salut are matured longer and because they contain less moisture, are slightly firmer, and hold their shape when cut.

HARD CHEESES

Often high in fat, though low in moisture, these long matured cheeses have flavors ranging from mild to sharp and textures from "flexible" to crumbly. Some cheeses in this category such as Emmenthal, have characteristic holes, caused by the gas-producing bacteria introduced within the ripening cheese. **HARD-GRATING CHEESES**, such as Italian Parmesan and Pecorino, are the driest of the hard cheeses. Aged until they have a dry, granular texture, they will keep for months in the refrigerator if wrapped tightly. Taste the cheese before buying if you can and reject any that taste over-salty or bitter. The rind should be hard and yellow and the paste yellowish white.

FRESH CHEESES

These are unripened, rindless cheeses which range in consistency from the creamy and smooth – fromage frais, cream cheese and mascarpone to thicker curd mixtures – ricotta, pot cheese and cottage cheese. The fat content varies, with many low-fat, skimmed-milk versions available. It is very important to use fresh cheese within the "use-by" date on the packaging.

BLUE CHEESES

These have had a bacteria culture introduced which creates their characteristic blue-green veining. Immature blue cheeses have little veining near the rind. Look for a firm, crusty rind with no signs of discoloration underneath. Blue cheeses may smell strong but should not smell of ammonia. Sample before purchase if possible, and avoid cheeses that taste over-salty or chalky.

HARD BLUE CHEESE should have even veining throughout and a creamy-yellow paste

FRESH CHEESE should be moist and white, with no sign of mold

SOME SOFT CHEESE has a "washed" orange rind. This should be evenly colored with no visible cracks.

GOAT CHEESE RIND varies with age. The more mature cheese has surface mold

GOAT AND SHEEP CHEESES

Curds made from goat's milk are lightly packed into small molds to produce cheese in a variety of shapes and sizes. They can be sold at any stage of the maturing process, the age determining the character of the cheese. Initially soft and mild, they mature to become firm with a tangy, strong flavor.

Buy goat cheese from a shop with a rapid turnover to ensure freshness. When fresh, goat cheeses should be moist with a slightly sharp, but not sour, flavor.

Of a medium fat content most ewe's milk cheeses are milder in taste than those of cow's milk. Famous exceptions include Roquefort, Pecorino and ewe's milk feta.

TESTING A SOFT CHEESE FOR RIPENESS

When a soft cheese develops its characteristic texture, flavor and aroma it is deemed ripe. Eat soft cheeses at their peak, because they deteriorate very quickly, especially after cutting.

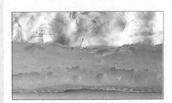

A Brie that is just ripe should feel spongy in the center and be creamy throughout.

Overripe Brie has thin, patchy rind, a bitter flavor, smells of ammonia and "oozes" excessively.

FRESH CHEESE

Characterized by a mild, clean, taste and soft texture, fresh cheese is simple to make. Here the technique of making a fresh cheese is demonstrated, plus ways to enhance fresh cheeses with coatings, marinades and flavorings.

FRESH CHEESES

The following varieties offer varying degrees of texture and richness. Most fresh cheeses are soft enough to eat with a spoon, however some are dried and as moisture evaporates, they thicken. Fat content varies, as they can be made from whole or skimmed milk, or even cream.

- Fresh chèvre cheese is made from 100 percent goat's milk.
- Cottage cheese is made from whole or skimmed milk curds.
- Mascarpone is a high-fat, soft Italian cream cheese with a rich, smooth texture.
- Ricotta is an Italian unripened whey cheese with a mild, almost bland flavor.
- Fromage frais is a soft, slightly acidic curd cheese often enriched with cream.

COATINGS FOR FRESH CHEESE

When fresh cheese is 2-3 days old it is usually firm enough to form into loose rounds. Coating the rounds with herbs, spices or nuts will add interest to the mild flavor of the cheese. The following coatings are suitable.

- Cracked mixed peppercorns.
- Paprika or cayenne pepper.
- Toasted sesame seeds.
- Snipped chives.
- Lightly crushed dried chilies.
- Coarsely chopped walnuts or hazelnuts.

MAKING FRESH CHEESE

Pasteurized milk is warmed to a temperature of 80°F, then buttermilk is added to provide the bacteria necessary for curds to form. Once the whey is drained off, use the cheese within a day; if salt is added, it will keep in the refrigerator for 2–3 days.

1 Combine 1 cup each buttermilk and warm milk; let stand at room temperature for 24 hours until curd forms.

2 Line a bowl with a double thickness of sterilized muslin. Carefully spoon in the curd and cover.

3 After about 5 hours, gather up the muslin and tie with string. Squeeze the whey out firmly with your hands, then hang above the bowl to drain.

4 Let drain for 1–4 hours until firm. Cut the string, turn the cheese onto a plate and peel off the muslin.

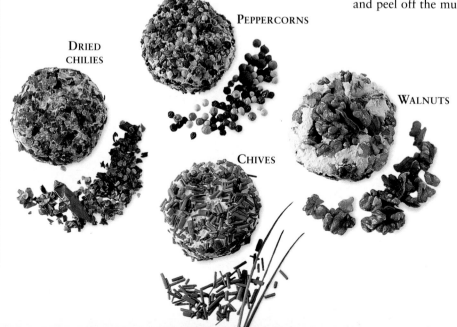

PEPPERCORNS

DRIED CHILIES

WALNUTS

CHIVES

FLAVORING FRESH CHEESES

Firm fresh cheeses gain flavor from a marinade (see box, right). They can be marinated for just a few hours, or refrigerated in sterilized glass jars for 2–3 weeks. Small round goat cheeses (crottins de Chavignol) are used here; cubes of Greek feta cheese are also suitable.

1 Place discs of cheese in a sterilized glass jar. Add flavorings of your choice (see box, right).

2 Pour olive oil over the cheeses until they are completely covered. Seal the jar tightly.

3 Store in the refrigerator for up to 2–3 weeks, turning the jar occasionally to redistribute the flavorings.

PIPING FRESH CHEESE

Fresh cheeses are extremely versatile because they are soft enough to be piped. Here homemade fresh cheese (see opposite page) is mixed with herbs and piped into an array of vegetables – hollowed-out cherry tomato halves, blanched and scooped-out pattypan squash, blanched and opened-out snow peas.

1 Mix cheese with chopped fresh herbs and seasonings to taste until evenly blended.

2 Put cheese in a piping bag fitted with a star tube and pipe into prepared vegetables.

MARINADES FOR FRESH CHEESES

Fruity extra-virgin olive oil makes the best base for a marinade; it also acts as a preservative. Add one or more of the following:

• Fresh herb sprigs, especially rosemary, thyme, oregano or marjoram.
• Whole peppercorns.
• Dried chilies or halved fresh chilies.
• Bay leaves.
• Fennel seeds.
• Pared lemon or lime zest.
• Whole cinnamon sticks.
• Bruised garlic cloves.
• Sun-dried tomatoes.

FLAVORINGS FOR FRESH CHEESE

When flavoring cheese, you can choose contrasting tastes and textures. Try the following:

• Chopped toasted pine nuts and chopped basil.
• Finely chopped scallions and fresh ginger.
• Chopped fresh cilantro and Thai curry paste.
• Ready-made tapenade and chopped fresh parsley.

USING CHEESE

Cooking with cheese requires care. Consistency, fat content and flavor all influence how it will behave in a recipe. Here are hints for picking the right variety – and method – for what you are making.

ROTARY GRATER

Equipped with a selection of drums, this time-saving tool (also called a Mouli grater) grates hard cheese easily into shreds of various sizes.

GOOD MELTING CHEESES

Several cheeses are prized for their ability to achieve a specific consistency when heated. Soft cheeses such as mozzarella, for instance, melt easily when simply sliced. A hard cheese like Gruyère is best grated.

- Mozzarella is the traditional topping for pizza. It melts evenly to produce gooey "strings" of cheese.
- Fontina is a well-tempered, nutty-flavored cheese that withstands high temperatures. It can even be coated in bread crumbs and deep-fried.
- Gruyère, France's favorite cheese for gratins, is best grated for even melting. Use well-aged Gruyère for fondue.
- Goat cheese holds its shape well when warm, and colors to an appetizing golden brown. It is good on croûtes.
- Cheddar melts and browns well. It is excellent for broiling.

GRATING

Different graters can be used according to the type of cheese you are grating and the size of shreds required. Use cheese straight from the refrigerator for best results.

FINE SHREDS
A rotary grater (see box, left) makes light work of fine grating. Simply put the cheese in the hopper and turn the handle.

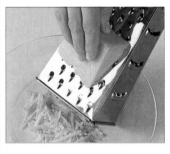

COARSE SHREDS
An upright grater creates thick shreds that hold up in a salad, or melt evenly.

PARMESAN
Use a special small Parmesan grater to grate this very hard cheese into tiny shreds.

MAKING A GRATIN TOPPING

Dishes that are to be finished by browning under the broiler or in the oven are often topped with grated cheese. The cheese melts quickly (see box, left) and forms a crisp, golden crust, making a delicious gratin topping.

Grated Gruyère is sprinkled on French onion soup (see page 20) and broiled 2 minutes before serving.

MELTING

Always melt grated cheese slowly over a low heat in a heavy-based pan. This will help prevent the melted cheese becoming stringy or grainy, or separating the oil. Not all cheeses melt well: each has a different fat and moisture level, which react differently to heat. For recommended melting cheeses, see box, left.

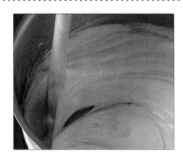

CORRECT
Cheese that is melted gently over a low heat is smooth and glossy.

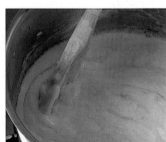

INCORRECT
Cheese that is melted too quickly over a high heat will separate into oily lumps.

MAKING SWISS CHEESE FONDUE

The word fondue *is French for melted, in this case for cheese melted in alcohol. Success depends on using a heavy-based pan and keeping the heat beneath it constantly low – the same technique that is essential for melting any cheese (see opposite page). Warm the wine before adding the cheese and stir until melted. Adding a little cornstarch will help to stabilize the mixture.*

1 To help prevent the mixture from sticking to the pan, stir constantly with a wooden spoon over a low heat.

2 Use long-handled forks for dipping bread into the fondue. Turn forks after dipping to stop fondue drips.

CHEESE FONDUE

1 tbsp. cornstarch
2 cups dry white wine
1 garlic clove, halved
½ lb. Emmental cheese, grated
½ lb. Gruyère cheese, grated
½ lb. Comté cheese, grated
Pinch of grated nutmeg
Salt and freshly ground pepper

Blend the cornstarch with 2 tbsp. of the wine. Rub the inside of a fondue dish with the cut side of the garlic and pour in the remaining wine. Bring to the boil, then lower the heat. Gradually add the cheeses, stirring constantly to ensure they have melted after each addition. Add the cornstarch mixture and stir until thick and creamy. Stir in the nutmeg and seasonings to taste. Serves 6–8.

BROILING

Broiled cheese on toast is a time-honored favorite. Here it's given a modern twist by using slices of fresh goat cheese cut from a log and basted with a spicy dressing of olive oil and peppercorns. If you like, you can use marinated cheese (see page 43), Italian mozzarella or Greek halloumi, varying the dressing by adding chopped herbs or ground spices to taste.

1 Put cheese on rack in broiler pan. Brush with dressing. Broil 1½ in. away from heat for 1–2 minutes.

2 Put the cheese on warm croûtes (see page 246) and serve on a bed of salad leaves, with more dressing.

DEEP-FRYING

This technique is perfect for individual portions of Camembert. The wedges are coated in beaten egg and breadcrumbs that become crisp during frying and protect the cheese from melting and oozing out into the oil. Use cheese that is ripe but firm, and chill it before frying so that it will retain its shape on the outside yet be perfectly runny in the middle.

1 Dip Camembert wedges in beaten egg, then in dried breadcrumbs. Chill for 1 hour in the refrigerator.

2 Deep-fry at 375°F for 2–3 minutes until crisp and golden. Drain on paper towels.

45

CREAMS

Milk products, such as cream, yogurt, buttermilk, crème fraîche, clotted cream and sour cream, have a myriad of uses in sweet and savory dishes. Though commercially available, the latter three are easily made at home.

CREME FRAICHE

This partially soured, tangy cream has the added bonus of not separating during cooking. It is made by mixing buttermilk, sour cream or yogurt with heavy cream, heating it, then letting it stand. Stir, cover and refrigerate crème fraîche after it has thickened. Use it as the French do – as a flavoring for soups, sauces and savory dishes. It is also delicious with fruits and sweet dishes.

1 Mix 2 cups buttermilk and 1 cup heavy cream. Put bowl over a pan of hot water and heat to 85°F.

2 Pour warm mixture into a glass bowl; partially cover. Let stand at room temperature for 6–8 hours.

CLOTTED CREAM

A specialty of England's West Country, this deep-yellow thick cream is made by gently heating the cream to scald it and make a crust. It will keep for up to 5 days in the refrigerator.

1 Pour 2½ cups heavy cream into a heavy-based pan. Heat gently until cream thickens, 25–30 minutes.

2 Chill the cream until it has set and a crust has formed on the surface.

3 Remove the crust of clotted cream with a large metal spoon. Reserve the cream and discard the liquid left underneath.

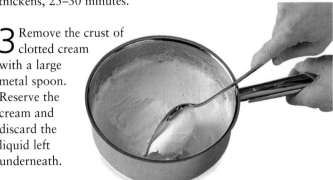

MAKING SOUR CREAM

This technique for making sour cream, a favorite with Mexican and Eastern European food, can also be applied to milk for making Devonshire scones.

Stir 1 tbsp. fresh lemon juice into 1 cup heavy cream in a glass bowl. Let the mixture stand at room temperature for 10–30 minutes or until it has thickened. Cover the bowl and refrigerate until ready to use.

FISH & SHELLFISH

CHOOSING FRESH SEAFOOD

Seafood falls into four categories: seawater, freshwater, preserved fish (smoked, salted and dried) and shellfish. All but preserved fish should be eaten as fresh as possible. It is only really possible to judge the freshness of a whole fish; fillets, steaks and pieces are more difficult to assess. Freshwater fish should smell fresh and clean, while marine fish should smell of the sea.

EYES should be full, moist, bright and bulging. Avoid fish with dull, dry, shriveled or sunken eyes

GILLS should be clean, red and bright, with no signs of graying or traces of slime

BODY should be firm, smooth and quite stiff, not limp, floppy or lumpy

BUYING FILLETS AND STEAKS

It is better to buy fillets or steaks that are cut from the whole fish while you wait, rather than pre-cut, or to buy the fish and cut or fillet it yourself (see pages 55 and 57). Very large fish, such as monkfish, shark, tuna and large cod, are almost always sold ready prepared. When judging the freshness of fillets and steaks, the smell and texture of the fish can be used as a guide. The fish should smell fresh (smelling of the sea in marine fish) and look moist, firm and springy, not dry.

HANDLING SEAFOOD

Fish and shellfish deteriorate much more quickly than meat, so they must be cooked on the day of purchase or as soon as possible afterwards.

Oily fish such as mackerel, herring and salmon, spoil more quickly than white fish because their natural oils turn rancid. If seafood has to be stored overnight, wrap it in damp cloths and keep it in the coldest part of the refrigerator. Whole fish will keep longer if gutted first.

BUYING SHELLFISH

LOBSTERS AND CRABS If you are buying live, choose an active specimen that feels heavy for its size. If buying cooked, check that the shell is undamaged and the claws intact. The smell should be fresh and not strong.

MUSSELS AND CLAMS Avoid those that are excessively covered in mud or barnacles, or that appear to be cracked or damaged. Discard any that remain open when tapped.

SCALLOPS These are most often sold opened, cleaned and trimmed rather in their closed shells. Check that they smell sweet; if so, they are fresh. The flesh of fresh scallops is slightly gray and translucent, not perfectly white.

OYSTERS The shells must be undamaged and tightly closed. When tapped they should sound solid. Traditionally, they were picked when there was an "r" in the month to avoid infection during warm weather. They are now generally sold all year round because of modern techniques of oyster farming and improved methods of transport.

SHRIMP These are sold in several ways: cooked in or out of their shells, or raw in their shells. Cooked shrimp should be bright pink and firm, not watery. Raw shrimp should also be firm, with shiny gray shells. Avoid any shrimp with black spots – a sure sign of aging.

SKIN should be shiny and damp to the touch, not dry or dull. Any natural markings and coloring should be undimmed. For example, red mullet and snapper should be a bright pinky red; trout, herring and mackerel should be iridescent; salmon a shimmering silver; and parrot fish a brilliant blue

UNUSUAL FISH

There are many exotic fish on sale at large supermarkets and city fish markets, many of them beautifully marked with spectacular, iridescent colors.

- Kingfish, also called *capitaine rouge*, *capitaine blanc* and *lascar*, has a strong flavor and is quite bony. Bake whole.
- Sea Robin is tasty and firm fleshed, good in fish stews and soups.

- Sea Bream or Porgy has sweet, firm flesh and is inexpensive. Gilt-head bream – *daurade* in French – is especially good. Bake whole with or without stuffing.
- Shark steaks are meaty and firm with very little bone. Good for chargrilling and in stews.
- Tilapia has firm white flesh and good flavor. It can be steamed, baked, broiled or barbecued, whole or in fillets.

USING FISH & SHELLFISH

Fish and shellfish are delicate foods to cook – they have fragile flesh that requires careful handling. Choose the freshest you can, and make sure they are thoroughly cleaned before use. Cook fish just long enough to set the protein and turn the flesh opaque; if overcooked, fish will become tough and dry. When substituting one fish for another, make sure it is of a similar structure, texture and flavor.

ROUND FISH

This variable family runs the gamut in size and shape. Their flesh is typically firm and "meaty" tasting, meaning they pair well with other assertive ingredients.

FISH	COOKING METHODS
BASS/ MULLET	Poach, steam, bake, barbecue
BREAM/PORGY	Bake, braise
CATFISH	Stew, braise, broil
COD/HADDOCK	Panfry, deep-fry, broil, poach, bake
EEL	Bake, stew, broil
HAKE	Bake wrapped, steam, panfry
MACKEREL	Panfry, broil, barbecue
MONKFISH	Panfry, bake, broil, barbecue
SALMON/TROUT	Panfry, poach, steam, bake, broil, barbecue
SARDINES	Grill, barbecue, panfry, bake
SNAPPER/ MAHI MAHI	Poach, panfry, broil, barbecue, bake
SWORDFISH/TUNA/ SHARK	Broil, barbecue, panfry, bake, stew, braise

FLAT FISH

To showcase the subtle flavor of these fine-textured varieties, choose for preference a swift cooking process that uses as few other ingredients as possible. Braising works particularly well because this moist-heat method tends to concentrate the natural, and often very delicate, flavor of the fish.

FISH	COOKING METHODS
BRILL	Bake wrapped and unwrapped, steam, poach, broil, panfry
GROUPER	Bake wrapped and unwrapped, steam, poach, broil, panfry
HALIBUT	Poach, panfry, braise
JOHN DORY	Poach, broil, pan-fry
FLOUNDER	Panfry, deep-fry, poach, steam, broil, bake
RAY/SKATE	Panfry, bake
SOLE	Broil, panfry, deep-fry, steam, bake
TURBOT	Bake wrapped and unwrapped, steam, poach, broil, pan-fry

SHELLFISH

Some mollusks require special attention. A live shellfish yields the best flavor, so store mussels or clams in salted water (4 tbsp. salt to 1 quart water) not fresh water, which will kill them. Bearding mussels more than a few hours before cooking can spoil them.

SHELLFISH	WHAT TO LOOK FOR	COOKING METHODS
CLAMS	*Shells should be tightly closed, not chipped or broken* *Shucked clams should be plump and smell fresh throughout*	Steam – in shell Broil, bake – half shell Stew, panfry – shucked
CRAB	*Active and heavy* *Shell undamaged and claws intact*	Boil, steam
LOBSTER	*Heavy for size* *Tail curled under* *Claws intact and undamaged*	Boil, steam – in shell Broil – split
MUSSELS	*Shells tightly shut and undamaged* *Not light and loose when shaken*	Boil, steam – in shell Broil, bake – half shell Panfry, stew – shucked
OYSTERS	*Shells tightly closed and undamaged* *Shucked oysters should be plump and uniform in size with clear liquid*	Serve raw Bake, broil – half shell Pan-fry, stew – shucked
SHRIMP	*Firm meat that feels full in the shell* *Moist appearance and fresh smell* *Avoid any that smell of chlorine or have black spots on the shell*	Panfry, deep-fry, stir-fry, broil, barbecue, bake, poach, steam
SCALLOPS	*Free of liquid with a sweet fresh odor whether on half shell or shucked* *Check the body section is plump and creamy white* *Coral pink and moist* *Avoid any with a sulphurous smell*	Bake, broil – half shell Poach, panfry – shucked
SQUID/ OCTOPUS	*Clear eyes, fresh smell* *White moist flesh*	Deep-fry, panfry, poach, bake, stew
WHELKS/ PERIWINKLES	*Should smell sweet* *Move into shell when prodded* *Lid should be moist and firmly in place*	Boil – in shell Stew – shelled

FISH ON THE MENU

From coast to coast, great cooks pair their region's catch with local ingredients and cooking techniques to create internationally appealing dishes.

FRANCE – *Bouillabaisse* (a lusty fish stew of Mediterranean fish and shellfish with saffron and fennel) originated in Marseille.
GREECE – *Kalamari* (squid deep-fried in a light batter and served with lemon wedges and chilled retsina) is a favorite midday snack on the Aegean.
ITALY – *Spaghetti alle vongole* (with clam sauce) is a staple in trattorias throughout Italy.
MEXICO – *Ceviche* (raw fish "cooked" not by heat, but by the acidity of lime juice) is refreshing with a tart tang.
SPAIN – *Paella* (shellfish and squid with saffron rice, tomatoes and garlic) is a favorite festive dish.
UNITED STATES – *New England Clam Chowder* (a soup made with potatoes, clams and cream) dates back to the early 1700s. *Manhattan Clam Chowder* (a spicy tomato- and clam-based soup) came to fame later in the 1930s.

PREPARING WHOLE ROUND FISH

Round fish are so named for their body shape – a round belly as opposed to a flat one, with an eye on either side of the head. Popular varieties include trout and salmon. Round fish yield two fillets, one from each side of the backbone. Though most often gutted before being sold, round fish can be cleaned at home if you like. Once gutted, round fish can be boned and stuffed or filleted.

VANDYKING

An English technique of preparing a fish to be served whole is to cut its tail into a "V." This is known as vandyking in honor of the painter's V-shaped beard.

Sir Anthony Van Dyck (1599-1641)

TRIMMING AND SCALING

Most fish, such as the salmon pictured here, have scales that need to be removed before cooking. Removing scales is a simple but messy task, so work as near to the sink as possible. Trimming any fins beforehand will make scaling more straightforward and, because some fins are spiny, will be gentler on your hands and make the fish easier to handle. Trim the fins with a pair of kitchen scissors but use a large chef's knife to remove the scales. Fish scalers are also available from specialist kitchen shops.

1 Cut off the three fins that run along the stomach of the fish from the head to the tail – the pectoral, ventral and anal fins – with kitchen scissors.

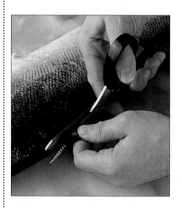

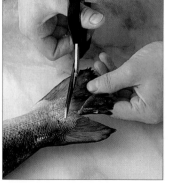

2 Turn the fish over and cut off the dorsal fins that run along the back of the fish with the kitchen scissors. It is important to cut off the fins as they harbor bacteria.

3 For fish that are to be served whole, you can make the tail look more attractive by cutting it into a neat "V" shape (see box, left) with kitchen scissors.

4 Hold the tail of the fish firmly. Scrape the scales off the fish with the back of a large chef's knife, working from the tail to the head. Rinse the fish thoroughly.

GUTTING THROUGH THE GILLS

Round fish that are to be served with their heads on should have their internal organs (innards) removed through their gills. This method retains their shape, ensuring a neat presentation. The fish can then be stuffed or left unstuffed. If the latter, bone the fish along its backbone (see page 55).

1 Locate and lift up the gill flap behind the head of the fish and cut out the gills with kitchen scissors. Discard the gills.

SCORING

Today's chefs dress up plain broiled, barbecued or steamed fish by making cuts in the flesh and inserting sprigs of herbs. Slices of garlic can also be inserted or, for an Asian dish, lemongrass, scallions and fresh ginger can be used. The flavors of the herbs penetrate the fish flesh during cooking.

2 Hold the fish belly up. Make a small cut at the bottom of the stomach and insert the points of the scissors or your fingers through it. Cut through the innards to loosen them from the fish.

3 Insert your fingers inside the gill opening. Grasp hold of the innards and pull them out. Check the hole cut at the bottom of the stomach, making sure no organs remain. Discard the innards.

4 Hold the fish under cold running water and let the water run through the inside of the fish from the gill opening to the tail. Rinse until the water runs clear. Pat dry with paper towels.

Make 2–3 slashes in one side of the fish, cutting through to the bones. Turn the fish over and repeat on the other side. Tuck the seasonings into the slashes. The fish is now ready for cooking.

GUTTING THROUGH THE STOMACH

The easiest and most common way to remove the innards from a fish is through its stomach. Use this method for fish that are to be served whole, stuffed or unstuffed, and where a pristine shape is not required, particularly if the fish is to be boned before or after cooking.

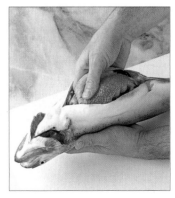

1 Cut out the gills behind the head and discard. Make a small cut at the bottom of the stomach, then cut along the underside, stopping just below the gills.

2 With your hand, grasp hold of the innards and pull them out. Discard the innards; they are not suitable for the stockpot.

3 Run along each side of the backbone with a tablespoon. This removes any blood vessels which detract from the fish's appearance and can make it taste bitter when cooked. Rinse the fish under cold running water, then pat dry with paper towels. The fish is now ready for cooking.

53

BONING SMALL ROUND FISH

Small, oily fish, such as the sardine shown here, have such soft bones that they can be boned with your fingers rather than a knife.

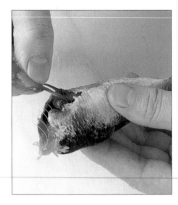

1 With your fingertips, break off the head of the fish behind the gills. Discard the head and gills. Insert your index finger into the head end of the fish and run it down the belly so that it slits open. Working from head to tail, pull out the innards and discard them.

2 Open the fish out and, working from head to tail again, pull out the backbone. Release the backbone at the tail end by snapping it off with your fingers. Rinse the fish thoroughly and pat dry with paper towels. The fish is now ready for cooking.

BONING THROUGH THE STOMACH

Once the innards have been removed through the opening in the stomach of the fish (see page 53), you should also remove the backbone through the stomach. Gutting and boning a fish through its stomach, as with the salmon shown here, creates a natural cavity for stuffings.

1 Hold the fish on its back and use a filleting knife to cut upwards between the rib bones and the flesh on one side of the backbone so that the rib bones are loosened.

2 Slide the blade of the knife down the rib bones close to the backbone so that all the ribs on this side are detached from the flesh. Repeat from step 1 to free the ribs from the other side of the flesh.

3 Cut the backbone from the fish with a pair of kitchen scissors, and discard along with the ribs.

4 Remove the fine pin bones from both sides of the fish's spine with a pair of tweezers. Run your fingers from the head to the tail, again on both sides, feeling for pin bones you may have overlooked. Wipe the fish dry with paper towels. The fish is now ready for cooking.

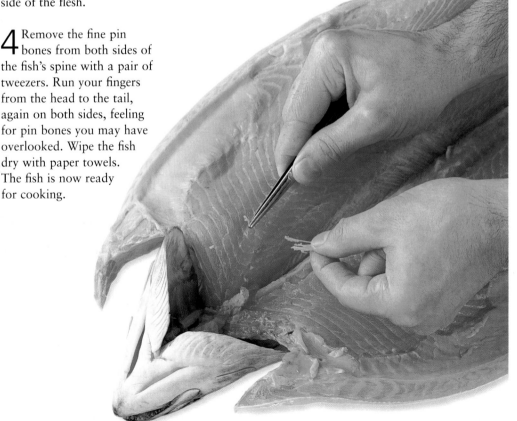

BONING ALONG THE BACKBONE

To preserve the shape of a whole round fish, leaving the stomach cavity intact for stuffing, bone it along the back. The fish, such as the trout shown here, should be gutted through the gills.

1 Working from the tail to the head, cut along each side of the backbone with a pair of kitchen scissors.

2 Carefully detach the backbone at both the head and tail ends of the fish, using a chef's knife. Lift out the backbone and discard. Wipe the fish thoroughly dry with paper towels. The fish is now ready for cooking.

FILLETING ROUND FISH

Once a fish has been scaled, trimmed and gutted through the stomach (see page 53), it can be filleted or cut into large boneless slices. Two fillets – one from each side – can be cut from round fish, such as the salmon shown here. Use a sharp, flexible filleting knife and work carefully to leave as little flesh on the bones as possible. Check the fillets for pin bones (see page 54).

1 Make a cut around the back of the head then, working from head to tail, using the rib bones as a guide, cut along one side of the backbone. Holding the knife flat use long, even strokes to cut the flesh away. Run the knife over the rib bones, holding the free flesh with the other hand.

2 Turn the fish over and repeat step 1 to remove the remaining fillet. The head and carcass will be left. Use the bones along with the head, but not the gills, to make fish stock (see page 17), if you like. The fillets may be skinned as for flat fish (see page 57) before cooking, depending on what the finished dish calls for.

BONING MONKFISH

If you buy monkfish on the bone you will need to know how to remove the bone if a recipe calls for fillets.

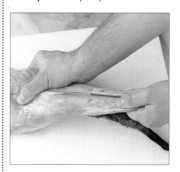

1 Lay the monkfish down, grasp hold of the skin and pull it back toward the tail of the fish.

2 Cut along both sides of the backbone with a chef's knife, separating the flesh of the fish into two fillets. The backbone can then be used to make fish stock (see page 17).

3 Carefully remove the dark membrane from the underside of each fillet. Wipe the fillets thoroughly with paper towels. They are now ready for cooking.

PREPARING WHOLE FLAT FISH

Flat fish are so named because they are flat-shaped. Popular varieties include flounder, sole, turbot and brill. Flat fish swim on their sides and have both eyes on their top side, or back, which is dark for camouflage. The underneath of flat fish is white. In order to preserve their shape, flat fish are always gutted, from behind the head and gills. Because gutting is done at sea, they are invariably sold ready-gutted.

SCALING

You will need to remove the scales from the skin of the fish if you are planning to serve the fish whole or if you have bought a fish that is not already scaled at the fish market.

This is a messy job, best done near the sink. Lay the fish dark-side up and hold the tail firmly. Working from tail to head with the back of a chef's knife, scrape the scales off the fish. Hold the fish by the tail under the cold tap and rinse it thoroughly, washing away the scales by rubbing the skin vigorously with your hands.

SKINNING

If you are serving a flat fish whole, only the dark skin needs to be removed – the white skin is left on to help hold the fish together during cooking. If you plan to serve the fish as fillets, you can remove both dark and white skins while the fish is whole, as with this Dover sole, or you can skin individual fillets.

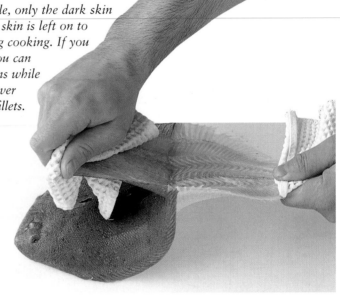

1 Working on the dark side first, scrape the skin away from the tail with a knife to loosen it from the flesh.

2 Grasp the skin and tail using a kitchen towel to prevent your hands from slipping. Pull the skin away from the tail and over the head, detaching it completely from the fish.

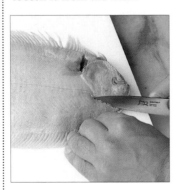

3 Turn the fish white-side up. Cut around the head of the fish to loosen the skin.

4 Working from head to tail on both sides, use your fingers to loosen the skin and pull it back from around the edge of the fish. Once the skin is quite loosened, grasp it at the tail end and pull it away from the flesh, detaching completely.

FILLETING

Depending on its size, a flat fish yields two or four fillets. Whether you are going to skin the fillets or not, you should always trim and scale the fish before filleting. Here a large brill is separated into four fillets.

1 Lay the fish dark-side up on a chopping board. Cut around the outside of the fish with a filleting knife where the flesh meets the fins, carefully tracing the shape of the fillets.

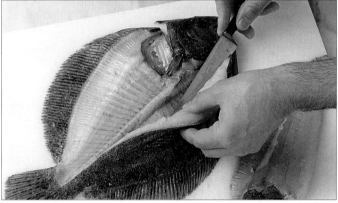

2 Cut down the center of the fish from head to tail with a sharp knife, cutting right down to the bone.

3 Working from the center of the fish to the edge, cut away one fillet with long, broad strokes of the knife. Take care to leave as little flesh still on the bones as possible. Turn the fish around and remove the second fillet in the same way.

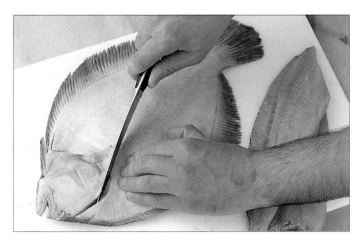

4 Turn the fish over. Make a cut around the back of the head and around the outside edge of the flesh. Cut down to the bone along the center of the fish, working from head to tail. Follow step 3 to remove the two remaining fillets.

SKINNING A FISH FILLET

Even when bought packaged from the supermarket, fish fillets most often come with their skins on – which helps them to maintain their shape. The technique of skinning a fish fillet is important; if the skin and the flesh are not separated properly, the flesh may come away with the skin or be ragged and torn.

Lay the fillet skin-side down and make a cut across the flesh at the tail end. Dip your fingertips in salt to help you get a good grip, grasp the tail end and insert the knife in the cut. Working away from you and using a sawing action, hold the knife at a shallow angle. Move the knife between the flesh and skin until you reach the other end of the fillet.

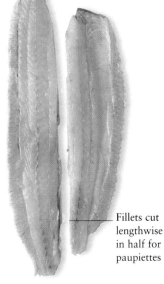

Fillet from one half of a Dover sole

Fillets cut lengthwise in half for paupiettes

Szechuan Fish

A Chinese classic, your choice of a whole, firm-fleshed fish such as red snapper, sea bass or grey mullet, is deep-fried in a wok, then braised in an aromatic sauce flavored with garlic, ginger and chili.

SERVES 4

*1 whole fish,
weighing about 2 lbs.*

Salt

2 cups peanut oil

1 tsp. cornstarch

2–4 garlic cloves, shredded

*1 in. piece of fresh ginger,
peeled and cut into very fine
shreds*

*2 tbsp. Shaoxing rice wine or
dry sherry*

1–3 tbsp. chili bean sauce

2 tbsp. light soy sauce

⅔ cup fish stock or water

*2 scallions, cut into very fine
shreds*

*2 fresh red chilies, deseeded
and cut into julienne*

1 tsp. sugar

1 tsp. Oriental sesame oil

*Fresh cilantro sprigs,
to garnish*

CHILI BEAN SAUCE

Commercial chili bean sauces range from mild to very hot, so add the amount you favor according to the brand used and your taste. You can make your own sauce by mixing dried red chilies, ground in a food processor or pestle and mortar, and yellow bean sauce. A ratio of one part ground chilies to two parts bean sauce will produce a moderately hot result.

Prepare the fish and remove any scales if necessary. Score both sides of the fish with three diagonal cuts, spacing them evenly along its length. Sprinkle the fish with salt on both sides.

Heat a wok over a high heat until it is hot, then slowly pour in the oil down the side. When the oil is very hot, carefully add the fish and deep-fry, turning once until golden brown on both sides, about 4 minutes.

Carefully remove the fish with two wide spatulas and allow to drain on paper towels. Pour off the hot oil, leaving about 1 tbsp.

Mix the cornstarch to a paste with 2 tsp. water; set aside. Add the garlic and ginger to the hot wok and stir-fry briefly, then add the rice wine, chili bean sauce and soy sauce and stir to mix. Pour in the stock and add the cornstarch paste. Bring to the boil, stirring. Reduce the heat, slide the fish back into the wok and braise gently for about 5 minutes.

Remove the fish. Stir the scallions, chilies, sugar and sesame oil into the sauce and simmer until reduced. Return the fish to the wok, spoon over the sauce and garnish with fresh cilantro.

Deep-frying and Braising

Because of its gently sloping sides, a wok is an excellent vessel for deep-frying a whole fish in hot oil, and then braising it in a sauce. For safety's sake, use a two-handled wok – it will be more stable than the type with one handle.

Heat the oil in the wok until it is just smoking (about 375°F). Slide in the fish and deep-fry until golden brown on both sides, turning it over with two wide spatulas.

Braise the fish in the sauce, basting it constantly, until it is cooked through. If the fish is very thick, turn it over with two wide spatulas halfway through cooking.

FISH STEAK & FILLET PREPARATIONS

Steaks and fillets can be cut from both round and flat fish. The French distinguish between *darnes*, steaks cut from round fish, and *tronçons*, steaks cut from large flat fish. Fish steaks are cut thicker and are quite robust; fish fillets are thinner than steaks and therefore more fragile.

CUTTING SCALLOPS

Large round fish fillets, such as the salmon illustrated here, can be cut into thin slices or scallops for use in a variety of preparations. Scallops can be cut from a fillet with or without its skin and should be about ½ in. thick. Often, they are then pounded between sheets of baking parchment to flatten them, making them even thinner. Check for pin bones and remove any you find before you start (see page 54).

Starting near the tail end of the fillet and working your way toward the head, with a sharp, thin-bladed knife, cut evenly sized pieces. Keep the knife almost flat against the fillet as you cut, and always face the tail.

CUTTING STEAKS

Steaks cut from a round fish are made by cutting across one that has been scaled, trimmed and gutted. Use a chef's knife or cleaver. Steaks are usually cut 1 in. thick and can be panfried, broiled, roasted or poached. Sea bass is shown here.

 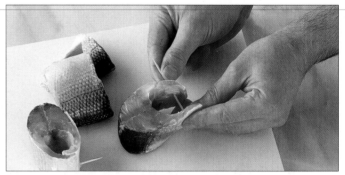

1 Make evenly spaced marks along the side of the fish. Cut down forcefully through the flesh and backbone at each mark with the knife.

2 Fold the ends of each steak in toward the center; secure the ends with a wooden tooothpick to keep the ends from curling during cooking. The steaks are now ready to cook and they can be served with or without the backbone.

MAKING PACKAGES

Thin pieces of fillet called scallops (see left) can be wrapped around a filling to make a savory package. Fish packages are fragile and are best poached or carefully panfried. Salmon is illustrated here.

1 Put the scallop between two sheets of baking parchment. Pound with a cleaver's flat edge until flat.

2 Wrap the scallop around your chosen filling, making as neat and square a package as possible.

3 Turn the package over seam-side down, and secure it by tying a strip of scallion around it.

MAKING PILLOWS

A pillow is a piece of fillet in which a pocket is cut to contain a stuffing. Any thick, firm fish, like the salmon shown here, can be used. Cut fillets into 3 x 1½ in. pieces to accommodate the stuffing. Because they are fragile, pillows are best poached.

1 Starting and ending ½ in. in from each side, cut a pocket in the front of the fillet (do not cut through the back, top or bottom).

2 Hold the pocket open with one hand and spoon the stuffing into the pocket. Do not overfill or the stuffing may burst out during cooking.

3 Secure the opening by tying a strip of scallion around it. The pillow is now ready for cooking.

MAKING BRAIDED FISH

A variety of round and flat fish fillets with contrasting flesh and thin colorful skins, such as the mackerel, snapper and sole shown here, can be used to good effect in this easy but impressive presentation. To preserve the delicate texture of the fillets, steaming is the best cooking method.

1 Cut each fillet into strips about 8 x 1 in. Lay three strips, one from each fillet, skin-side up on the chopping board. The strips should be close together.

2 Interweave the strips, keeping the braid as even as possible. Braid the strips loosely because they shrink a little when cooked.

3 Steam the braids (see page 70) over simmering *court bouillon* (see page 66) or fish stock (see page 17).

MAKING PAUPIETTES

For this technique, skinless fish fillets are halved lengthwise and rolled. They are stuffed before cooking, either by spooning the stuffing on one end of the fish and then rolling it up, or by spooning in the stuffing when the fish rolls are upright. Any flat fish fillet can be used, but the sole shown here, is a classic. Paupiettes are best poached, steamed or baked.

Coil the fillet, skinned-side in, into a turban – the tail end on the outside. To hold the coil, stand them close together during cooking or secure them with wooden toothpicks.

FILLINGS FOR FISH PACKAGES, PILLOWS AND PAUPIETTES

Vegetables, fish mousse, soft cheese and herbs are all appropriate. Try one of these:

- A fine julienne (see page 166) of blanched carrots and leeks tossed in vinaigrette.
- Soft cheese and chopped fresh herbs such as parsley or dill.
- A brunoise (see page 166) of mango, cucumber and fresh ginger with baby shrimp.
- Mushroom duxelles (see page 170).
- A light, creamy risotto with a hint of lemon.

Sushi & Sashimi

These well-known Japanese dishes are much enjoyed in the West.
Sushi is based on vinegared rice rolled in seaweed, with strips of raw fish or
a vegetable such as cucumber or avocado hidden in the center. Sashimi is
simply very fresh raw fish, served with a horseradish paste called wasabi.
Both are exquisitely presented, and are eaten with chopsticks.

....

Sushi Rolls

MAKES 32 SLICES

1 piece of very fresh tuna fillet, about ½ lb, skinned

4 sheets of nori seaweed, each measuring 8 x 7 in.

Rice vinegar

1½ lb. vinegared rice (see page 197)

Wasabi (see box, right)

TO SERVE

Pickled ginger roses (see page 69)
Cucumber crowns (see page 139)
Japanese soy sauce

Cut the tuna crosswise into strips, each ½ in. wide.
If the nori is not labeled "yakinori" – pre-toasted – hold each sheet with tongs and wave one side over a gas flame for a few seconds until crisp (see page 329).

Place a rolling mat flat on the work surface and put a sheet of nori on top, close to one of the short edges of the mat. Dip your fingers in water mixed with a dash of rice vinegar, and spread a layer of vinegared rice over the nori. Make a line of wasabi paste in the center of the rice and cover with tuna.

Roll the nori around the rice with the mat. Press the mat around the roll to keep the shape tight. Run a wet fingertip along the exposed edge of the nori to seal it. Using a moistened chef's knife, cut the roll across into eight pieces. Repeat four times.

Arrange the sushi rolls, cut-side up, on a platter. Serve with ginger roses, cucumber crowns and soy sauce.

Sashimi

SERVES 4

1 piece of very fresh red mullet fillet, about ½ lb, scaled but not skinned

1 piece of very fresh salmon fillet, about 1 lb, skinned

About ¾ lb. very fresh mackerel fillet, unskinned, with membrane removed

TO SERVE

Cucumber crowns
Wasabi (see box, right)
Japanese soy sauce

Before cutting the fish, check that all bones, especially fine pin bones, have been removed. The fish will be much easier to cut thinly if it is very well chilled.

Cut the piece of red mullet fillet into very thin slices against the grain.

Cut the mackerel fillets lengthwise in half. Holding the halves together, skin-side up, cut the fish across into thin slices, the same thickness as the red mullet and salmon.

Arrange the mullet, salmon and mackerel slices on plates, keeping them separate. Serve with cucumber crowns, wasabi and soy sauce.

WASABI

Known as Japanese horseradish because of its hot, pungent flavor, wasabi comes from the root of an Oriental plant. It is used freshly grated in Japan, but in the West it is normally sold as a paste, ready prepared in tubes. Look for it in large supermarkets.

Making Sushi Rolls

Individual sushi rolls are cut from one long roll to reveal the filling hidden in the center.
For shaping the long roll you need to use a mat. Special bamboo rolling mats can be found in Oriental shops, or you can use an undyed, flexible straw place mat.

Lay tuna over the line of wasabi paste to cover it completely. You may need more than one strip of tuna.

Lift up the short end of the mat nearest to you and roll the nori around the rice, rolling it away from you.

Cut the long sushi roll across into four equal lengths, then cut each length in half to make eight pieces.

STEAMING FISH

The vapor produced by a simmering liquid cooks fish by steaming. This method is ideal for delicate fish, such as sole and flounder, and shellfish. Water can be used, but a vegetable or herb broth adds flavor.

FLAVORING THE FISH

Steamed fish can be bland so give flavor to it by adding vegetables, herbs and spices, and other seasonings to the liquid in the wok or steamer, or by sprinkling them over the fish itself.

- Chop a mixture of herbs and vegetables – onions, carrots, celery, fennel, parsley stalks or cilantro leaves – and add to the steaming liquid.
- Place the fish on the steaming rack on a thick bed of fresh fennel fronds and fresh sprigs of thyme or dill.
- Cover the fish with chopped scallions, slivers of fresh ginger or garlic and slices of lemon and a sprinkling of fennel seeds.
- Marinate the fish before steaming. Olive oil, combined with lemon juice or white wine, or soy sauce are all good marinades for fish.

STEAMING TIMES

Fish is cooked when opaque throughout and the flakes separate easily with a fork. If overcooked, the fish will be dry and fall apart.

- FILLETS
  3–4 mins
- BRAIDS
  8–10 mins
- WHOLE FISH
  6–8 mins (up to ¾ lb.)
  12–15 mins (up to 2 lbs.)

CONVENTIONAL METHOD

Metal steamers contain perforated baskets that sit above the simmering liquid at the bottom. Steam filters through the perforations and cooks the fish. Here, braided mackerel, snapper and sole (see page 61) are steamed over a simmering court bouillon.

1 Add *court bouillon* to cover the bottom of the steamer and bring to a simmer. Arrange the fish in a single layer in the basket. Place the basket over the simmering liquid. Cover and steam (see chart, below left).

2 The fish is ready when it is opaque. Test it with a fork: the flesh should feel moist and tender.

BAMBOO STEAMER METHOD

A woven basket can be placed in a wok over simmering broth. The aromatic steam helps flavor the fish, while herbs, spices and other seasonings can be added to the fish itself. Steaming preserves the attractive color of fish, such as the red snapper shown here.

2 Score the fish and insert flavorings of your choice (see page 53) so the flavors enter the flesh. Lay the fish flat in the basket and sprinkle more flavorings over it. Place the basket in the wok.

1 Half fill a wok with water and bring to a simmer. Add chopped vegetables (see box, above left).

3 Place the lid on the basket to intensify the flavor imparted by the vegetables and other additions. Steam according to the times given in the chart, left. Serve with the steamed vegetables and seasonings.

BROILING FISH

The high heat of the broiler and barbecue cooks fish quickly which is by far the best way. Fatty fish such as sardines and mackerel are ideal, their natural oils help keep the flesh moist during cooking.

BROILING SMALL WHOLE FISH

Skin and bones keep fish moist so it is best to broil fish whole. Trim, scale and gut the fish (see pages 52–53) before cooking and score (see page 53) if you like. For additional flavor, marinate in olive oil, crushed garlic and chopped parsley as shown here with the sardines.

1 Remove the fish from the marinade and place on an oiled broiler rack. Broil under a high heat for 2 minutes.

2 Turn the fish over and brush with the marinade, or with olive oil if a marinade was not used. Broil for another 2 minutes, or until the skin is crisp and golden.

BARBECUING WHOLE FISH

The heat of the barbecue sears the fish keeping the flesh moist and flavorful. Trout is shown here but other suitable fish include mackerel, shark, tuna and bass. For even cooking, score the fish (see page 53), and for ease of handling, use a fish rack (see box, above right).

Place the fish in an oiled rack, with sprigs of fresh herbs or vine leaves if you like, and close the rack tightly. Place the rack on the grid of a hot barbecue. Cook the fish for about 3 minutes on each side, basting frequently with olive oil or marinade. Check for doneness: the skin should be crisp and golden and the flesh forktender.

FISH RACKS

Whether barbecuing whole fish, fillets or steaks, a special hinged fish rack can make the job more manageable. Brush the fish rack with olive oil to prevent the fish from sticking to it.

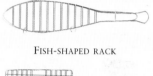

FISH-SHAPED RACK

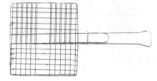

SQUARE RACK

SALSA FOR FISH

Contrast a cooked fish straight from the barbecue with a chilled spicy salsa.

A traditional accompaniment in Mexican cooking, *salsa* combines pungent garlic, onion and chilies with the sharp tang of lime. Served chilled *salsa* brings out the subtle flavors of hot fish.

71

BAKING

This is an excellent method for cooking large and medium-sized whole fish and for thick steaks and fillets. Fish can be baked without a covering, or wrapped in parcels of foil, paper or leaves or, for a whole fish, baked with a salt crust. For a more substantial dish, fish can be stuffed before baking; this will also give the fish more flavor.

FLAVORINGS FOR OPEN BAKING

The simplest flavoring is fresh herbs pushed into the stomach cavity. Some alternatives are:

- Asian flavorings such as fresh ginger and lemongrass.
- Fresh bread crumbs with herbs, spices or chopped nuts bound with egg.
- Shrimp with garlic or parsley.

OPEN BAKING

Medium-sized whole fish such as red snapper are ideal for cooking this way.

Place a single layer of fish in a greased roasting pan. Sprinkle over flavorings (see box, left) and just cover with liquid. Bake, uncovered, at 350°F for 30 minutes or until the flesh is opaque and the skin crisp. If you like, strain the pan juices and serve with the fish.

STUFFING AND BAKING IN FOIL

A foil wrapping allows fish to cook in its own juices, keeping it deliciously moist. The fish can be wrapped unstuffed or, depending on the boning method can be stuffed through the stomach or back. Stuffed fish take a little longer to cook.

1 Spoon your chosen stuffing into the stomach cavity of the fish. Secure the stomach opening with 1–2 wooden toothpicks.

2 Wrap fish individually in oiled or buttered foil. Seal the foil tightly to prevent juices escaping during cooking.

3 Bake in a roasting pan at 350°F, 25 minutes for a small fish, 35–40 minutes for a large fish. Open the foil wrapping at the table.

STUFFING THROUGH THE BACK BEFORE BAKING

Though the back cavity is smaller than the stomach, stuffing the back enables the fish to maintain a good shape. For the technique of boning a whole fish through the back, see page 55.

Spoon the stuffing into the cavity in the back of the fish. Wrap and bake as for the fish shown left.

BAKING EN PAPILLOTE

The term en papillote *is French for "in a paper bag." This technique protects the fish (brill is shown here) and helps keep it moist. The topping of herbs, vegetables and white wine adds flavor during cooking. For maximum effect, open the parcels at the table.*

1 Cut a heart shape, 2 in. larger than the fish, out of baking parchment or foil, and oil it.

2 Put the fish on one half with 4 sprigs of cilantro, 2 carrots, julienned (see page 166) and 4 tbsp. white wine.

3 Fold over the other half of the paper and twist to seal the edges. Place on a baking sheet and bake at 350°F for 15–20 minutes, until puffed.

BAKING IN LEAVES

Vine and banana leaves keep fish moist during cooking and they also flavor the fish.

Set the fish in the center of a leaf. Roll and wrap the leaf around the fish. Tie in place with a blanched strip of leek if necessary.

BAKING IN A SALT CRUST

Fish baked in this way will have a crispy skin and moist flesh – without being over salty. The salt crust will help the fish to retain moisture and add flavor. Before cooking, trim, scale and gut, then wipe the fish dry with paper towels.

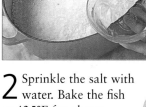

1 Spread a 2 in. layer of kosher or sea salt evenly over the bottom of a heavy-based casserole dish. Lay the fish on top of the salt and cover with another salt layer (3 lbs. salt will cover 2 lbs. fish as shown here).

2 Sprinkle the salt with water. Bake the fish at 425°F for about 30 minutes.

3 Chip through the top layer of salt with a small hammer. Remove the fish, keeping it in one piece. Brush away the excess salt and serve immediately.

TRICK OF THE TRADE

BRAIDED MONKFISH

Braid rindless bacon strips around a monkfish fillet, tucking in a few thyme leaves as you go. Bake at 350°F for 20 minutes. During baking the bacon imparts flavor to the fish and forms a crunchy coating; the fat seeps into the fish to moisten it.

FRYING

Choose pieces of fish of equal thickness to ensure even cooking. The temperature of the fat, whether oil or butter, is vital – too low and the coating will be soggy and fall apart, too high and it will cook too quickly.

COATINGS FOR FISH

A light coating protects delicate fish fillets and helps keep them moist during frying.

- Make a dry blend of Cajun herbs and spices – paprika, onion and garlic powder, dried thyme and oregano, white, black and cayenne pepper and salt.
- Mix fragrant herbs and spices such as chopped fresh dill, crushed fennel seeds and coarsely ground pepper.
- Mix snipped chives and a little grated lemon zest into fine bread crumbs or flour.

SHALLOW PANFRYING

Use equal parts butter and vegetable oil for successful panfrying. Season and coat the fish first (see box, left) and ensure the butter is foaming before adding fish.

1 Place the fish, skin-side down, in foaming butter and oil. Fry for 5 minutes then turn the fish over.

2 Fry the fillets for another 3–5 minutes, until golden brown. Insert a fork into the thickest part of the flesh – it should feel firm and be opaque throughout.

NUT-BROWN BUTTER

Called beurre noisette *in French, this is the classic butter for frying white fish, especially skate wings. Remove the dark skin and coat with seasoned flour.*

Heat 4 tbsp. butter in a frying pan until it turns a light nutty brown. Add the skate wings and fry for 8–10 minutes, turning once.

CAJUN-STYLE

Fish fried Cajun-style, from New Orleans and the states around the Gulf of Mexico, has a dark, peppery-hot crust. This comes from the special coating that is generously rubbed over it before cooking (see box, above left).

Place coated fish fillets (red snapper is shown here) in hot fat. Fry until the coating is charred, about 6 minutes, turning once.

COATING WITH AN HERB CRUST

This technique creates an attractive crust, which adds contrast in flavor and texture to the moist fish. Use firm textured fillets such as salmon, cod or monkfish. A non-stick pan reduces the oil required, allowing the crust to "toast."

1 Spread a mixture of fragrant herbs and spices (see box, above left) over a plate. Press skinned fish fillets, skinned-side down, into the mixture to ensure an even coating.

2 Panfry the fillets, crust-side down, in a little hot oil for 7–10 minutes without turning. Press firmly with a metal spatula to encourage the juices to rise to the surface and the heat to penetrate upwards into the flesh.

DEEP-FRYING FISH IN BATTER

Batter provides a protective coating, which keeps fish succulent and moist. A high cooking temperature (350–375°F) is necessary for the best result, and the oil should be carefully chosen, both for its ability to reach the required temperature and how it affects the flavor of the fish; vegetable oils are best. Cut the fish into even pieces or use steaks or fillets.

1 To test the temperature of the oil, drop in a cube of white bread, it should brown all over in about 30 seconds. Remove the bread and discard.

2 Lower the batter-coated fish into the hot oil. Cook large pieces of fish one at a time for 7–10 minutes to ensure even cooking.

3 When golden and crisp, lift the basket out of the fryer. Shake the basket to remove excess oil, then drain the fish onto paper towels. Season before serving.

MAKING GOUJONS

Cut strips from skinned fish fillets, working across the grain of the flesh: this helps the goujons retain their shape. The oil will rise in the pan, so fill to the recommended level – a deep pan should be filled to one-third of its capacity.

1 Cut the skinned fish fillets into ½-in. strips, working across the grain and using a chef's knife.

2 Put the strips of fish in a plastic bag containing seasoned flour. Twist the top to seal, and shake to coat evenly.

3 Heat the oil to 350–375°F. Lower the goujons into the oil using a slotted spoon or fryer basket. Deep fry for 3–4 minutes until golden. Remove and drain on paper towels.

DEEP-FAT THERMOMETER

This has a hook to fix it to the side of the pan, avoiding the need to have your hands over hot oil. Position it when the oil is cool and wait until the reading is correct before immersing food.

BATTERS FOR FISH

The mixture should be smooth (see page 39) and lightly coat the fish. Change cooking oil regularly as flavorings may taint the batter.

- Add a little oil or melted butter to enrich batter.
- Use beer instead of milk for a light coating with added color.
- Flavor flour with cayenne, chili or curry powder.
- Use tempura batter (see page 269) to coat shrimp or goujons and serve them with soy sauce.

FISH MIXTURES

Many fish can be puréed or flaked and the resulting mixtures have many applications. Fish mousse can be molded, layered or shaped into dumplings, and flaked fish can be formed into cakes. Enliven the basic fish mousse shown here with chopped herbs, ground spices or other seasonings.

FISH MOUSSE

1 lb. fish fillets (whiting, flounder, sole or salmon)
Salt
2 egg whites
1½ cups heavy cream
Ground white pepper or cayenne

Trim and skin the fish fillets and remove all of the bones, checking carefully for any pin bones. Purée the flesh in a food processor with salt to taste, then add the egg whites. For a velvety texture, pass this mixture through a fine sieve into a bowl (this will also help eliminate any fine pin bones that may remain). Gradually fold in the cream over an ice bath to prevent the mixture from splitting. Season with salt and pepper. Makes about 2 lb.

WHAT'S IN A NAME?

QUENELLES: The word derives from the German word for dumpling, *Knödel*, but it now means any egg-shaped sweet or savory mixture such as mousse and sorbet. Small quenelles can be used to garnish clear soups.
TIMBALES: This is the name given to small, round, deep molds and also to any food that is shaped or baked in them, as long as it forms a single serving. The name can be applied to fish, meat or vegetable preparations.

MAKING A FISH MOUSSE

Chilling the mixture over an ice bath when adding the cream prevents the mixture from separating.

1 Chop the fish into chunks and purée evenly with the salt in a food processor fitted with the metal blade. Add the egg whites and process until evenly incorporated.

2 Work the mixture through a sieve into a bowl, then set it over a bowl of water and ice cubes. Fold in the cream with a rubber spatula.

MAKING FISH TIMBALES

One of the simplest ways to use the fish mousse above is to bake it in dariole molds.

1 Divide the mousse between 6 chilled dariole molds. Cover with buttered baking parchment. Set in a roasting pan and pour in hot water almost to the top of molds.

2 Bake in a *bain marie* at 325°F until firm, about 25 minutes. Turn out onto individual plates.

MAKING FISH QUENELLES

These dumplings, made from the fish mousse above, are shaped with tablespoons that have been dipped in water.

1 Take one spoonful of mousse and round each side with another spoon until smooth and egg-shaped. Repeat to make 18 quenelles.

2 Poach the quenelles until firm, 5–10 minutes. Remove with a slotted spoon, and drain on paper towels.

MAKING FISH CAKES

These can be made from a variety of different raw fish: white fish such as cod or hake, or oily fish such as mackerel or salmon. A mixture of fresh and smoked fish is also good, and the fish can be coarsely flaked or finely ground, whichever you prefer.

Leftover cooked fish can also be used in fish cakes, using equal quantities of fish and potatoes.

1 Flake raw fish with a fork. Mix with mashed potato and enough egg to bind, using a spatula. Add chopped parsley and seasonings and blend into the mixture.

2 Form the mixture into balls, flatten them and coat in dried bread crumbs. Let chill for 30 minutes. Panfry in hot oil for 5–6 minutes on each side or until golden.

MAKING A LAYERED FISH TERRINE

Here the basic fish mousse (see box, opposite page) is given an elegant treatment in a terrine with three layers. One layer uses the basic mixture, another uses the basic mixture with liquefied herbs, and spinach-wrapped prawns are sandwiched in between. If you like, add contrast by making half the mousse with salmon or trout. The terrine can be served hot or cold.

1 Line a buttered terrine mold with blanched spinach leaves, making sure that there are no gaps.

2 Roll up the shrimp in blanched spinach leaves and place on top of the plain mousse in three rows.

3 Cover the spinach-wrapped shrimp with the fish mousse to which liquefied herbs have been added. Pipe it in even rows so that the finished texture will be smooth. Once baked, turn out and serve sliced. If serving the terrine cold, as shown here, serve slices on a saffron sauce garnished with saffron strands.

FISH TERRINE

2 lbs. fish mousse
  (see opposite page)
¾ lb. cooked peeled shrimp
12–15 large spinach leaves,
  blanched
2 tbsp. chopped chervil and dill

Liquefy the chopped chervil and dill in a food processor. Divide the mousse in half and add the liquefied herbs to one half until the mousse is a rich green colour.

Line a buttered 1½ quart loaf pan or terrine with blanched spinach. Pipe a layer of the plain fish mousse in the terrine. Wrap the shrimp in blanched spinach, arrange on the plain mousse and pipe a layer of the herb mousse on top. Cover with baking parchment. Bake in a *bain marie* at 300°F for about
1 hour or until a knife inserted in the center comes out clean. Turn out and serve sliced, hot or cold.

LOBSTER

A lobster's flesh is meaty, sweet and delicate. For absolute freshness, lobsters are best bought live and prepared at home. Choose active ones that feel heavy for their size.

HUMANE KILLING

Some chefs recommend placing the live lobster in the freezer for an hour to desensitize it before killing.

Hold the lobster, back up and claws bound, firmly on a chopping board. Locate the center of the cross-shaped mark on the back and pierce through to the board with the point of a chef's knife. This kills instantly, but there may be some twitching from the severed nerves. You can now cut the lobster as required.

COOKING A LIVE LOBSTER

Lobsters are usually bought with rubber bands tied around the claws and the tail braced with string tied to a piece of wood.

1 Leaving the body support intact, plunge the lobster into a deep pan of boiling *court bouillon* (see page 66).

2 Bring back to the boil and cook until the shell turns red, 5 minutes per initial 1 lb, plus 3 minutes for each extra 1 lb. Transfer the cooked lobster with a slotted spoon to a colander. Drain and let cool.

REMOVING THE TAIL MEAT FROM ITS SHELL

Cooked lobster can be served in numerous ways. The tail meat, one of the most succulent parts, is generally removed in one piece and sliced into neat pieces known as medallions.

1 Remove body support. With the lobster belly-side up, cut through the shell along each side of the tail.

2 Pull the shell back, exposing the meat of the lobster tail.

3 Pull tail meat from shell, keeping it whole. Make a shallow cut along the inner curve. Remove dark vein.

4 Cut away the white flesh from the top of the tail meat, then cut the remaining flesh into even slices. Present them overlapping along the back of the lobster – when glazed with aspic this presentation is called *en bellevue* (see box, left).

REMOVING MEAT FROM THE HALF-SHELL

The orangey-red shell of a cooked lobster makes an attractive serving "dish." The entire tail section can be detached from the head, rinsed out and used for serving. Alternatively, and especially when the lobster is intended for two, you can serve the meat on the half-shell.

LOBSTER CRACKERS

Lobster claws are especially tough. To remove their meat, use a cracking tool or small hammer.

Lobster crackers are similar to the hinged type of nut crackers but are rather sturdier. The inner edges near the hinge are ridged to provide grip on the smooth shells. Some have a prong at the end to pry out the claw meat. You can also buy lobster pincers designed to crack the claws and extract the meat.

2 Spoon out the green liver, or tomalley, and reserve. Female lobsters may contain roe, or coral, which is pink when cooked and should be saved. Discard the gravel sac.

1 Cook the lobster as described on the opposite page. When it is cool enough to handle comfortably, cut the string and remove the body support. Hold the lobster with its back uppermost, and cut it in half lengthwise from head to tail with a large chef's knife.

3 Gently pull the tail meat from each side of the shell. Remove and discard the intestinal vein.

4 Crack each claw just below the pincer, without damaging the meat. Remove meat from base of claw shell.

5 Pull the small pincer away from the rest of the claw, bringing with it the flat white membrane. Remove the meat from this part of the claw. Pull the meat from the large pincer shell, keeping it in one piece.

PARTS OF A LOBSTER

The lobster's shell accounts for two-thirds of its weight, but very little of the rest is inedible. Blue-black when raw, the shell turns scarlet when cooked.

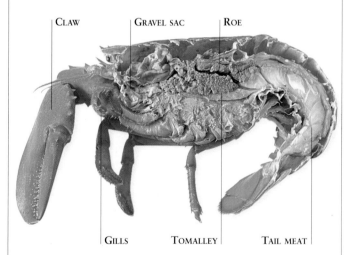

CLAW | GRAVEL SAC | ROE

GILLS | TOMALLEY | TAIL MEAT

EDIBLE PARTS
- The most meaty part is the lobster tail.
- The two claws are also full of delicious flesh.
- The green, creamy liver (tomalley) is a delicacy.
- In the female, the roe can be eaten. It is black when raw and scarlet when cooked.

INEDIBLE PARTS
- The shell and legs.
- The bony membranes in the two claws.
- Small gravel sac (the stomach).
- The intestinal channel which runs down the back to the tail.
- The feathery gills in the body section between the lobster's head and tail.

CRAB

There are over twelve edible varieties of crab, the large-bodied species being the most common in the kitchen. You can buy crab whole, alive or cooked – live ones should be active and feel heavy for their size. Crabs are usually cooked whole and then cut up afterward.

LOUISIANA CRAB BOIL

As an alternative to a traditional *court bouillon*, consider a Louisiana crab boil, which gives the meat a peppery flavor. In this unique cooking method, crab is cooked in a fiery herb broth made heady with lemon, allspice, thyme, chilies, onion, garlic and peppercorns. The recipe stems from states around the Gulf of Mexico, which are rich in Creole and Cajun tradition. Creole cooking, a sultry blend of French, Spanish and African influences, is considered to be the more refined of the two. Cajun cooking, inspired by French settlers is spicier than Creole.

HOW TO DRESS CRAB

This classic presentation turns the large shell into an elegant container for the crab. Remove meat, keeping pieces as large as possible. Pick over crab and remove any membrane or shell. Cut around the line rimming the edge of shell. Scrub out shell and dry. Arrange white meat in one half of shell. Mix any brown meat with a little mayonnaise and pile into the other half. Garnish with finely chopped fresh parsley, finely chopped hard-boiled egg white and sieved hard-boiled egg yolk; serve with additional mayonnaise.

BOILING A CRAB

The cooking liquid can vary from water or the classic court bouillon (see page 66) to a spicy broth (see box, left). Before you start, put the live crab in the freezer for 1 hour to desensitize it. The crab will then be easy to handle.

1 If not already done at the fish market, tie the crab with string to keep its claws still. Fill a pan with enough *court bouillon* to cover the crab. Bring to the boil.

2 Add the crab and cover the pan; bring back to the boil and cook until the shell of the crab turns red, about 5 minutes per 1 lb.

3 Remove the cooked crab from the pan with a slotted spoon. Transfer to a colander to drain. Let cool, then remove the cooked meat from the shell (see below).

REMOVING COOKED CRABMEAT FROM THE SHELL

Although size and shape vary from one species to another, the essential parts of the body need a similar approach. The larger the crab the easier it is to remove the meat. A variety of utensils are available to extract the meat. For the legs, snip open the shell and remove the meat with a pick. Use a spoon to scoop out the yellowish-brown meat from the shell. Opt for a skewer or larding needle to poke out the white fibers from the central body. To dress a crab, see box (left).

1 Hold the legs and claws close to the body and twist to remove. Discard the legs.

2 Crack the claws without damaging the meat inside. Remove the meat in large chunks.

3 Remove the pointed tail or apron flap by snapping it back with your fingers.

4 Break the shell by pressing down each side of the body with your thumbs. Lift out the body section. Scrape away the soft brown meat from the shell, keeping it separate from the white claw meat.

5 Discard the stomach sac and soft gills (also known as dead man's fingers) as they are inedible. If you intend to use the shell for serving, clean it thoroughly.

6 Cut the body of the crab in half lengthwise with a chef's knife. Remove the meat from the body of the crab with the handle of a small spoon or a chopstick, keeping it separate from the brown shell meat.

SHRIMP

The different varieties and sizes of shrimp available are enormous, but no matter what sort you buy, the techniques for dealing with all of them are the same. Whether raw or cooked, you need to know how to shell them and how to remove the dark intestinal vein.

PREPARING SHRIMP

Most large shrimp have a black intestinal vein running along their backs. This is unsightly, and its gritty texture is unpleasant to eat, so it should be removed. If you buy raw shrimp, remove these veins before cooking.

1 Peel off the shell, being careful to keep the shrimp intact and leave no flesh on the shell. All the shell can be removed, including the tail end, or you can leave the shell on the tail for an alternative presentation.

2 Make a shallow cut along the back of the prawn with a small knife, to expose the dark vein. Carefully loosen any overhanging membrane that may tether the vein to the prawn.

3 Remove the dark intestinal vein with the tip of the knife. Discard the vein. Rinse and pat dry with paper towels.

CRAYFISH

Although crayfish resemble tiny lobsters, they are in fact prepared and cooked in a similar way to shrimp. The intestinal vein is best removed before cooking. Twist the center section of the tail, then pull it away from the body – the vein will come away too.

TRICK OF THE TRADE

KEEPING SHRIMP STRAIGHT
Oriental chefs use this simple technique to prevent shrimp from curling during cooking.

Before cooking, insert a long wooden toothpick through the center of each shrimp. Remove the picks before serving.

MUSSELS

Choose undamaged, fresh-smelling mussels. Avoid those that feel heavy – they may be full of sand – or light and loose when shaken – they are probably dead. Ensure all are tightly closed; reject any that do not shut when tapped.

MOULES A LA MARINIERE

2 tbsp. butter

2 shallots, chopped

2 garlic cloves, chopped

1 cup dry white wine

1 tbsp. chopped fresh parsley, plus extra for garnishing

1 lb. live mussels, cleaned

Salt and freshly ground pepper

Melt the butter in a large, deep pan and sauté the shallots and garlic for 5 minutes or until soft. Add the wine and parsley, bring to a simmer, then add the mussels. Cover the pan tightly and steam for 6 minutes or until the mussels open. Discard any that remain closed. Lift out the mussels, draining their liquid back into the pan. Strain the liquid to remove any sand; rinse out the pan. Return liquid to pan and boil to reduce; season. Serve with the liquid poured over and garnished with parsley. Serves 4.

CLEANING

About three-quarters of mussels on sale today are cultivated. The rest are harvested from the wild. Mussels filter seawater through their bodies to extract nutrients and may pick up any toxins in the water. Whether cultivated or wild, they must be carefully cleaned before being cooked.

1 Scrape off any barnacles from the outsides of the shells with the back of a small knife.

2 With your thumb against the blade, pull out and detach any hair-like "beards" from the hinges of the shells.

3 Scrub each shell briskly under cold running water with a stiff brush. This will remove any sand and thoroughly clean the mussels before cooking. Discard any mussels with cracked shells and any that do not close when tapped. Place cleaned mussels in a bowl of lightly salted cold water for about 2 hours or until ready to use.

From left to right: New Zealand green-lipped mussel; mature marine mussel; young marine mussel

SAFETY FIRST

- Do not collect mussels from the wild unless you are certain the water is not polluted, and never collect them in the summer.

- If possible cook mussels on the day of purchase or picking – keep them in a bowl of lightly salted cold water for 2 hours, fresh water will kill them.

- If shells are muddy, or you want to cook them the next day, soak them overnight in cold water with 1 tbsp. flour and 3–4 tbsp. salt.

- Discard mussels that stay open when tapped or are cracked.

- Discard all mussels that do not open when cooked.

STEAMING OPEN

To open mussels, and cook the meat at the same time, they are steamed in a small amount of liquid with flavorings such as shallots, garlic and herbs. You can use water for the liquid, but fish stock or cider will give a better flavor. Another choice is dry white wine, as in the steps here for moules à la marinière *(see recipe, opposite page). Always clean the mussels well.*

REMOVING THE RUBBERY RING

The rubbery ring that forms a brown edge to the mussel flesh should be removed.

1 Clean the mussels (see opposite page), then add to the hot wine mixture.

2 Cover pan and steam the mussels for 6 minutes. Shake the pan occasionally to ensure even cooking.

3 Remove the mussels using a slotted spoon; discard any that are shut. Serve with the strained, reduced liquid.

1 Clean mussels and steam them open. Remove them from the cooking liquid and then from their shells.

SERVING ON THE HALF-SHELL

Once opened, the meat of the mussels can be removed from the shells and used in recipes, or left in and served in the shells with a sauce, or topped with herb butter or bread crumbs mixed with chopped fresh herbs. If they are large mussels, their tough, rubbery rings should be removed (see right).

1 Clean mussels (see opposite page) and steam them open as above, with liquid and flavorings of your choice. Remove them from the liquid and let cool, then pry them open with your fingers and discard the top shells. Loosen the mussels from the bottom shells.

2 Carefully pull off the rubbery ring that surrounds the flesh with your fingers and discard it.

2 Arrange the shells on sea or kosher salt in a heatproof dish. Top each with ½ tsp. pesto (see page 330) or garlic and herb butter (see page 127), and broil for 2–3 minutes. Garnish with a *concassée* of tomatoes (see page 178) and basil leaves.

OYSTERS & CLAMS

Both oysters and clams can be eaten raw, or removed from their shells and simmered in soups and stews, baked, or deep-fried. Left on their half shells, they can be topped with a sauce or stuffing and broiled.

SHUCKER

To open live oysters or other shellfish you need a short strong knife. A shucker is specially made for this task. The blade is sharply pointed, tapering on two sides. A prominent guard serves to protect your hand from the blade and the equally treacherous edges of the oyster shells.

OPENING CLAMS

There are many varieties of clam, from the small ones called vongole *in Italy, which can be steamed open like mussels (see page 83), to the larger* palourdes, *or Venus clams, and the huge hard clams or* quahogs *essential to American clambakes and chowders. Scrub all clams well before opening to remove grit and sand, and discard any open or damaged ones.*

1 Hold the clam firmly and insert the knife blade between the shells. Twist the knife to pry open the shells and sever the hinge muscle.

2 With a spoon, loosen the muscle in the bottom shell. If serving clams without their shells, tip both the meat and juices into a bowl.

SHUCKING OYSTERS

Oysters are usually eaten raw and should be opened (or shucked) just before eating. Discard open or damaged ones. Scrub the shells well before opening.

1 Using a cloth, hold the oyster, rounded-side down, in your hand. Insert the shucker just below the hinge.

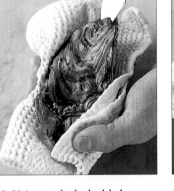

2 Work the shucker further between the two shells. Twist the shucker to separate the shells.

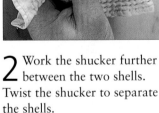

3 Carefully scrape the oyster from the top shell, cut the muscle and remove the top shell. Detach the oyster from the muscle underneath the meat on the bottom shell. Serve on the half-shell on a bed of crushed ice with lemon halves for squeezing. Garnish with blanched samphire, if you like.

SCALLOPS & WHELKS

Scallops can be bought on the shell or ready cleaned and shucked. They do not have to be live when cooked, but they should be very fresh and sweet smelling. So too should whelks, although they are not eaten raw.

OPENING AND PREPARING SCALLOPS

In Europe, shelled scallops are available with their orange roe (coral) intact; in the United States this is usually absent. Scallops on the shell must be opened and trimmed before cooking. To open scallops, split them with a shucker as shown here, or with a small knife.

1 Hold the scallop with its rounded side down in the palm of your hand. Insert an oyster shucker (see opposite page) between the shells close to the hinge.

2 Work the shucker further between the shells. Twist the shucker to separate the shells. Cut the scallop from the flat top shell by scraping it with the shucker.

PILGRIM SCALLOPS

Fan-shaped scallops are also called pilgrim scallops or *coquilles Saint-Jacques* in French. This is because the shell is the badge of the pilgrims who worship at the shrine of Saint Jacques, patron saint of Spain; the badge is always pinned to their wide-brimmed hats. Pilgrims travel to Santiago de Compostela in northern Spain, where legend has it that the saint is buried.

WHELKS

These must be cooked in their shells because their meat is difficult to extract while they are still alive. Bring a pan of court bouillon (see page 66) to the boil and add the whelks. Simmer until they are firm but tender.

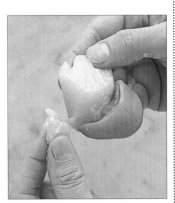

3 Carefully detach the scallop from the muscle underneath the meat in the bottom shell with a spoon. Scoop the scallop out; set the shell aside if you are going to use it in the presentation.

4 Pull away and discard the dark organs from the white muscle and the orange coral with your fingers. Rinse scallop under cold running water.

5 Pull off and discard the crescent-shaped muscle on the side of the scallop. The scallop may be cooked with or without the coral. If using the shells for serving, scrub and boil them for 5 minutes.

Lift the whelks out of the pan with a slotted spoon. Remove the whelk from the shell with a fork. Clean the whelk if there is any sign of sand.

SQUID

With a sweet flavor and pleasantly firm bite, squid has long been prized in coastal cuisines. The following techniques prepare squid for numerous dishes, including pasta, stir-fries and seafood salads.

PREPARING

When cleaning whole squid, you need to deal with all of its parts. The pouch, fins, tentacles and ink are all edible; the rest should be discarded. In addition to being used in soups and fish stews, the various parts of the squid can be stir-fried, deep-fried, poached, broiled and even eaten raw in Japanese sushi.

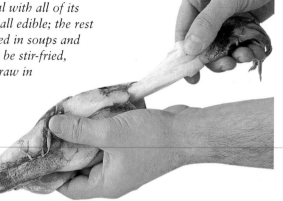

1 Hold the body firmly in one hand and pull off the head and tentacles. Drain the ink and set it aside if you are going to use it in cooking (see box, below).

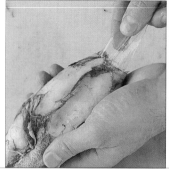

2 Pull out the "pen," which looks like a long piece of clear plastic, and discard.

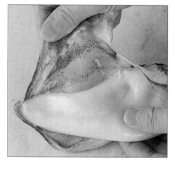

3 Peel off all of the purple skin covering the body (pouch) and the fins; discard the skin.

4 Remove the fins from the pouch with a chef's knife and reserve. Cut the tentacles from the head and reserve.

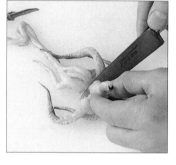

5 Squeeze the tentacles to remove the beak; cut off and discard. Cut off eyes and mouth; discard.

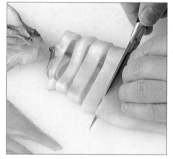

6 After cleaning, cut the pouch into rings or leave it whole for stuffing. Chop the fins and tentacles.

SQUID INK

Black ink is contained in a sac inside the squid. If the sac doesn't break during cleaning, remove it, pierce it and reserve the ink. Sacs can also be bought separately from some fish markets.

In Italy, squid ink is used to color and flavor pasta; in Catalonia it is used with rice, especially paella. The Spanish dish *calamares en su tinta* is squid cooked in its own ink.

STUFFING

When left whole, the pouch, or body, of the squid makes a perfect natural container for stuffing. Leave a little room at the top because the stuffing swells during cooking. Use the chopped tentacles in the filling, along with other full-flavored ingredients. A popular Spanish stuffing includes ham, onions and bread crumbs. A Middle Eastern mixture of couscous, sausage, red pepper and mint makes a delicious alternative.

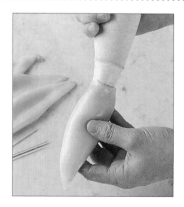

1 Hold the pouch in one hand. Pipe or spoon the stuffing into the pouch with a large tube.

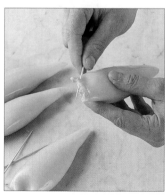

2 Secure openings with wooden toothpicks or sew closed with a trussing needle and string.

POULTRY & GAME

CHOOSING POULTRY

Whether fresh or frozen, look for well-shaped plump birds that have blemishfree, light, even-colored skin. Fresh birds should look moist but not wet; wetness can indicate that the bird has been partially frozen. Feed and breed can affect the color of the skin and the flavor of the meat.

MAKE SURE the legs are pliable and the skin intact

SELECT BIRDS with moist, even-colored skin. There should be no signs of bruising or feathers

WHEN SELECTING younger birds, gently bend the tip of the breastbone – it should be flexible

THE BODY SHOULD be compact, well rounded in shape with plump, firm breasts

THE BIRD SHOULD smell fresh; any smells from the wrapping should disappear quickly

BUYING POULTRY

Most supermarket birds are conventionally reared and have a consistently bland taste. Free-range birds, which are more expensive, are more flavorful as a result of their varied diet and free roaming conditions. Corn-fed chickens are another option – their diet gives them an attractive yellow color and good taste.

When choosing frozen birds, make sure the wrapping is sealed and intact and that there are no ice crystals or discoloration – a sign of freezer burn on the skin. Use the chart on the opposite page to select an appropriate bird for each occasion and to check the suitable cooking methods. When considering game, domestic rabbit is generally included with wild birds.

HANDLING POULTRY

Remove the original packaging from a fresh bird then place on a rack over a plate. Cover loosely and store in the refrigerator (34–40°F) away from cooked meats. Store any giblets separately in a covered bowl.

Always check the label on frozen birds and portions for freezer storage times. Frozen poultry must be defrosted completely before cooking. Thaw in the original packaging on a plate in the refrigerator, allowing 3–5 hours per 1 lb. Remove any giblets as soon as possible. Cook the bird within 12 hours of thawing and do not refreeze. Raw poultry is susceptible to bacterial growth, so clean work surfaces, chopping boards and utensils after use. To store cooked poultry, cool it quickly, then cover and store in the refrigerator for 2–3 days.

POULTRY & GAME

Chicken and turkey suit everyday and special occasion meals, while other birds are generally reserved for the latter. Select young, tender birds for quick cooking such as stir-frying, broiling and stovetop grilling and older birds for slow, moist methods, like stewing, which will help to tenderize the flesh and draw flavor from the bones. Ask your butcher for help with selection advice.

BIRD	WHAT TO LOOK FOR	COOKING METHODS
STEWING FOWL	Lean breast with firm breastbone Slightly mottled skin Flesh a little darker than chicken	Braise, stew, casserole, boil, poach, steam
CHICKEN	Creamy white smooth skin, should look fresh and moist	Roast, pot roast, braise, casserole, steam, poach, broil, panfry, deep-fry, stir-fry
DUCK	Supple, waxy-looking skin Dry appearance Long body with slender breasts	Roast (whole) Panfry, broil (breasts) Use fat for roasting potatoes
GOOSE	Plump breast with flexible backbone Light colored waxy skin Yellow fat in body cavity	Roast, pot roast Braise, stew (portions)
GROUSE	Moist, fresh-looking skin Deep red flesh, with no "shot" damage	Roast, pot roast, braise, casserole, stew
SQUAB/PIGEON	Tender, deep red meat Dry appearance Plump breasts	Roast, panfry (breast) broil, casserole
PARTRIDGE	Plump, pale-colored, soft flesh Obvious gamey aroma	Roast, pot roast, braise, casserole, stew
PHEASANT	Good even shape with no "shot" damage Limbs intact and not broken Strong gamey aroma	Bard and roast, stew, braise
CORNISH GAME HEN	Moist, creamy-white skin Plump legs and lean breasts	Roast (whole) Broil, barbecue (split)
QUAIL	High proportion of meaty flesh to bone Good round shape and plump flesh	Roast, pot roast, braise, casserole, broil, barbecue (split)
RABBIT	Even covering of flesh and rounded back Lean, moist, pale pink flesh Very little visible fat	Panfry, broil roast, braise, stew, casserole
TURKEY	Plump, well-rounded breast and legs Moist skin with no blemishes Very little odor	Roast (whole) Roast, braise, casserole (portions) Stir-fry, panfry (breast meat)

CHICKEN ON THE MENU

Inexpensive, easy to prepare and perfect with a vast range of seasonings and accompaniments, chicken is a popular dish worldwide.

CHINA – *Bang Bang Chicken* (shredded, poached chicken served with cucumber shreds and a spicy dressing) is a favorite appetizer dish.

EASTERN EUROPE – *Chicken Paprikash* (chicken pieces cooked in a tomato and paprika-flavored sauce) is a Hungarian classic, while *Chicken Pojarski* (deep-fried minced chicken and brioche balls in a tomato-mushroom sauce) was once a favorite of the Russian royal family.

FRANCE – *Coq au vin* is a slowly simmered chicken that gets its rich flavor from red wine, bacon, and mushrooms.

GREAT BRITAIN – *Hindle Wakes* (chicken with a fruit, vinegar and mustard stuffing) is a time-honored Yorkshire classic.

INDIA – *Tandoori Chicken* is marinated in spicy yogurt and cooked in a clay oven.

ITALY – *Chicken Cacciatore* (or "hunter's style") is made with a mushroom and wine-infused tomato sauce.

UNITED STATES – *Southern-Fried Chicken* (chicken pieces dipped in milk and seasoned flour and deep fried) is a popular picnic and easy dinner dish.

PREPARING WHOLE BIRDS

All birds, both domestic – chickens, ducks and geese – and game birds such as pheasant and grouse, need careful preparation, in order to keep their shape during cooking and to make carving easier. Before trussing, clean away feathers and down, rinse inside and out, and dry with paper towels.

GIBLETS

The giblets consist of the neck, gizzard, heart, and liver of the bird as well as the lungs and intestines (though the last two are generally not included in ready-prepared birds). Unless you clean the bird yourself, you will usually find the giblets packed in a plastic bag inside the body cavity, but often they're omitted from ready-prepared birds. You can also buy them separately– either fresh or frozen – from some large supermarkets or from a butcher. To make stock for gravy (see page 101), trim the giblets, discarding the membrane and yellow gall bladder from the liver. Simmer them with a few tablespoonfuls of chopped onion and carrot, a bouquet garni (see page 185) and a few black peppercorns.

The livers of poultry (see page 94) and some fresh game birds are delicious in their own right, although the giblets of well-hung game birds are best discarded.

Handle and cook giblets as you would poultry. Store them separately, in a covered container away from cooked meats, in the refrigerator for 1–2 days. Always cook thoroughly before eating.

REMOVING THE WISHBONE

The wishbone is located at the neck end of the bird. It is not necessary to remove it, but if you do it will be easier to carve the breast. This is particularly important if you are dealing with a large chicken or a turkey. Use a small, pointed knife.

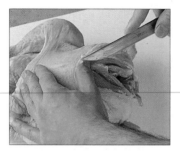

1 Pull back the skin from the neck cavity of the bird. Cut around the wishbone.

2 Scrape the meat from the wishbone, then cut away at the base.

TRUSSING SMALL BIRDS

Trussing gives the bird a neat shape and helps keep stuffing in place. Use a string to tie quite small birds, such as Cornish game hens, partridges, pheasants, grouse, quails, and squab, around their legs and bodies. Before you begin to tie up the birds, tuck the wing tips and the neck flap underneath.

1 After seasoning, with the bird breast-side up, tie string around the legs and under the skin flap at the tail.

2 Bring the string toward the neck end of the bird, passing it down between the legs and body.

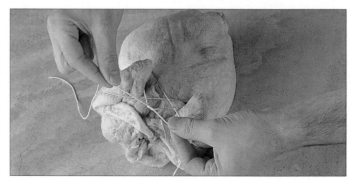

3 Turn the bird over. Cross the string over the center of the bird. Wrap the string around the wings to keep them flat against the bird.

4 Pull the string to bring the wings together, and then tie a firm, double knot. The bird is now ready for cooking – roasting, potroasting, barbecuing or casseroling.

TRUSSING LARGE BIRDS

Trussing with a needle and thread is best for large birds, and professional chefs always truss birds this way to ensure a neat, compact shape. Trussing helps the bird retain its natural juices, keeping the flesh moist and flavorful.

1 With the bird breast side up, push the legs back to the center of the breasts. Insert the needle through the joint in one of the legs, push it through the body, and out through the other leg. A 6 in. piece of string should remain where the needle first entered the bird.

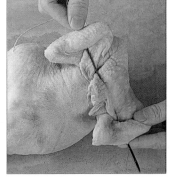

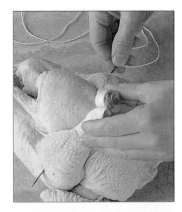

2 Tuck the wing tips under the body, and fold over the flap of skin from the neck. Thread the string through the wings and flap of skin.

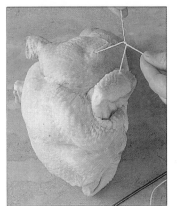

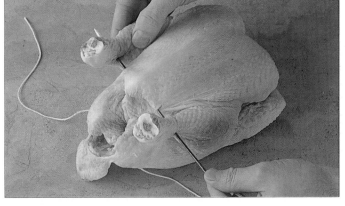

3 Make a double knot by tying the end of the string threaded through the wings with the end left at the leg. Trim both ends of the string.

4 Thread the needle under the legs through the tail end, leaving a 6 in. piece of string where the needle first entered the bird. Insert the needle through the end of one leg, push it through the breast, and out through the other leg.

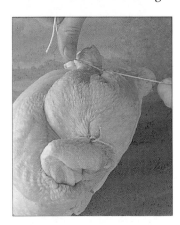

5 Make a double knot by tying the end of the string that has been threaded through the legs with the end left at the tail. Cut both ends of the string.

6 Turn the bird breast side up. It is now ready for cooking – roasting, poaching, barbecuing or pot roasting (see pages 100, 110, 113 and 114 respectively).

TRUSSING NEEDLE

To truss a large bird you need a special trussing needle. These are available in various lengths from specialist kitchenware shops. Make sure you use one which is long enough to pierce the bird fully through both legs and body. A small turkey, for example, will require a trussing needle of about 10 in. in length.

Trussing needles have very sharp points and eyes large enough to allow easy threading. The thread should be black, to show up on the cooked meat, and not plastic-coated or otherwise treated.

TRICK OF THE TRADE
●

QUICK TRUSSING
Large birds that are to be roasted without a stuffing or barbecued can be quickly and simply secured by the insertion of two large metal skewers. One is pushed through both sections of the wing, into the neck skin and out through the other wing. The other skewer is pushed through the thighs and tail cavity. Secured this way, the bird will hold its shape and is ready for cooking.

JOINTING & CUTTING

Birds are usually left whole for roasting, potroasting and poaching, but for most other cooking methods they are cut up into pieces, unless they are small birds such as Cornish game hens or quail. The number of pieces depends upon the size of the bird. Some small birds may be spatchcocked (split) or cut in half. Others are cut into four, six or eight pieces.

SPATCHCOCKING

The derivation of this very strange sounding culinary term is slightly obscure. Dating back to the 16th century, and most likely of Irish origin, the word is said to have come from the habit of catering for unexpected guests by speedily killing a bird and roasting it over the fire – "despatching the cock" – hence spatchcock. The term has now come to mean cutting and removing the backbone so that the bird can be cooked flat – and therefore more quickly.

SPATCHCOCKING A BIRD

Small birds are perfect for barbecuing or broiling. To make them the same thickness throughout so that they cook quickly and evenly, the backbone is removed, then the birds are flattened and secured with metal skewers – called en crapaudine *in French.*

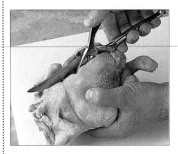

1 Tuck under the wings and remove the wishbone. Turn the bird over; cut along each side of the backbone with poultry shears and remove it.

2 Push down on the bird to break the breastbone, flattening it against the chopping board.

3 Keeping the bird flat, push a metal skewer through the wings and breast. Push another metal skewer through the thighs.

CUTTING A DUCK INTO FOUR PIECES

Ducks are less economical than chickens, because they have less meat in proportion to their weight, and more fat stored under the skin. They are also a different, more awkward shape to cut up, and therefore it is better to cut them into four pieces so that each portion contains a good amount of meat to bone. The joints can be roasted or casseroled.

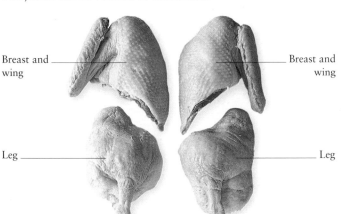

Breast and wing

Leg

Breast and wing

Leg

1 Trim wing tips and remove wishbone (see page 90). Cut breast in half from tail to neck, splitting the breastbone with poultry shears.

2 Separate the bird into two halves by cutting along each side of the backbone and removing it.

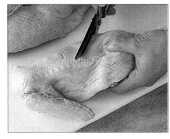

3 Cut each piece of duck diagonally in half with poultry shears. The duck is now ready for cooking.

CUTTING A BIRD INTO EIGHT PIECES

A medium-sized or large bird can be jointed into four, six or eight pieces. For some dishes you may want to keep the breasts and/or the legs intact, but to ensure there is some white and dark meat for each serving, breasts are cut in half with the wings attached and the legs are split into thighs and drumsticks.

1 Place the bird breast side up and cut away one leg. Cut through the thigh joint to separate the leg from the body. Repeat.

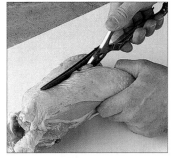

2 Holding the wing, cut the breast in half, splitting the breastbone. Turn the bird over and cut alongside the backbone to separate the body.

3 Cut out the backbone with the poultry shears – reserve it to make stock (see page 16). Leave the wing joints attached.

4 Cut each breast in half diagonally with the shears, so that one piece of breast has the wing attached.

5 Cut each leg in half through the knee joint, following the line of white fat on the underside. Cut off the wing tip at the first joint.

POULTRY SHEARS

Professional chefs joint poultry with a large knife, but for cutting the breastbone and backbone, you may find poultry shears easier.

Poultry shears have strong, upward-curving blades, one with a straight edge and one with a serrated edge. Some have a notch in the lower blade which helps get a grip on bones. The handles are strongly sprung and are closed with a loop that holds the blades shut when not in use.

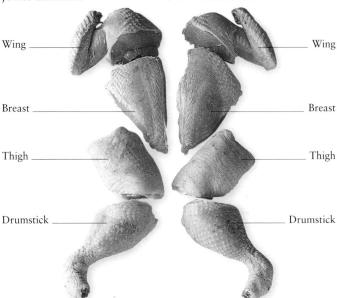

Wing — — Wing

Breast — — Breast

Thigh — — Thigh

Drumstick — — Drumstick

CUTTING UP A RABBIT

Rabbits can be roasted whole, but it is more usual to portion them for slow cooking in casseroles and stews. You may only need to joint wild rabbit since domestic rabbit is mainly sold cut into pieces. A whole rabbit, depending on size, can be cut into six to nine pieces which will feed three to five people. Boneless rabbit meat is a good choice for pâtés and terrines (see page 116).

1 Cut the back legs from the carcass with a large chef's knife. Cut down the center to separate. Cut each leg in two.

2 Cut the body crosswise into three or four pieces with the knife, making one cut below the rib cage.

3 Cut the rib section in half through the breastbone and backbone with the knife or kitchen scissors.

PREPARING PIECES

Poultry is immensely versatile: it can be cut into suprêmes and scallops for panfrying, chargrilling, stuffing and poaching, and into strips for stir-frying. Thighs provide lean, chunky pieces for casseroles and kebabs.

MAKING SUPREMES

These are skinless, boneless chicken breasts. Traditionally, they include the wing bones, but are often prepared without. Although available ready-prepared, preparation at home is more economical. Joint the bird (see page 93), cutting off both wings but keeping the breasts whole.

1 With your fingers, pull the skin and membrane away from the chicken breast. Discard skin and membrane.

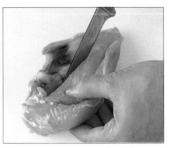

2 Turn the breast over and cut away the rib cage. Remove the tendons from the breast (see below).

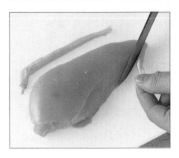

3 Turn the breast over, skinned-side up, and trim away fat and rough edges. The suprême is now ready.

PREPARING POULTRY & GAME LIVERS

Poultry livers and those of some fresh game birds can be gently sautéed and served on toast or with dressed salad leaves; they are also very good in pâtés and terrines.

Poultry livers consist of smooth lobes surrounded by membranes and sinews. Trim the livers, removing all tubes, membrane and fine, stringy sinews that would be unpleasant in the mouth. Remove the gall bladder and cut away any dark brown or yellowish patches around it.

REMOVING THE TENDONS

There are two tendons in a chicken breast, one in the small fillet and one in the main breast. Removing them is not essential, but it does make for easier slicing and eating. In step 2, the main sinew is removed prior to slicing strips for stir-frying.

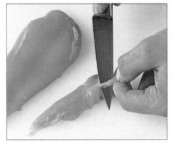

1 Pull away the small fillet. Cut out the tendon with a chef's knife.

2 Cut away the tendon from the breast, using a cleaver or chef's knife.

MAKING SCALLOPS

A chicken breast provides two scallops; a turkey breast, three or more. Scallops can be panfried plain or coated (see page 108), chargrilled (see page 109), or made into pinwheels (see page 111).

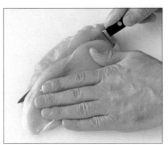

1 Remove the skin and tendons (see above). Split in half horizontally with a knife.

2 Place each piece of chicken between two sheets of baking parchment. Pound all over with a rolling pin until flattened.

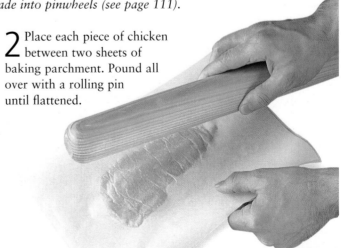

CUTTING POULTRY FOR STIR-FRYING

Poultry meat is ideal for stir-frying because it cooks rapidly, quickly becomes tender, and teams well with the strong flavors of Asian cooking. Skinless, boneless breast of chicken, turkey, and duck are most often used, and the strips marinated to heighten flavor. For the technique of stir-frying poultry, see page 109.

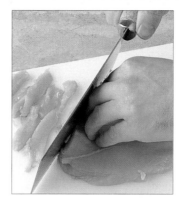

Trim the breasts of any fat and remove the tendons (see opposite page). Put the breasts between two sheets of baking parchment and pound with the flat side of a cleaver. Remove the paper and thinly slice the breasts, working diagonally across the grain of the meat (see box, right).

GOING AGAINST THE GRAIN

Meat that is cut "cross-grain," as the Chinese call it, has three advantages: a greater cut surface area is exposed to the heat, making cooking very quick; long fibers are cut which makes the flesh more tender; and the strips hold their shape during cooking.

PREPARING THIGH MEAT FOR KEBABS

Thigh meat is good for kebabs as it is firmer than breast. A marinade adds flavor and moisture – the meat should be soaked at least an hour before cooking, preferably overnight. Another trick is to leave the skin on for cooking, then remove it just before serving.

3 Marinate the meat if you like, then fold the pieces in half and thread onto skewers. Alternate the meat with cubed or sliced vegetables, to add color and make the meat go further.

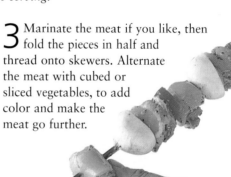

1 Remove the skin. Cut the flesh from one end of the thigh bone. Lift the bone and scrape away the flesh. Cut the bone from the meat.

2 Cut the thigh into large pieces, across the grain of the meat. Cut away any sinew or bone that may be attached to the meat.

PREPARING A WHOLE BREAST OF DUCK

The breasts are the best part of the duck. They are long, thick, meaty, and boneless, and can be panfried, roasted, broiled or chargrilled whole and carved crosswise into neat, elegant slices to serve. The French word magret *is used to describe any duck breast, although it originally only related to Barbary duck. Breasts can be cut from a whole duck (before it is jointed) using a boning knife, or can be bought ready-cut. They are not usually skinned.*

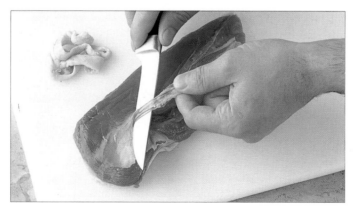

1 Trim away the rough edges of skin from the duck breast. Turn the breast onto its skin and trim away the tendon from the flesh with a boning knife.

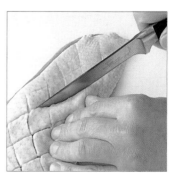

2 Score a diamond pattern in the skin. This makes it more attractive for serving, and helps release fat during cooking (see page 108).

MAKING A BALLOTINE

The word ballotine comes from the French *ballot*, meaning bundle, a neat parcel of stuffing encased in lean, boneless poultry meat. Here, a whole bird is boned and then stuffed with a forcemeat mixture. Poultry breast meat or truffles are sometimes included in stuffings for ballotines, as are whole or chopped nuts or pitted olives.

FORCEMEAT STUFFING

12 oz. skinless, boneless chicken
*   breasts, cut into pieces*
½ cup fresh bread crumbs
2 tbsp. milk
1 tbsp. butter
1 shallot, chopped
1 garlic clove, chopped
1 egg white
1 tbsp. mixed fresh thyme and
*   tarragon, chopped*
Salt and freshly ground pepper

Grind the chicken in a food processor or grinder and place in a bowl. Soak the bread crumbs in the milk until the liquid is absorbed, then squeeze out the excess milk and add the bread crumbs to the chicken. Melt the butter in a pan and sauté the shallot and garlic until softened, about 5 minutes. Let cool, then add to the chicken and bread crumbs and mix well. Bind the mixture with the egg white, then add the chopped herbs and salt and pepper to taste. Makes enough stuffing for a 2½ lb. bird.

BONING THE BIRD

Ballotines are usually made with duck, turkey, or, as here, chicken, but game birds such as pheasant or grouse are also suitable. You can ask your butcher to bone the bird for you, or do it yourself following the techniques shown here. Reserve the carcass for stock (see page 16). A ballotine is almost always served cold, so start making it the day before you want to serve it to allow time for the meat to settle and cool after cooking.

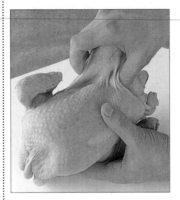 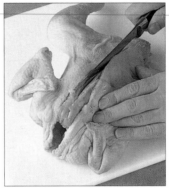 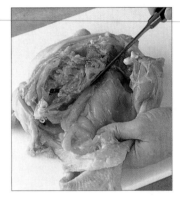

1 Dislocate each leg by breaking it at the thigh joint. Carefully remove the wishbone with a boning knife (see page 90).

2 With the bird breast-side down on the chopping board, cut down the center of the backbone from the neck to the tail end.

3 Working from the front of the bird to the back, carefully scrape away the flesh on one side of the backbone, cutting into the bird to expose the rib cage.

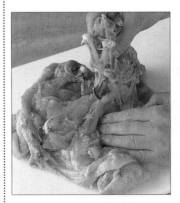  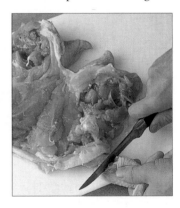

4 Repeat on the other side of the backbone, being careful not to pierce the breast skin with the knife. Pull the rib and backbone from the flesh of the bird.

5 Scrape away the flesh from each thigh bone and cut away the bone at the joint with a knife or poultry shears. Scrape all the flesh away from the wings up to the first joint.

6 Remove the exposed wing bone by cutting away the rest of the wing at the joint. Cut away the tendon from each fillet and breast. The chicken is now ready for stuffing and rolling.

STUFFING AND ROLLING

After careful boning and stuffing, the bird is rolled into a neat cylinder, wrapped in baking parchment, then foil, and tied securely with string. This holds the meat and stuffing tightly and makes a neat shape for easy slicing.

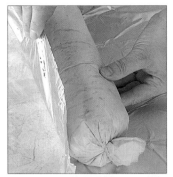

3 Dampen a large piece of baking parchment with water. Place the stuffed bird parallel to one long end of the paper, and roll the paper tightly around it, to make a cylinder. Twist the ends to seal. Place the wrapped bird on a large piece of foil and roll up in a similar way.

1 Season the inside of the whole boned bird with salt and pepper. Spread the stuffing (see page 96) evenly over the inside of the bird; pull up the sides of the bird to cover the stuffing.

2 Stitch the bird closed from the tail to neck end with a trussing needle (see page 91) and thread. Season the outside of the bird by rubbing the skin with salt and pepper.

4 Cut a piece of kitchen string about 1 yard long. Wrap the string first around the length of the cylinder, then several times around its width at regular intervals, securing the ends of the string with double knots.

POACHING AND SLICING

Ballotines are usually poached very slowly in water, stock or another flavored liquid, then left overnight and served cold. Cooling the meat in its wrapping allows it to set in the cylinder shape and as a result makes slicing easier. Ballotines can also be braised on a bed of vegetables, in which case they are rolled and tied but left unwrapped and generally served hot.

1 Weigh the ballotine and calculate the cooking time, allowing 20 minutes per 1 lb. Place in a pan, cover with stock and weight it down if necessary. Bring to the boil, then lower heat and poach for the calculated time.

2 Let the ballotine cool in the liquid. Lift out of the pan, cut string and unwrap. Snip one end of the thread and pull it out. Slice the ballotine and serve cold, with a garnish of your choice (see page 104).

Cailles Rôties Farcies Madame Brassart

This wonderfully rich dish of stuffed quails is named after the founder of Le Cordon Bleu, Madame Brassart. Boned quails, filled with a mixture of wild rice, foie gras, and cepes, are roasted and served with two sauces.

SERVES 4

4 quails

Goose fat or a mixture of butter and oil

Salt and freshly ground pepper

FOR THE STUFFING

3 oz. wild rice

1¼ cups chicken stock

4 oz. foie gras, cut into small cubes

5 oz. fresh cepes, cleaned and finely chopped

2 shallots, finely chopped

⅔ cup mixed fresh herbs (parsley, chervil, basil), chopped

1–2 tbsp. port or cognac

Pinch of quatre-épices or ground mixed spice

Fresh parsley and rosemary, to garnish

Bone the quails whole (see box, below). Roast the carcasses at 400°F for 10 minutes, then use the bones to flavor the port sauce (see box, right).

Make the stuffing: simmer the rice in the stock for 30–40 minutes until tender, and set aside. Season the foie gras with salt and pepper and sauté in a hot frying pan until the cubes are sealed on all sides. Add to the rice.

Heat 1 tbsp. goose fat in the frying pan and sauté the cepes until wilted. Add the shallots and herbs and sauté until the shallots are soft. Reserve a few cepes for

garnish; add the rest to the rice with the port and spice. Check seasoning and let cool.

Season inside the quails; fill them loosely with stuffing and truss. Heat 3 tbsp. goose fat in a roasting pan, and brown the quails on all sides. Roast the quails at 400°F for 15–20 minutes, basting occasionally. Remove from the oven and arrange the birds on a platter.

Reheat the port sauce and spoon some sauce around the quails. Garnish with parsley, rosemary, and the reserved cepes. Serve crème d'ail (see box, below left) and remaining sauce separately.

PORT SAUCE

7 oz. shallots, sliced

2 oz. butter

4 roasted quail carcasses

¼ cup sherry vinegar

1 cup port

3 cups chicken stock

1 sprig of fresh thyme

Sweat the shallots in butter. Add the carcasses and vinegar and boil until almost evaporated. Stir in the port and reduce by half, then add the stock and thyme and simmer for 20 minutes. Strain and season to taste.

CREME D'AIL

12 garlic cloves, peeled

¾ cup heavy cream

Blanch garlic cloves, drain and refresh. Put in a pan with cream. Cook for 10 minutes until garlic is soft. Continue cooking until reduced by half, then purée in a blender. If too thick, thin with chicken stock. Check seasoning.

Boning a Quail Whole

This clever technique removes the carcass from a tiny bird leaving it whole with its skin intact, and enabling it to retain its shape when it is stuffed. Because quails are so tiny, use a small pointed knife and your fingertips.

Remove the wishbone (see page 90). Loosen the leg bones from the carcass. Cut the wings from the carcass.

Insert a small knife between the rib cage and the flesh and scrape all around to free the flesh from the carcass.

When the carcass is free, pull it out with your fingers and roast the bones for using in the port sauce.

ROASTING BIRDS

Use a roasting pan that is only a little larger than the bird and cook on a rack or a bed of vegetables to prevent it from being fried underneath. Cover large birds halfway through cooking to prevent overbrowning.

ROASTING TIMES

The following roasting times are approximate, so test for doneness (see page 101) to be absolutely sure the bird is properly cooked. Before cooking, weigh the bird and calculate the total cooking time.

- CAPON
  375°F for 25 mins per 1 lb.

- CHICKEN
  400°F for 18 mins per 1 lb. plus an extra 18 mins

- GUINEA FOWL
  400°F for 15 mins per 1 lb. plus an extra 15 mins

- CORNISH GAME HEN
  400°F for 25–40 mins

- TURKEY
  350°F for 20 mins per 1 lb. under 10 lb.
  16–18 mins per 1 lb. over 10 lb.

ROASTING A WHOLE BIRD

Poultry and game birds have little natural fat, so to make sure the meat stays moist during roasting place fat on the skin before putting it in the oven. Butter gives a good flavor and blends with sediment in the pan to make rich-tasting juices or gravy (see opposite page).

 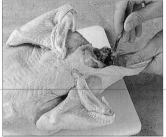 

1 Wipe the bird inside and out with paper towels. Season the cavity and insert flavorings (see below, right).

2 With the bird breast-side down, season the neck end and spoon in stuffing if you like (see below left).

3 Tuck drumsticks under tail skin, then put the bird on a rack in the pan. Cover breast generously with butter.

4 Roast the bird (see chart, left), basting frequently. Start cooking the bird on one of its sides for 15–20 minutes, then turn it over and cook on the other side for the same amount of time. Turn breast-side up for the remainder of the roasting time.

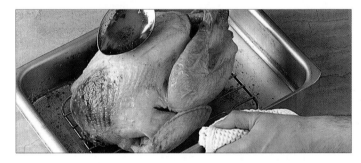

STUFFINGS FOR POULTRY

Sausage meat, bread crumbs and cooked rice are all good stuffing bases. Add seasonings and, for different textures, nuts and dried fruit. Prepare about 8 oz. for a 5 lb. bird and chill for at least 2 hours. Loosely stuff the neck end. Stuffing the body cavity can prevent heat from penetrating the center and is not recommended for large birds. Stuff the bird just before you roast it, and let it come to room temperature to ensure even cooking.

For a tasty meaty stuffing, mix sausage meat, chopped onion, nuts, parsley, raisins, apricots and bread crumbs. Bind with egg and season.

KEEPING POULTRY MOIST

When roasting any bird, but especially the drier kind like turkey and pheasant, it is important to keep the meat as moist as possible. Placing softened butter under the skin can help, or you can cover the bird loosely with buttered paper or foil. To brown the skin, remove the paper or foil for the last 20–30 minutes of cooking time. You can also cover the breast with bacon slices (see page 103) or with back fat, as the French do.

Another method to help keep a bird moist during roasting is to insert half of an onion or a lemon wedge inside the cavity of the bird before roasting.

TESTING FOR DONENESS

After roasting a bird for the recommended time, always check it for doneness.

Hold the bird above the pan. If the juices run clear, not pink, it is fully cooked.

CUTTING UP A ROASTED BIRD

Before cutting up small and medium-sized birds, let them rest for about 15 minutes under a loose tent of foil so the meat can relax and the juices settle. This will make carving easier. After resting, remove any trussing string and cut up the bird using a large chef's knife or carving knife. A two-pronged carving fork can be used to steady the bird.

1 Place the bird breast-side up. Cut each leg from the bird and then in half to separate the drumstick and thigh, following the line of white fat on the underside.

2 Hold the bird steady on the chopping board with a two-pronged fork. Carefully cut the breast in half by splitting the soft breastbone and backbone.

3 Cut each breast piece in half diagonally, leaving a good part of the breast meat attached to the wing. Arrange the pieces on a warmed serving platter.

CARVING A ROASTED BIRD

Turkeys and large chickens are best served with their meat carved into neat slices. Before carving, let the bird rest, as above, then snip away any trussing string and carve. The dark meat can also be sliced from the drumstick if you like.

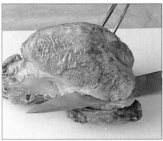

1 Remove the legs, cut them in half, and transfer to a warmed platter. Hold the bird steady with a fork and make a horizontal cut into the breast above the wing, cutting all the way to the bone.

2 Carve neat, even slices from the breast, holding the knife parallel to the rib cage. Repeat on the other side.

3 Arrange the slices of white meat, overlapping, on the platter with the drumsticks and thighs.

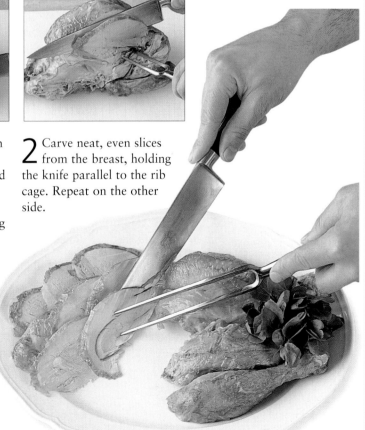

MAKING GRAVY

In France the juices (jus) from the pan are served with the bird; here they are thickened to make gravy.

Remove the bird from the pan and pour off all but about 1 tbsp. fat. Put the pan over a low heat, sprinkle in 1 tbsp. all-purpose flour and stir well.

Gradually whisk in 2 cups hot stock or water. Increase the heat and bring to the boil. Simmer, whisking, for 1–2 minutes. Check seasoning. Serves 6–8.

ROASTING TIMES

- DUCK
  350°F for 30 mins per 1 lb.

- GOOSE
  400°F for 15 mins per 1 lb.
  plus 15 mins

- GROUSE
  400°F for 35 mins

- PARTRIDGE
  400°F for 40 mins

- PHEASANT
  450°F for 10 mins, then 400°F
  for 30 mins

- QUAIL
  375°F for 15–20 mins

PREPARING A FATTY BIRD FOR ROASTING

When roasting a fatty bird such as a duck (shown here) or goose, remove as much fat as possible beforehand and place the bird on a rack so that it does not sit in melted fat during roasting. Cooking times are given in the chart, left.

1 With bird breast-side up, cut away excess fat from tail and tail cavity. Remove the wishbone (see page 90).

2 Season inside the tail cavity with salt and pepper, then insert 1–2 bay leaves and an orange wedge.

3 Place the bird breast-side up on a rack in a roasting pan. Pierce the bird all over with a metal skewer.

ROASTING AND CARVING DUCK

Weight for weight, duck serves less people than chicken, but because of its rich flavor, portions can be smaller. Small roast ducks are difficult to carve; they are best cut into four pieces as for an uncooked bird (see page 92).

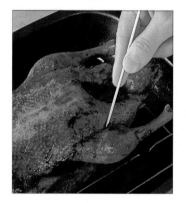

1 Roast the bird (see chart, above left) first on one of its sides, then on the other. Turn it breast-side up for the remainder of the time until the juices from the thickest part of a leg run clear. Let the duck rest, loosely covered with foil, for 15 minutes.

2 Place the duck breast-side up and cut the legs from the bird with a large chef's knife or carving knife. Cut down through the thigh joints to separate the legs from the body. Cut each wing away from the body of the duck at the shoulder joint.

3 On the main body of the bird, cut away one side of the breast meat in slices, moving inwards toward the breastbone. Repeat on the other side of the breast. Arrange the sliced breast, legs and wings on a warmed serving platter.

PREPARING AND ROASTING A GAME BIRD

The meat of young game birds is very lean, and therefore it tends to dry out easily during roasting. Barding the bird with fatty bacon helps make the flesh moist and flavorsome. A simple recipe for roast pheasant, using the techniques shown here, is given in the box, right.

1 Remove the wishbone (see page 90) before roasting so that the breast of the bird will be easy to carve.

2 Trim the wings by cutting through the second joint. Rinse the cavity, then wipe dry with paper towels. Truss the bird (see page 90).

3 Season the skin if you like, then cover loosely with bacon slices around the breast and thighs.

4 Roast the bird (see chart, opposite page) until the juices from the thickest part of a leg run clear, and the tip of a knife feels warm to the touch when withdrawn. Leave to rest, covered loosely with foil, for 10–15 minutes before carving.

ROAST PHEASANT WITH WINE GRAVY

2 lb. pheasant
Salt and freshly ground pepper
3–4 slices centercut bacon
2 tsp. all-purpose flour
1 cup red wine

Prepare the pheasant for roasting (see steps 1–3, left), then place on a rack in a roasting pan. Roast at 450°F for 10 minutes, then at 400°F for 30 minutes.

Remove the bird, cover loosely with foil, and let rest for 10–15 minutes. Place the pan on top of the stove. Sprinkle in the flour, stir over a low heat for 2 minutes, then gradually whisk in the wine. Increase the heat and bring to the boil, then simmer, whisking, until thickened. Check seasoning. Serve the pheasant hot, with the gravy and accompaniments (see box, below). Serves 2.

ACCOMPANIMENTS FOR GAME BIRDS

There are many traditional accompaniments for game birds, and these are given in the box on page 104. Here are some additional ideas that can also be used to highlight the texture and flavor of the bird.

• Glazed carrot bâtons.
• Roast parsnips.
• Bunches of fragrant fresh herbs.
• Garlic flowers (see page 189).
• Watercress bundles.
• Braised sliced red cabbage, onion and apple with port.

ORIENTAL ROAST DUCK

Based on Chinese tradition, a duck is often hung to dry, glazed, and then roasted. Peking duck with its crispy, lacquered skin is the most famous example of this roasting method. There are various stages to the technique.

MAKING CHINESE SEASONING MIX

An aromatic mixture of garlic, ginger, chilies, and scallions is combined with spices and herbs to impart a delicate Oriental flavor to roast duck.

Heat a wok until hot. Add 2 tsp. vegetable oil and heat until hot but not smoking. Add 3 finely chopped garlic cloves, 1 tbsp. crushed fresh ginger, 2 finely chopped and seeded fresh red chilies and 2 sliced scallions and stir-fry until fragrant and just soft, about 2 minutes. Add 2 tsp. toasted and crushed Szechuan peppercorns, 2 tbsp. each yellow bean sauce and soy sauce and stir-fry to mix, then remove from the heat and let cool. Stir in 2 tbsp. chopped fresh cilantro. just before applying to the skin of the bird to be roasted.

PREPARING THE DUCK

Before roasting, boiling water is poured over the duck. This tightens the skin and seals the pores so that the skin will be crisp when cooked.

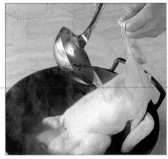

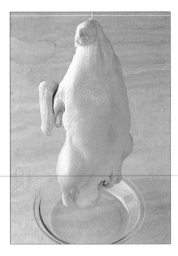

1 Trim away the excess fat from the tail end of the duck. Cut a long piece of kitchen string and tie it in a double knot around the fat at the neck end of the duck.

2 Bring about 2 quarts water to the boil in a wok. Hold the duck in the water and ladle it over the duck until the skin becomes taut. Remove the duck and pat dry.

3 Hang the duck over a dish to catch the drips. Leave in a cool (50°F), airy place until the skin is dry, about 3 hours.

ROASTING THE DUCK

Once the duck is dried, the cavity is stuffed with Chinese seasoning mix and the skin is basted with maltose mixed with water. During roasting the flesh of the bird will take on the flavor of the Chinese seasoning and the skin will become crisp and dark in color.

1 Soak a bamboo skewer in water for 30 minutes. Cut the string from the air-dried duck. Put the duck on a rack over a roasting pan. Spoon Chinese seasoning mix (see box, left) into the body cavity.

2 Thread the soaked bamboo skewer through the skin at the tail end of the duck to ensure that it remains closed while cooking. Roast the duck in a 400°F oven for 15 minutes.

3 Remove the duck from the oven and brush with maltose (see opposite page) and water. Lower the heat to 350°F and continue to roast, basting every 15 minutes, until the duck is dark brown, 1½–1¾ hours.

CARVING THE DUCK

This is the classic Chinese method for carving roast duck. The pieces are reassembled on the serving plate in the shape of the bird. Garnish with sprigs of fresh cilantro, if you like.

MALTOSE

This dark syrupy sugar solution is made from the fermented grains of barley, wheat or millet in a process sometimes called malting. It has been produced in China since the 2nd century BC and is commonly used in Chinese cooking for darkening the skin of roasted poultry and meat. Kept sealed, it will last indefinitely. Look for it at Oriental stores and large supermarkets.

To use it for Oriental roast duck, mix 1 tbsp. maltose with 4 tbsp. boiling water. If maltose is not available, you can use molasses instead.

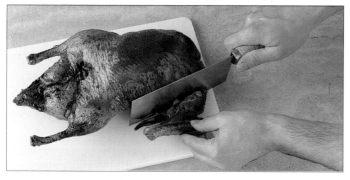

1 Let the duck rest for 15 minutes to allow the meat to retain its moisture and then place, with the breast-side up, on a chopping board. Carefully remove the bamboo skewer from the tail flap. Cut each wing away from the body at the shoulder joint with a cleaver or large chef's knife. Cut each wing in half at the middle joint.

2 Remove each leg from the bird, cutting down through the thigh joint with a cleaver to separate it from the body. Cut the thigh from the drumstick at the joint between them.

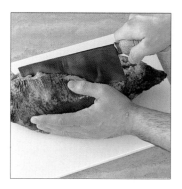

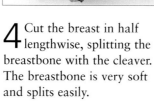

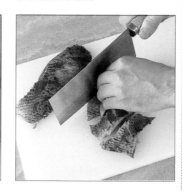

3 Turn the duck on its side and cut away the whole breast from the body, cutting through the rib bones and leaving the backbone behind. Cut the backbone and the meat still attached to it across into pieces.

4 Cut the breast in half lengthwise, splitting the breastbone with the cleaver. The breastbone is very soft and splits easily.

5 Cut each half breast across into roughly equal pieces, cutting down through the breastbone.

6 Arrange the meat on a warmed platter in the shape of the duck, starting with the wings, thighs and drumsticks. Pile the pieces of back on top, followed by the pieces of breast.

FRYING

Pieces of poultry and game can be panfried, deep-fried, sautéed or stir-fried. These are all quick-cooking methods so small pieces or breasts are the most suitable. The pieces can be fried plain, coated or stuffed.

PANFRYING A BREAST OF DUCK

Duck breasts can be "dry-fried" in their own fat and juices because they are so fatty. For successful results, trim and score the fat first (see page 95). Begin skin-side down, in a dry pan over a moderate heat, so the fat runs into the pan.

1 Season the duck breast. and place skin-side down in a frying pan. Cook for 3–5 minutes, pressing with a spatula to extract the juices and keep the breast flat.

2 Turn the breast and cook for another 3–5 minutes (duck breast is best medium rare). Remove from the pan and let rest, covered. With the skin-side up and knife at a slant, cut thin, diagonal slices.

MAKING SCHNITZELS

Scallops cut from the breast (see page 94) can be panfried plain or coated with seasoned flour. Coating them in egg and bread crumbs protects the delicate flesh. If you refrigerate them, uncovered, for one hour before panfrying, the coating will harden to give a crisper result.

1 Season each scallop; dip in flour and beaten egg, then coat in fresh or dried bread crumbs, pressing them firmly onto the meat.

2 Make criss-cross scores on the scallop with the back of a chef's knife. Heat enough oil and butter in a frying pan to just cover the bottom.

3 When the butter is foaming add the scallop. Cook over a moderate heat for 2–3 minutes on each side. Drain on paper towels. Serve.

STUFFING AND FRYING A CHICKEN BREAST

Boneless chicken breasts make perfect pockets for holding stuffings. Butter or soft cheese mixed with crushed garlic and/or herbs is the classic stuffing; chopped mushrooms, garlic and fresh herbs also work well, as do chopped spinach and ricotta. Take care not to overfill the pocket or it may burst during cooking. The parcels can be fried plain or coated as for schnitzels above.

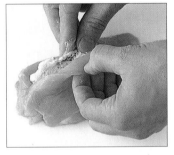

1 Cut a pocket 1–1½ in. deep in the side of the breast, without puncturing the base of the pocket. Fill with stuffing.

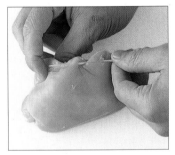

2 Secure the opening by threading a soaked wooden toothpick through the cut edges of the breast.

3 Heat a little olive oil in a nonstick frying pan – just enough to cover the bottom of the pan. Add the parcels and cook, turning once, until golden on both sides, about 15 minutes. Remove the toothpicks before serving.

CHARGRILLING SCALLOPS

One of the simplest ways to fry scallops is on a ridged cast-iron stovetop grill pan. The ridges on the pan give the meat a striped "chargrilled" effect, which is very attractive and looks as if the meat has been barbecued. The scallops are best simply fried in a good quality virgin olive oil or a nut oil, or a mixture of oil and butter if you like. Deglazing the pan with balsamic vinegar adds to the flavor and is one of the simplest ways to make an instant sauce.

1 Brush a little olive oil over the pan and heat until hot but not smoking. Add the scallops and cook over a moderate heat for 5 minutes, turning once. Add 1–2 tbsp. balsamic vinegar and stir into the pan juices to make a tasty sauce.

2 Serve the scallops on a bed of crisp rocket, as shown here, or on other leaves such as baby spinach or oakleaf lettuce. Spoon the pan juices over the top of the scallops and salad leaves as a dressing.

SAUTEING PIECES

Sautéing is the technique of turning joints or pieces in a pan over a high heat to seal and brown the skin. Turning prevents the meat from burning on the outside before the inside is properly cooked. Use a good quality virgin olive oil or a mixture of oil and butter. Duck can be sautéed in its own fat.

In a flameproof casserole or sauté pan, heat about 2 tbsp. oil to a high heat. Add the poultry pieces and cook until they begin to brown, turning them frequently with a fork or tongs to ensure they color evenly. Reduce the heat to moderate and cook for 25–30 minutes or until done – the juices should run clear.

STIR-FRYING STRIPS OF POULTRY

Cut skinless, boneless breasts of chicken, turkey or duck across the grain into strips (see page 95). Coat and stir-fry as shown here, then stir-fry vegetables, liquid and flavorings in the wok according to your chosen recipe. Finally, return the strips to the wok and toss with the other ingredients.

1 Stir the poultry strips in a mixture of egg white and cornstarch until evenly coated. For ½ lb. chicken use 1 egg white and 1 tbsp. cornstarch, mixed until smooth.

2 Heat a wok until hot. Add 2 tbsp. vegetable oil and heat until hot but not smoking. Add the poultry. Toss over a moderate heat for 5 minutes, or until tender. Remove with a slotted spoon or spatula.

POACHING

A whole chicken poached in a flavorsome broth is one of the most delicate dishes. You can also poach chicken breasts or thighs, with or without stuffing. Poached chicken meat is perfect for potpie fillings and sandwiches.

POACHING A WHOLE BIRD

Gentle poaching is one of the classic ways of cooking a chicken. It leaves the meat tender and juicy, and produces a delicious broth. Trussing the chicken first (see page 90) ensures it retains its shape during cooking, while the weight of the bird determines the poaching time – allow 20 minutes per 1 lb, poaching over a gentle heat on top of the stove.

1 Truss the chicken, including the neck end if you like, and place in a large pan. Pour over enough cold water just to cover the chicken. Bring the liquid slowly to the boil over a moderate heat.

2 Skim the surface with a slotted spoon. Lower the heat and add sliced carrots, onions and a bouquet garni. Poach, partially covered, for the calculated cooking time.

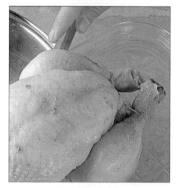

3 When the chicken is tender, remove from the poaching liquid, holding it over the pan so that as much liquid as possible drains from the bird. Remove the trussing string and cut the chicken into pieces (see page 93). Use the poaching liquid as a basic chicken stock or reduce and thicken to make a sauce.

SHREDDING POACHED POULTRY

The firm breast meat is best suited to this technique. Remove the breasts from the carcass while still warm – they will come away more easily. Begin shredding at the tip of the breast and work along to the other end, using a fine-pronged large fork.

Place the chicken breast side up on a chopping board and pull off the skin. Remove the breasts from the carcass and shred the meat with the prongs of a fork. Remove the leg and wing meat from the carcass with your fingers; use as bite-sized pieces or shred if you like.

POACHING PINWHEELS

This clever technique is surprisingly simple – chicken breasts are cut open, then rolled around a filling. After cooking, the rolls are sliced crosswise to reveal pinwheel shapes. For the filling, use colorful, juicy ingredients, such as bell pepper strips, spinach, herbs, and soft cheese. Here the rolls are foil-wrapped and poached; they can be wrapped in bacon and roasted.

1 Cut through one long side of a skinless, boneless chicken breast, leaving it attached on the opposite side. Detach the fillet and set aside.

2 Open the breast out flat, cut-side up. Put it between two sheets of baking parchment and pound with a rolling pin or meat mallet to flatten and stretch it. Remove the top sheet of parchment. Spread your chosen stuffing (in this case goat's cheese and chopped spinach) evenly over the cut side.

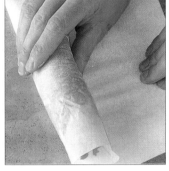

3 Replace the fillet in the center of the breast, parallel to the long sides. Starting from one long side, roll the meat into a cylinder.

4 Roll the paper around the cylinder, pulling it tightly as you go, and twist the ends to seal. Wrap in foil and twist the ends as before.

5 Bring a pan of water to the boil and add the roll. Poach, covered, over a gentle heat for 15 minutes or until a metal skewer feels warm when withdrawn from the center. Remove from the pan, unwrap, and slice crosswise on the diagonal.

THE ASIAN ALTERNATIVE

Asian chefs often prefer to retain the succulence of chicken breasts by poaching or steaming them in wrappers that also enclose flavor-imparting ingredients, such as lemongrass.

1 Cut a banana leaf into four squares, each one large enough to enclose a chicken breast. Brush each center with a 1:1 hoisin and soy sauce mix. Place a chicken breast on each and top with lemon grass and a few slices of fresh ginger. Spoon over more soy sauce.

2 Wrap each leaf square around the chicken breast to make a neat parcel and secure with string if necessary. Place 1–2 packages at a time in a steamer basket over simmering water and cook for 15 minutes. Serve the chicken breasts in their banana leaves to be unwrapped at the table.

CASSEROLING & POT ROASTING

These are long, slow-cooking methods that give depth of flavor and unrivalled tenderness to any type of poultry or game, both whole birds and pieces on the bone. Cooking can be on top of the stove or in the oven.

COQ AU VIN

2½–3 lb. chicken, cut into
  6 serving pieces (see page 93)
4 tbsp. vegetable oil
1 tbsp. all-purpose flour
9 oz. carrots, sliced
1 onion, chopped
2 bay leaves
Salt and freshly ground pepper
6 oz. mushrooms, sliced

MARINADE
3 cups red wine
1 carrot, chopped
1 onion, chopped
2 garlic cloves, chopped
1 bouquet garni
4–5 juniper berries
1 tsp. whole black peppercorns
¾ cup red wine vinegar

Cook marinade ingredients, except vinegar, for 15 minutes. Transfer to a bowl and let cool. Stir in the vinegar; add the chicken. Sprinkle over half the oil; cover and refrigerate overnight.

  Remove the chicken and strain the marinade. Heat the remaining oil in a flameproof casserole; add the chicken. Sauté until brown. In another pan, boil the marinade. Skim any blood from the surface.

  Sprinkle the chicken with flour, add the remaining ingredients and stir over a moderate heat for a few minutes. Add the marinade and bring to the boil. Cook in a 350°F oven for 1 hour or until tender. Add the mushrooms for the last 15 minutes. Check seasoning. Serves 4–6

MARINATING AND CASSEROLING IN WINE

Poultry pieces are tenderized by being steeped and slowly simmered in a concentrated cooked red wine marinade. This is the technique behind the classic French coq au vin *(see box, left). For a fuller flavor, let the casserole go cold, preferably overnight. Reheat well before serving.*

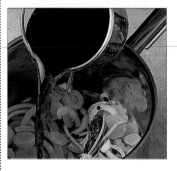  

1 Cook the vegetables for the marinade in wine so that they will soften and impart flavor.

2 Let the marinade cool before adding the chicken or the chicken will begin to cook before marinating.

3 Sprinkle oil over the surface of the marinade to help contain strong odors during marinating.

4 Make sure the chicken pieces are thoroughly dry before adding them to the hot oil, otherwise they will not brown evenly.

5 Add the strained marinade to the casserole after it has been boiled and skimmed; this will eliminate any coagulated blood.

6 When the chicken is done, the sauce will be thick and rich and the chicken will feel tender when pierced with a skewer. Let stand for 10–15 minutes before serving, to allow the flavors to mellow and the fibers in the meat to settle.

POT ROASTING TOUGH GAME BIRDS

Small game birds, such as quail and grouse, can be dry and tough, so they are suited to slow, moist methods of cooking. Wrapping the birds in bacon adds flavor and protects the flesh; tying helps to keep the birds in a neat shape. Marinating before cooking (see box, right) will help moisten, flavor and tenderize the flesh.

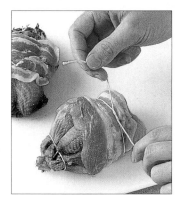

1 Tuck the neck skin and wings underneath the birds and tie the legs together with string. Season the birds, then wrap bacon slices around them, and tie in place with kitchen string.

2 Heat 2 tbsp. oil in a large, flameproof casserole. Brown the birds, turning them occasionally by hooking a two-pronged carving fork under the trussing string.

3 Add carrots and onions to the pan, with salt and pepper to taste. Sweat the vegetables for 5 minutes over a gentle heat, stirring with a wooden spoon to incorporate any sediment from the bottom of the pan.

4 Pour enough red wine to cover the birds halfway. Cover and simmer very gently until the birds are tender and the sauce reduced, about 30 minutes on the stovetop, or 1 hour in a 350°F oven. Check seasoning and serve.

MARINADES FOR TOUGH BIRDS

Marinades add flavor to meat, and help tenderize it. This is because most marinades contain an acid such as wine or fruit juice which helps break down tough fibers. Fresh pineapple juice is most effective as it contains a special enzyme that breaks down proteins and tenderizes meat.

- Fresh pineapple juice mixed with grated lemon zest.
- Lemon juice, crushed garlic and dried red pepper flakes.
- Red wine, cranberry juice and juniper berries.
- Orange juice, lime juice, cracked peppercorns, coriander seeds and chopped fresh chili.
- White wine, cider vinegar, cumin seeds, allspice berries and cinnamon stick.
- Red wine, cinnamon stick and cracked cloves.
- Sherry vinegar, oil, thyme, sage and bay leaf.
- Red wine, rosemary and marjoram.

TERRINES & PATES

Any bone and sinew free poultry or game meat can be ground up and turned into a spreadable pâté, or molded and cooked as a terrine. Don't overcook the meat; pâtés and terrines are best when moist and juicy.

CHICKEN LIVER PATE

9 oz. chicken livers
4 tbsp. unsalted butter, softened
2 tbsp. brandy
Salt and freshly ground pepper
2–4 tbsp. lukewarm liquid clarified
    butter (see page 227)

Toss chicken livers in about one-third of the butter until they change color, about 5 minutes. Remove from the pan and purée in a food processor with the remaining butter and the brandy. Add seasonings to taste. Transfer the pâté to four ramekins, smooth the surface, then cover with clarified butter. Cool, then chill in the refrigerator. Serves 4.

MAKING A PANFRIED LIVER PATE

One of the easiest ways to make a pâté is by panfrying livers quickly, working them to a fine or coarse purée in a food processor, then chilling until firm in the refrigerator. Chicken livers are favored because of their mild flavor and soft texture. Take care not to overcook them or they will toughen.

COOKING THE LIVERS
Keep them moving in hot butter in the center of the pan, so they do not stick or burn, until pink tinged.

ADDING CLARIFIED BUTTER
Spoon liquid clarified butter over the pâté to keep it airtight – the mixture may discolor in contact with air.

MAKING A RABBIT TERRINE

The technique here is to contrast a creamy, smooth farce with thin slivers of tender meat to make an easy layered terrine. The addition of aspic after baking helps keep the terrine moist. It also gives the terrine a professional-looking finish.

FARCE FOR RABBIT TERRINE

3 lb. rabbit
2 shallots, roughly chopped
2 eggs
¾ cup heavy cream
2 tbsp. shelled pistachios
1 tbsp. dried cranberries
2 tbsp. chopped fresh parsley
Freshly grated nutmeg
Salt and freshly ground pepper

Cut up the rabbit (see page 93), then remove the meat from the bones. Set aside the best pieces, and grind the rest in a food processor with the shallots. Work in the eggs and cream, then turn the mixture into a bowl and mix in the nuts, dried cranberries, parsley and seasonings to taste.

1 Line a 9 x 5 x 3 in. loaf pan or 1½ quart terrine with about 15 bacon slices. Make sure there are no gaps and allow the ends to overhang.

2 Put half the farce (see box, left) in the terrine, cover with pieces of rabbit in an even layer, then spoon in the remaining farce.

3 Fold over the overhanging bacon slices, arranging them in a pattern. Cover the mold and bake in a *bain marie* at 400°F for 2 hours.

4 Slowly pour 1¼–1½ cups liquid aspic (see page 19) over the terrine. Add it a little at a time so that it soaks in. Let cool, then refrigerate until set before slicing.

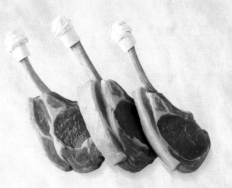

MEAT

•

CHOOSING BEEF & VEAL

Buy your meat from a reliable source, a high turnover will help to indicate fresh stock. Look for good butchering techniques – large cuts should follow the contours of the muscle and bone. Smaller cuts should be neat and well trimmed with little sinew, and any bones should be smooth with no sign of splinters.

SMOOTH fine-grained flesh that is creamy white with a pale grayish-pink tinge is best. Any outer fat should be firm and white.

AN EVEN marbling of fat in the meat is a good indication of high quality.

OUTER LAYER of fat should be creamy white and smooth; yellow fat can indicate the meat is past its best except in grassreared beef.

LOOK FOR deep red, moist-looking meat with a generous marbling of fat throughout.

BUYING BEEF AND VEAL

Though the age of the animal from which it came, and its breed and feed will be reflected in the meat, the best beef and veal will smell fresh and have clean looking flesh that is not too bright in color. Meat with a greenish-gray tinge and an "off" smell should be avoided.

Look for cuts that are uniform in thickness to aid even cooking, and that have a moist, freshly cut surface; avoid wet meat that is slimy to the touch. Always check the "use by" dates to ensure freshness. Leaner cuts last longer than fatty cuts because fat goes rancid before meat.

Buying the freshest and best quality meat is always worthwhile, but you must be prepared to pay a little more for organically-raised beef.

HANDLING BEEF AND VEAL

Remove meat from its original wrapping as soon as possible after purchase and place on a plate or in a dish to catch any blood. Loosely cover, then store in the coldest part of the refrigerator (34–40°F) away from cooked meats.

Ground meat and small cuts of veal are best eaten on the day you buy them. Smaller roasts, chops and steaks will keep for 2–3 days and large roasts up to 5 days.

Freezing beef and veal quickly reduces the chance of damage to the texture or succulence of the meat; smaller pieces freeze more successfully than large cuts. For convenience, freeze cuts tightly wrapped in individual portions; use veal within 6 months and beef within 1 year. Defrost, loosely wrapped, in the refrigerator allowing 5 hours per 1 lb.

BEEF & VEAL CUTS

Beef cuts are the most variable of meats and offer the cook the greatest culinary scope. Milk-fed veal is very delicate in flavor and texture and should be cooked in ways that preserve these qualities such as broiling or barbecuing. Calves that are fed both milk and straw will have darker pink flesh but this does not alter the eating quality. Choose cuts suitable for the chosen cooking method – leaner cuts benefit from quick cooking, tougher cuts require long, slow cooking to tenderize them.

BEEF CUTS	WHAT TO LOOK FOR	COOKING METHODS
CHUCK	*Large lean joint, with some connective tissue* *Marbled with some outer fat* *Also sold boned or cubed*	Stew, braise
FILLET/TENDERLOIN	*Lean with light marbling* *No outer layer of fat*	Roast (whole), broil, panfry, barbecue (smaller cuts)
RIB	*Lean meat with obvious layers of fat and some marbling* *Creamy white bone* *Even layer of outer fat*	Roast, braise, pot roast (boned and rolled).
GROUND MEAT	*Pale meat indicates high fat content; darker color means leaner meat* *Look for % fat declared on package*	Use for pasta sauces, potpies, burgers, stuffings
SIRLOIN	*Lean with light marbling* *Even outer layer of creamy white fat*	Roast (with bone or boned)
STEAK	*Lean meat with light marbling* *Creamy white bone with no splinters*	Broil, panfry or barbecue
TOP ROUND	*Lean with little marbling* *Separate layer of fat tied around outside*	Braise, pot roast, roast

VEAL CUTS

BREAST	*Lean meat with light marbling* *Thin even outer layer of white fat*	Roast, pot roast, braise, stew, roast, braise (boned and stuffed)
RIB CHOP	*Very light marbling, smooth, white bone* *Even outer layer of white fat*	Broil, barbecue
FORESHANK	*High proportion of white bone – smooth, no splinters* *Pink lean flesh, some connective tissue*	Braise (osso buco), stew
LOIN	*Lean meat, bones smooth and white* *Thin uneven outer layer of white fat*	Roast (whole), panfry, broil, barbecue (chops)
POTPIE/STEWING	*Lean with some connective tissue* *Usually cubed*	Stew, casserole
SHOULDER	*Clear pink flesh with light marbling* *Visible connective tissue, white outer fat*	Roast, braise
BOTTOM ROUND (SCALLOPS)	*Very lean, pale pink* *No outer fat*	Lard and braise or roast (whole), broil, panfry, barbecue

BEEF AND VEAL ON THE MENU

Generally more expensive than poultry, there are beef and veal classics that range from the rustic to the divine.

FRANCE – *Boeuf Bourguignon* (a slowly simmered beef stew flavored with smoked bacon, red wine and mushrooms) creates a deliciously tender meat in a rich sauce.

HUNGARY – *Goulash* (cubes of chuck steak simmered in a paprika-scented stock) is thickened with sour cream and sprinkled with additional paprika before serving.

ITALY – *Osso Buco* (veal braised in a rich vegetable, tomato and wine stock) was originally created by chefs in Milan.

JAPAN – *Teriyaki Beef* (steak with a soy sauce, sherry and sugar marinade) is stir-fried with peppers and onions.

MEXICO – *Fajitas* (steak marinated in spices and lime juice) is served in *tortillas* with avocado, sour cream and *salsa*.

UNITED STATES – *Chili con carne* (cubed chuck steak, beef stock and red kidney beans. Modern variations may include tomatoes, peppers, black beans, cilantro and sour cream) may have a Spanish name, but the flavors are pure Texas.

PREPARING FOR COOKING

Beef and veal offer a wide range of cuts from lean, tender steaks that need only brief cooking, to tougher, but flavorful cuts such as shin that benefit from slow braising. Correct and careful preparation is essential.

WHAT'S IN A NAME?

Very lean meat requires extra fat to help keep it moist as it cooks. Use chilled pork fat to make handling easier.

LARDING: This technique is used for moistening lean meat flesh from the inside during cooking. Small pieces of pork fat (lardons) inserted into the flesh will melt, making the meat more succulent. To add extra flavor, season the fat or marinate it for at least 1 hour before larding.

BARDING: Lean meat can be wrapped in pork fat to keep it moist and help retain the shape of the meat. The barding fat will disappear during cooking; if any remains it should be discarded before serving, unless decoratively applied (see right).

PREPARING ROASTS

Some cuts, such as the rib shown here, have thick outer layers of fat which need trimming before cooking.

Trim the fat from the underside of the meat. Leave a thin layer on the surface to help keep the flesh moist.

PREPARING STEAKS

Steaks need to be trimmed and scored before cooking. First cut away some of the excess fat, leaving an even layer sufficient to flavor the meat during cooking, then cut through the fat into the thin membrane at regular intervals. This prevents the steak from curling as it cooks. Sirloin steaks are illustrated here; round steaks require the same technique.

1 Trim off the outer layer of fat with a boning knife, leaving ½ in. fat next to the meat. Discard the fat.

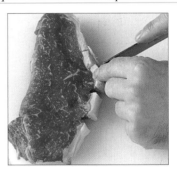

2 Cut through the fat at regular intervals with a chef's knife or snip with kitchen shears.

LARDING AND BARDING

Some cuts lack natural fat, and if they are to be roasted or braised it may be necessary to add fat to keep them tender and succulent. This can be done internally by larding, or externally by barding.

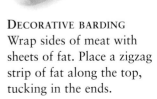

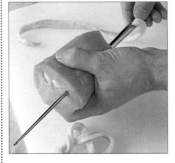

LARDING
Insert a larding needle into the meat following the grain. Thread the needle with chilled pork fat, then pull through.

SIMPLE BARDING
Wrap a thin layer of fat around the outside of the meat and tie in place with string (see opposite page).

DECORATIVE BARDING
Wrap sides of meat with sheets of fat. Place a zigzag strip of fat along the top, tucking in the ends.

BONING A BREAST OF VEAL

Roasts can be cooked with the bone in or out. Boned roasts cook more evenly and are much easier to carve into neat slices. After boning, the meat is ready for rolling and tying, with or without a stuffing, or for cutting into pieces.

1 Outline the rib bones, with the tip of a boning knife. Cut the bones away from the meat beneath.

2 Cut through the cartilage and around the breast-bone. Remove the bone.

3 Remove the rib bones. Trim the breast of any cartilage, sinew or excess fat.

ROLLING, STUFFING AND TYING

Boneless meat can be tied to make neat packages for roasting or braising, hold barding fat in place (see opposite page) or keep a rolled stuffed roast together. Stuffings add flavor and help lubricate the meat from inside; they also help "stretch" the meat and make it go further.

1 Place the boned breast, skin-side down, on a board. Spread the stuffing evenly over the surface.

2 Starting from the thick end, roll up the meat, smoothing it into a neat shape for tying.

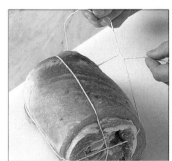

3 Wrap the string twice around the length of the roll. Tie off, but do not cut.

4 Wrap the string around one hand and tuck the end of the string over it to create a loop. Slip the loop on to the meat and tighten. Repeat along the roll. Knot the ends to secure.

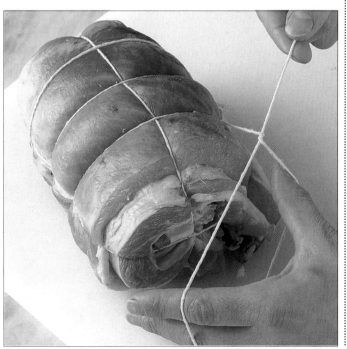

(see opposite page)

TRICK OF THE TRADE

SIMPLE TYING

Instead of the butcher's technique in steps 3 and 4 left, you can use a series of knots to tie a whole beef fillet into a neat shape for even cooking.

Wrap a length of kitchen string lengthwise around the fillet, tie it securely and trim the ends. Tie another piece of string around the center of the meat. Secure this piece with a double knot and trim the ends. Starting at one end, work toward the center of the fillet, tying pieces of string at about 1 in. intervals knotting and trimming the ends as you go.

121

BEEF CARPACCIO

1¼–1½ lb. fillet of beef in one
 piece
Salt and freshly ground pepper
⅓ cup extra virgin olive oil
Juice of 1 lemon
Shredded fresh basil
A few capers
Parmesan curls
 (see box, page 236)

Trim the beef of any excess fat
and membrane (see right), then
wrap in foil, freeze and slice very
thinly (see right).

  Arrange the slices of beef on
individual serving plates, slightly
overlapping them so they
completely cover the surface.

  Just before serving, lightly
season the slices with salt and
pepper, drizzle with the olive oil
and lemon juice and sprinkle with
shredded basil, capers and
Parmesan curls. Serves 4

TRICK OF THE TRADE

TENDER STEAKS
*Meat that is to be cooked
quickly can be tenderized
by pounding, which helps
break up the connective
tissues. A rolling pin can
be used instead of the
cleaver shown here.*

Place the steak on a chopping
board. Pound the steak all over,
using the flat side of a cleaver.

TRIMMING AND SLICING A FILLET OF BEEF

*The fillet is the finest cut of beef – lean and meltingly tender.
It is a classic cut for roasting, either plain or stuffed, with or
without a pastry casing (see page 125). Sliced, it can produce
tournedos or fillet steaks, châteaubriand, very thick steak from
the center of the fillet, or strips for stir-frying.*

1 Remove the chain muscle
from the side of the main
fillet. Cut away the sinewy
membrane, sliding the blade
of the knife underneath and
holding the membrane away
with the other hand.

2 Slice the fillet crosswise
into slices about 1 in.
thick. Cut them thicker at the
narrow end, then pound them
with the flat side of a cleaver
or meat mallet.

SLICING BEEF WAFER THIN

*Placing meat in the freezer
firms up the fibers and makes
it very easy to slice. Use this
technique for carpaccio (see
box, left) or stir-fries.*

Wrap a piece of trimmed beef
fillet tightly in foil and place
in the freezer for 1–4 hours,
depending on size. Remove
from the freezer and slice
very thinly using a sawing
action. Allow to thaw.

CUTTING MEAT FOR STEWING

*For long, slow cooking, such as stewing and braising, you can use cuts like the chuck steak
shown here, skirt or shin of beef or shoulder or breast meat of veal. During the cooking process
the tough muscle should soften and the gelatinous tissues break down and melt into the sauce,
making it rich and velvety. For this to happen the meat must be cut into even-sized pieces,
either cubes or strips, so that they cook evenly.*

1 Trim any excess fat and
sinew from around the
meat using a boning knife.
Discard the fat.

2 Cut the meat across the
grain into 1–2 in. wide
slices, using a chef's knife.
Turn each slice on its side and
cut in half lengthwise.

3 Cut across each slice of
meat to give 1–2 in. cubes.
The meat is now ready for
stewing or braising.

GRINDING

Although ground meat can be bought already prepared, grinding your own means you can choose the cuts you use. Lean cuts with a little marbling are the most suitable. This simple technique can be done using a grinder or by hand, using a pair of heavy chef's knives with very sharp blades that will cut the meat cleanly. For burgers, meat can also be chopped (see page 152).

BY MACHINE

This is suitable for large amounts and for tough cuts such as neck or flank. It produces a smooth texture ideal for sausages or burgers. Cube the meat (see opposite page) and feed small amounts at a time through the machine. Process a slice of bread at the end to ensure all the meat is pushed through.

BY HAND

This is the best method for small amounts or prime cuts such as round or fillet (it is always used for steak tartare in France). With a chef's knife in each hand, chop cubed meat using a rhythmic action.

ROLLING VEAL SCALLOPS

Scallops are lean pieces of veal cut at an angle from the leg fillet; the large, even slices require a light pounding before being coated and panfried. When rolled around a filling they are called paupiettes *in French,* saltimbocca *in Italian. The same techniques can be applied to beef fillet and top round.*

1 Lightly pound the scallop on a board between two pieces of baking parchment. Remove the paper and cut the scallop crosswise in half.

2 Place the filling of your choice (see box, right) on the meat, then roll the meat up around it and secure with a wooden toothpick. The meat is now ready for panfrying (see page 126).

STUFFINGS FOR VEAL SCALLOPS

Choose stuffings that are moist and provide a contrast in flavor and texture to the meat.

- For *saltimbocca* (see page 126), roll the veal around Parma ham and fresh sage leaves.
- Spread veal with a mixture of ricotta cheese and chopped spinach moistened with a little cream, sprinkle over a few toasted pine nuts and roll up.
- Mix strips of roasted peppers with fresh bread crumbs and shredded basil leaves.
- Combine ground veal with raisins, chopped chestnuts and chopped fresh herbs.
- Mix together equal quantities of cream cheese and crème fraîche and flavor with a few capers and grated lemon zest.

QUICK COOKING

Methods of quick cooking include roasting, for large prime cuts of meat such as rib or fillet of beef, and panfrying or broiling for small, tender pieces such as steaks and scallops. For roasting, bones can be left in, or they can be removed and the meat stuffed and rolled. The high heat sears the roast and produces a glossy crust, which seals in the juices.

MEAT THERMOMETER

The best way to tell if a roast is done is to use a meat thermometer. After searing the meat, insert the spike of the thermometer into the thickest part of the meat. Be careful not to touch any bone as this will give you an inaccurate reading. The reading should be 140°F for rare, 160°F for medium and 170°F for well-done.

ROASTING TIMES

All timings are approximate, and are based on minutes per 1 lb. at 350°F

- BEEF ON THE BONE
Rare	20 mins plus an extra 20 mins
Medium	25 mins plus an extra 25 mins
Well-done	30 mins plus an extra 30 mins

- BEEF OFF THE BONE
Rare	15 mins plus an extra 15 mins
Medium	20 mins plus an extra 20 mins
Well-done	25 mins plus an extra 25 mins

- VEAL ON/OFF THE BONE
  25 mins plus an extra 25 mins

ROASTING A RIB OF BEEF

Before cooking, let the meat come to room temperature for about 2 hours, then trim (see page 120). Weigh the meat, calculate the cooking time and preheat the oven (see chart, bottom left). Season the meat. Coat the bottom of the pan with oil, and heat on top of the stove until hot but not smoking. Place the roast in the pan and sear on all sides, about 5 minutes. If using a meat thermometer, insert it in the thickest part of the meat (see box, left).

1 Roast the meat in the preheated oven for the calculated cooking time, basting occasionally with a large metal spoon.

2 If no thermometer is used insert a skewer in the meat for 30 seconds. If cool when withdrawn the meat will be rare; if warm, medium.

CARVING A RIB OF BEEF

After removing the roast from the oven, cover it loosely with foil and let it rest for 10–15 minutes. This allows the juices on the surface to be reabsorbed into the flesh. When carving, use a two-pronged fork just to steady the roast; take care not to let it pierce the meat.

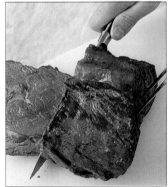

1 Place the rib upright on a board and steady it with a fork. Cut down along the bone between the meat and the ribs. Remove the bones.

2 Turn the roast on its side. Holding the roast with the fork and without piercing the meat, carve thin, even slices across the grain.

CARVING A ROLLED JOINT

Boned and rolled roasts, such as the breast of veal here, are very easy to carve. Rest the joint 10–15 minutes, then remove the string and carve.

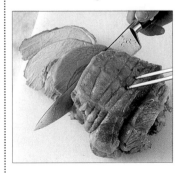

Place the roast seam-side down on a board. Holding it steady with a fork, carve the meat crosswise into slices with a sawing action.

ROASTING A WHOLE FILLET OF BEEF

Sear the trimmed and tied meat in hot oil before roasting to seal and brown the outside, then insert a meat thermometer, making sure the tip of the spike is in the center of the meat. A 3 lb. beef fillet roasted at 425°F should take about 20 minutes for rare meat, 25–30 minutes, medium-rare.

1 Season meat, then sear in hot oil, turning with tongs. Insert thermometer and place in preheated oven.

2 Baste frequently during roasting to keep meat moist. Check thermometer reading; remove from oven.

ROASTING A WHOLE FILLET OF BEEF EN CROUTE

This French technique produces rare beef in the center and crisp pastry on the outside. The secret lies in first seasoning and searing the fillet as in step 1 above, partially roasting it at 425°F for 20 minutes until just rare, then letting it cool and encasing it in crêpes to prevent the meat juices leaking into the crust.

1 Press *duxelles* (see page 170) around cooled 3 lb. beef fillet. Wrap in three 10 in. thin herb crêpes.

2 Roll out 1½ lb. puff pastry to ¼ in. thickness, then wrap around the fillet to enclose it completely.

3 Place parcel seam-side down and decorate the top and sides with a lattice of pastry trimmings.

4 Place the parcel on a dampened baking sheet and brush with egg wash (see page 31). Bake at 400°F for 10 minutes, then lower the heat to 350°F and bake for another 20 minutes until golden and crisp. Let rest for 10 minutes, then cut into slices to serve.

TRICK OF THE TRADE

STUFFING A FILLET

Professional chefs often slice and stuff a whole fillet of beef before roasting. This adds flavor and helps the meat retain moisture during cooking.

Sear the fillet (see step 1, above left) and let cool. Slice thickly, almost all the way through, then spoon *duxelles* (see page 170) or the stuffing of your choice between each slice. Reform the fillet, wrap in thin herb crêpes and pastry and roast (see left).

BEEF WELLINGTON

Filet de boeuf en croûte (fillet of beef in pastry) was a French culinary classic long before Wellington's time, but in honor of the English hero of the Battle of Waterloo it was renamed Beef Wellington – and the name has stuck. The dish was popular at early 19th-century banquets, and was known to be a particular favorite of the Duke of Wellington. Traditionally it is made with a mushroom stuffing mixed with diced bacon and fresh chopped herbs.

Duke of Wellington (1769–1852)

SLOW COOKING

Tough, sinewy cuts of meat require gentle slow cooking in aromatic liquids to allow time for fibrous tissues to soften and flavors to develop. Large and small pieces of meat can be cooked using this technique. For maximum flavor and tenderness, cool the meat in the liquid and reheat the next day.

POT ROASTING

Less prime cuts benefit from slow cooking in liquid. This tenderizes sinews and imparts a rich flavor to the meat. Suitable cuts are boned and rolled brisket, top and bottom round of beef; foreshank and round of veal. A 2 lb. boned and rolled roast takes about 2¹/₂ hours to cook.

1 For a good flavor and color at the end of cooking, first sear the meat over a high heat in a little oil, turning until evenly browned.

2 After browning, add stock or wine or a mixture of the two, chopped vegetables such as onions and leeks, plus a bouquet garni and seasonings. Simmer gently or cook at 325°F until tender. Add root vegetables about 30 minutes before the end of cooking.

MAKING A STEW

Stewing or casseroling is a very moist method of cooking, perfect for less prime meat such as flank, shin and chuck. For best results, trim meat of excess fat and sinew and cut into equal-sized cubes, then brown in a flameproof casserole. Add liquid just to cover and cook in the same casserole, either on top of the stove or in a 325°F oven. A stew made with 2 lb. meat takes 2–2¹/₂ hours to cook.

1 If the meat has been marinated, dry thoroughly on paper towels, then brown in batches over a high heat to seal in juices and add color to the sauce.

2 Test for doneness by inserting the point of a small knife into one of the pieces of meat. The blade should slide easily through the fibers.

BRAISING SINEWY CUTS

When choosing beef or veal for braising, select tough cuts with a good amount of bone but not too much fat, such as the shin of veal shown here. Sinew and gristle break down during cooking to enrich the sauce. Only a small amount of liquid is used, so keep the dish tightly covered. A simple recipe for osso buco, *using the techniques shown here, is given in the box, right.*

1 Brown the veal in hot oil. The coating of flour will form a crust around the meat and help thicken the sauce.

2 Turn the meat once or twice during braising so that it cooks evenly and takes on the flavor of the sauce.

COOKING SALT BEEF

Before refrigeration, meat was preserved by drying or salting in brine flavored with herbs, spices and sugar. Today this is not necessary, but salt beef is still popular for its unique flavor and attractive pink color. It is available at specialist butchers and some supermarkets.

Before cooking, soak salt beef in cold water overnight to remove excess saltiness. Drain and rinse in cold water, then place in a pan with roughly chopped vegetables, such as carrots, parsnips and potatoes, and freshly ground pepper. Cover with water and bring to the boil, then cover and simmer gently for 2 hours or until tender.

COOKING IN A CLAY POT

In the Middle East meat is often slow cooked in a clay pot – the steam condenses inside the tight-fitting lid of the pot, drips back into the stew and makes the meat wonderfully moist. The conical lid of the pot shown here, a Moroccan tagine, *is especially effective for this cooking method.*

1 First brown cubes of beef in hot oil in a frying pan, then place in the bottom of the pot with dried fruit such as prunes or apricots, thinly sliced lemon or orange zest, hot beef stock and seasonings.

2 Cover the pot tightly with its lid, sealing it with a flour and water paste if you like. Cook in a 325°F oven for 2 hours. Serve hot, sprinkled with chopped fresh herbs.

OSSO BUCO

2 lb. shin of veal, sawn into
  2 in. pieces
1 tbsp. plain flour
2–3 tbsp. olive oil
2 carrots, diced
2 onions, chopped
½ cup dry white wine
½ cup brown stock (see page 16)
13 oz. can tomatoes
1 tsp. dried mixed herbs
Salt and freshly ground pepper
Gremolata (see page 330)

Toss the meat in the flour. Heat the oil in a flameproof casserole and brown the meat. Remove, then add carrots and onions and sweat for 10 minutes. Return the meat to the pan and add the wine, stock, tomatoes, dried herbs and seasonings to taste. Cover and cook at 325°F for 2 hours or until tender, turning occasionally. Check the seasoning. Serve hot, sprinkled with gremolata. Serves 4.

Thai Beef

A salade tiède, or warm salad, this stunning dish is made with lean, tender beef in a zesty Asian dressing, garnished with crisp cucumber and sweet mango, and served with rice cooked in coconut milk.

SERVES 4

1½ lb. piece of rump steak, cut 1 in. thick

Vegetable oil

½ oz. fresh cilantro leaves

½ oz. fresh mint leaves

3 stalks of lemongrass, trimmed and finely chopped

FOR THE DRESSING

2 small fresh chilies, halved, deseeded and chopped

2 garlic cloves, peeled

1½ in. piece of fresh ginger, peeled and chopped

Juice of 1 lime

3 tbsp. light soy sauce

2 tbsp. vegetable oil

2 tsp. light brown sugar

TO SERVE

1 fresh red chili, halved lengthwise

1 cucumber, scored lengthwise and thinly sliced

1 large ripe but firm mango, peeled and sliced

Coconut rice (see box, below)

Heat a stovetop grill pan over moderate to high heat until very hot but not smoking.

Lightly brush the steak with oil and place on the hot pan. Grill for about 3 minutes on each side; the steak should be rare to medium-rare (it will continue to cook a little after it is removed from the heat). Move steak to a plate. Let rest while you make the dressing.

Put the dressing ingredients in a blender and blend until they are quite fine.

Chop the cilantro and mint leaves, keeping a few leaves whole for garnish.

Cut the beef into thin slices. Put in a bowl, add a few spoonfuls of the dressing and toss together with the chopped herbs and lemongrass.

Pile the beef mixture on a platter, top with the pieces of chili and arrange the cucumber and mango decoratively around the edge. Serve with the remaining dressing and the coconut rice.

COCONUT RICE

2½ cups coconut milk

1¼ cups water

1 stalk of lemongrass, bruised

½ tsp. salt

9 oz. Thai jasmine rice

Put the coconut milk and water in a saucepan and add the lemongrass and salt. Bring the mixture to the boil, add the rice and stir. Half cover the saucepan with the lid and simmer very gently for 20 minutes. Remove from the heat, cover tightly and let stand for 5 minutes. Discard the lemongrass and fluff up rice with a fork.

Cooking and Shredding Thai Beef

If the steak is pressed constantly during chargrilling this will loosen the fibers in the meat and make the meat easy to slice.

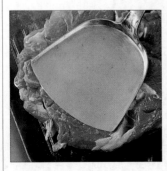

While chargrilling the steak, press it constantly with a wok scoop to keep it flat.

Cut the steak across the grain into slices about ½ in. thick, using a cleaver.

CHOOSING LAMB

Modern methods of breeding and farming have improved the taste and texture of lamb and fulfilled the demand for leaner, less fatty cuts. Meat from milk-fed baby lamb is very pale and looks similar to veal; meat from sheep less than a year old (spring lamb) has slightly darker pink flesh with a delicate flavor. Although not readily available, mutton (meat from sheep over two years old) has a stronger more gamey taste and darker colored flesh.

MEAT should be firm, with a fine-grained velvety texture

GENEROUS marbling denotes succulent pieces of lamb

FAT should be white, firm and waxy

BUYING LAMB

Lamb freezes well with little damage to the meat so that frozen lamb is a good choice when fresh meat is unavailable.

Choose firm, pinkish meat with visible marbling, avoiding meat that appears dark, wet and mushy. As a general rule, the pinker the flesh the younger the lamb. Don't choose cuts that are surrounded by yellow fat; check for an even layer of creamy white, firm fat.

Large cuts are often sold with the papery outer skin – this should feel fresh, moist and pliable, not dry or wrinkled. Also called the "fell," this skin should be removed from steaks and chops before cooking, but left on roasts because it helps keep the meat moist and imparts a stronger flavor.

HANDLING LAMB

Store lamb in its original wrapping, tightly sealed, in the coldest part of the refrigerator (34–40°F), away from cooked meats. Always check the "use by" dates. Chops and steaks will keep 2–4 days, large roasts up to 5 days. Ground lamb deteriorates quite quickly, so use within 24 hours.

Cooked lamb will keep in the refrigerator for up to 2 days. Make sure it is thoroughly cooled before putting it in the refrigerator. Store, wrapped in foil, within 2 hours of cooking.

Lamb freezes well – store tightly wrapped small cuts for 3–4 months and large cuts 6–9 months. To defrost, place the lamb on a plate to catch the drips and thaw slowly in the refrigerator allowing about 6 hours per 1 lb, use within 2 days.

LAMB CUTS

Ranging from inexpensive cuts, that are best braised, stewed or casseroled to moisten and tenderize their less succulent meat, to exquisite chops, cutlets and elegant crown roasts and guards of honor for special meals, there is a cut of lamb to suit every culinary occasion. Grain-fed domestic lamb tends to have a milder flavor than most grass-fed imports. Domestic cuts are also meatier and nearly twice the size of imported lamb. Although lamb is available year-round, new-season lamb is the sweetest and most tender. It is a traditional Easter dish in many countries where it heralds the arrival of spring.

LAMB CUTS	WHAT TO LOOK FOR	COOKING METHODS
SHOULDER	*Moist, pink meat with obvious marbling* *White moist bone surrounded by visible connective tissue* *Thick layer of outer fat*	Roast, braise, stew (boned and cubed)
RIB	*Even layer of creamy white outer fat* *Marbling throughout meat* *Bone moist with no splinters*	Roast, casserole, broil (chops and cutlets)
CROWN ROAST/ GUARD OF HONOR	*Fat trimmed away from rib bones* *Bones clean but moist; "chine" bone may be sawn* *Moist lean meat*	Roast
LOIN		
Sirloin loin chops	*Lean meat with light marbling* *Bones red and moist – "T" bone in loin, round bone in sirloin* *Creamy white layer of fat around edge of chop*	Broil, barbecue, panfry, braise
Noisettes	*Very lean moist flesh* *Thick layer of creamy white fat tied around outside*	Panfry, broil, barbecue
Saddle	*Pink lean meat* *Lightly marbled* *Even layer of fat (may need trimming)*	Roast
LEG	*Fat and "fell" intact* *Cut end of bone red and moist* *Lean meat with some marbling* *Visible connective tissue*	Roast, broil, barbecue (boned)
FORESHANK	*White bone* *Creamy white fat* *Full of connective tissue*	Stew, casserole, braise
BRISKET	*Heavy marbling* *High ratio of creamy white fat to meat* *Some connective tissue*	Roast, braise

LAMB ON THE MENU

Whether it's delicately perfumed with fresh herbs or boldly seasoned with exotic spices, lamb is very much an international favorite.

FRANCE – *Gigot d'Agneau* (flavored leg of lamb) is prized throughout the country. In Provence it's typically flavored with garlic, rosemary and thyme and in Burgundy, juniper. At a Parisian bistro, it may be served on a bed of creamy white beans.

GREAT BRITAIN – *Shepherd's Pie* (ground lamb with carrots, mushrooms and onions and a mashed potato topping) is a consummate cold weather meal.

GREECE – *Moussaka* (ground lamb layered with sliced eggplants and a cinnamon-scented béchamel sauce) is a rich and satisfying dish.

INDIA – *Lamb Curry* (cubed meat with spices such as cumin and coriander) may also include vegetables, chickpeas, or even nuts.

MOROCCO – *Lamb Tagine* (cubed lamb gently simmered with onions, peppers, fennel, olives, preserved lemons, and nuts and raisins) is a delicious stew that is traditionally served with couscous.

PREPARING FOR COOKING

The techniques shown here may require a little skill, but the results are well worth the effort taken. A boned roast is easier to carve than one with the bones left in, and a spectacular crown roast is a must for special occasions.

BONING A SHOULDER

A shoulder of lamb is an awkward cut to carve; removing the blade and shoulder bones prepares the meat so that it can be rolled and tied with or without a stuffing, then roasted or braised. You will then find it easier to carve. Cut away excess fat as you bone the meat.

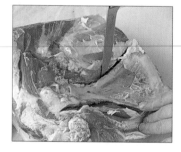

1 Cut through the meat on either side of the blade bone, using a boning knife.

2 Cut through the ball and socket joint to separate the blade and shoulder bones.

3 Holding the joint firmly, pull the blade bone sharply away from the meat.

4 Scrape the meat away from the shoulder bone; when free, pull the bone out.

TUNNEL BONING A LEG

This technique prepares a leg of lamb for stuffing, creating a neat pocket for the filling. It also makes carving easier. Trim off the fat from the outside of the leg and cut through the tendons at the base of the shank before you start boning.

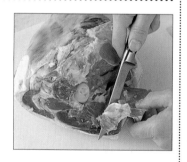

1 Cut around the pelvic bone and through the tendons. Remove the bone.

2 Scrape flesh from shank bone; cut tendons at leg joint and remove shank bone.

3 Cut around leg bone when exposed, twist and pull out to remove.

BUTTERFLYING A LEG

This technique prepares the leg for broiling or barbecuing. The term "butterfly" refers to the shape of the leg after it has been split and cut almost through. Before butterflying, tunnel bone the leg (see left).

1 Insert the knife into the leg bone cavity; cut to one side to split the meat open.

2 Open out the meat and make a shallow cut down the center to keep it open.

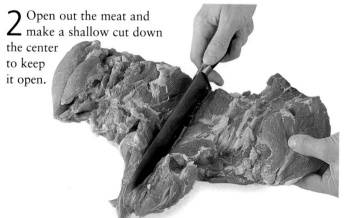

PREPARING A RACK

A rack of lamb is one side of the animal's rib cage. There are usually 6–9 cutlets in a rack, which can be roasted. Before preparing the rack, cut off the skin and all but ½ in. of fat.

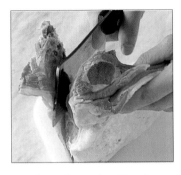 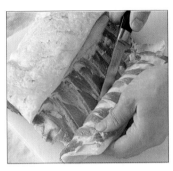 

1 Place the rack of lamb on its side. Cut off the chine (back) bone.

2 Cut fat from ribs 2 in. from bone ends. Turn over and score between bones.

3 Cut and scrape away the meat and tissue from between the bones.

WHAT'S IN A NAME?

French culinary terms are often confusing, and the names given to cuts of lamb are no exception. The following list includes the most commonly used cuts.

- *Carré d'agneau* is a rack of lamb.
- *Côte d'agneau* is a chop taken from the loin or rack.
- *Couronne* is a crown roast.
- *Gigot* is a leg of lamb.
- *Garde d'honneur* is a guard of honor.
- *Noisette* is a boneless cut from the saddle, tied with string.

MAKING A CROWN ROAST

This roast takes its name from the fact that when one or two racks are tied together they look like a crown. Before making the crown roast, prepare a rack following steps 1–3 above. Stuffing can be packed into the central cavity of the crown before roasting if you like, or it can be baked in a separate dish.

 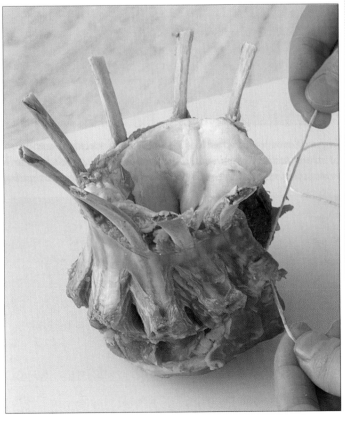

1 Cut the membrane between the ribs so the rack can be bent.

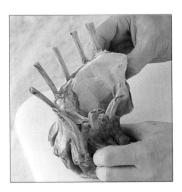

2 Stand the rack meat-side out; curve to form a crown shape.

3 Bend the ribs outward so the crown can sit upright. Tie string around the middle to hold the rack in place. Sew ends together, if you like. The crown is now ready for roasting.

MAKING A GUARD OF HONOR

When the bones of two racks interlock like swords, a "guard of honor" is formed.

Prepare two racks as in steps 1–3 above, removing all outside fat if you like. Holding one rack in each hand with the meat and ribs facing inwards, push the racks firmly together so the bones interlock. The joint is now ready for roasting (see page 136).

Noisettes d'agneau au thym, tian provençale

Boneless lamb noisettes, cut from the saddle, are succulent and tender. Here they are scented with thyme and served with individual gratins of zucchini, onions and tomatoes. These take their name from the French word tian, *for the earthenware dish in which they were traditionally baked.*

SERVES 4

1 saddle of lamb

¼ cup olive oil

1 bunch of fresh thyme sprigs

Salt and freshly ground pepper

2 oz. unsalted butter

FOR THE JUS

1 tbsp. olive oil

Lamb bones, chopped

6 oz. mirepoix of onion, carrot and celery (see page 166)

2 garlic cloves, crushed

1 quart veal stock

1 tbsp. tomato purée

1 bouquet garni containing a lot of thyme

TO SERVE

Petits tians (see box, above right)

Fresh parsley sprigs

Bone the saddle of lamb and cut into noisettes (see box, below); reserve the bones.

Put the noisettes in a dish, pour the oil over them and add the thyme sprigs and pepper. Turn the noisettes to coat with the oil and thyme, cover and leave in a cool place to marinate overnight.

To make the jus, heat the oil in a saucepan and brown the reserved lamb bones. Add the *mirepoix* and garlic and brown with the bones, then add the stock and stir well. Add the tomato purée, mix well, and cook for 1 minute. Add the bouquet garni. Bring to the boil, skimming the surface, then lower the heat and simmer gently for 30 minutes. Strain and season.

Melt the butter in a large frying pan, then increase the heat to high. Shake excess oil from the noisettes, season to taste and add them to the pan. Panfry for 4 minutes, turning once, until the noisettes are richly browned on both sides but still quite pink in the center.

Arrange the noisettes on warmed plates with the petits tians. Pour jus around the noisettes and garnish with parsley sprigs.

PETITS TIANS

Sweat 10 oz. finely chopped onions in ¼ cup olive oil. Put one quarter in a 3 in. metal ring on an oiled baking sheet. Slice and blanch 8 oz. zucchini. Slice 6 oz. cherry tomatoes. Arrange a few zucchini and tomato slices over the onions, alternating them in a circle; season. Remove ring and repeat to make 4 tians. Sprinkle with bread crumbs, chopped thyme and olive oil. Bake in a preheated oven at 350°F for 10 minutes.

Cutting Noisettes

The double loin of lamb, which is joined along the backbone of the lamb, is called the saddle. Once the saddle is boned, these two loins can be cut into 1 in. thick slices and chargrilled or fried. These slices are called noisettes *in French.*

Place the saddle fat-side down, and cut off the flaps on either side of the backbone with a boning knife.

Holding the knife close to the bone, cut and scrape down both sides of the backbone to release the two slender fillets.

Cut each fillet crosswise into 6 even slices using a chef's knife. Flatten each slightly using the side of the knife.

CHOOSING PORK

Once considered a fatty meat, pigs are now bred to produce much leaner meat.
In fact, some cuts are so lean that they require basting as they roast. Pork is sold
fresh as both large and small cuts and is also available cured and smoked.
Different curing methods produce variously flavored bacon and ham, which can
then be smoked. Bacon that is left unsmoked is often referred to as "green."

THERE IS GENERALLY little
marbling within pork meat

THE PALE PINK flesh will be
darker in the leg and
shoulder cuts

THE MAIN LAYER of fat
encases the flesh and should
be well trimmed by the
butcher before purchase

BUYING PORK

Larger roasts will often be sold with the papery outer skin – this
should feel fresh and moist and be free of hairs and elastic.
Always select pork that has smooth pink flesh that is moist but
not damp or oily looking. The fat should be firm and white.
Avoid cuts that have waxy, yellowing fat.

Bones may have a blue tinge and any cut ends should be red
and spongy – the whiter the ends the older the animal before
slaughter and as a result the meat may be less tender.

Ham is the cured hind leg of a pig, smoked or salted and
smoked. Ham is sold cooked or raw. When buying raw ham such
as Parma ham, choose pieces with creamy white fat and deep
pink flesh. Slices should look moist and lay flat, not dry and
curled at the edges.

HANDLING PORK

Because it can harbor a parasite that causes worms, pork must
be thoroughly cooked (see page 145). Store pork in its original
wrapping in the coldest part of the refrigerator (between
34–40°F), away from cooked meats. Always check the "use by"
dates. Fresh pork will keep for 2–3 days (smaller cuts do spoil
more quickly), cooked pork 4–5 days and ham up to 10 days.

Bacon is often vacuum wrapped and marked with a use by
date; in general, it will keep in the refrigerator for up to 3 weeks.

Bacon and ham do not freeze well – their high salt content
causes deterioration. Fresh pork, however, can be frozen, tightly
wrapped, for up to 6 months, though ground pork should be
used within 3 months. To defrost, place on a plate in the
refrigerator; allow about 5 hours per 1 lb.

PORK CUTS

Today's pork comes from a leaner hog than in the past. Such pork also tends to be trimmed much closer by butchers and supermarkets. All pork cuts are relatively tender but no matter the cooking method, the meat must be cooked until the juices are no longer pink and they run clear. Although today cases are rare, there is a danger of contracting trichinosis from undercooked pork. Use a meat thermometer (see page 124) when cooking roasts. The meat should register an internal temperature of 180°F on the thermometer to ensure that any bacteria in the meat is killed. Some hams produce an irridescent film on the surface which can be uninviting. This is a normal reaction between the natural fats and the curing process, which is harmless and does not affect the quality of the meat.

PORK CUTS	WHAT TO LOOK FOR	COOKING METHODS
SHOULDER BLADE STEAKS	Some marbling visible throughout Dark pink, moist flesh No outer fat or skin	Broil, fry, barbecue, stew, braise
SHOULDER ROASTS	Light marbling Some connective tissue Even outer layer of white fat Elastic skin	Roast, pot roast (whole) Broil, stew (boned and cubed)
LOIN	Very lean with no visible marbling Clean cut bone with no splinters Thin even outer layer of fat May have skin intact	Roast, pot roast, braise Broil, fry, barbecue, stew (chops)
TENDERLOIN/FILLET	Leanest cut, no visible fat Moist pink flesh	Roast, broil, fry, barbecue
RIB CHOPS/STEAKS	Very light marbling Thin layer of creamy white fat White bones with red spongy centre	Barbecue, broil, fry, roast, stew, braise
SPARE RIBS	Pink moist flesh with very light marbling Clean cut bones with no splinters	Broil, roast, barbecue
BACON	Clear, pink, moist meat An even layer of white fat	Broil, fry
SCALLOP	Deep pink flesh An even, smooth texture No outer fat or skin	Broil, fry, barbecue
HAM	Sweet smelling, moist, but not wet, meat	Roast
LEG	Lean moist meat with very little visible marbling Some connective tissue Even outer layer of fat under rind which should be hairless, elastic and scored	Roast, pot roast, braise
GROUND	Clear pink meat with specks of fat	Pasta sauces, stuffings, meatloaf

PORK ON THE MENU

From East to West, versatile pork pairs with a myriad of flavors to excite a multitude of cultural palates.

CHINA – *Sweet and Sour Spare Ribs* (ribs marinated in a savory soy, hoisin, sherry, ginger and garlic sauce) is a very popular, and highly exported, dish.

CYPRUS – *Afelia* (pork stew marinated then cooked in red wine) gets its distinctive flavor from typical island spices such as cumin, coriander and cinnamon.

GERMANY – *Knockwurst* (pork sausage with cumin and garlic) is a quintessential and much loved pork snack.

GREAT BRITAIN – *Roast Pork* (pork roasted and topped with crackling) is a comforting, old-fashioned favorite, usually served with sage and onion stuffing.

UNITED STATES – *Boston Baked Beans* (salt pork with beans, molasses, tomato and mustard) was introduced by Puritan settlers in New England.

PREPARING FOR COOKING

The correct preparation of pork is a very important part of a cook's repertoire, because so much of the pig is suitable for cooking and the range of pork dishes is vast. The techniques shown here include boning, stuffing and rolling a whole pork loin, cutting pockets in chops, and preparing and stuffing tenderloins.

STUFFINGS FOR A BONED LOIN

- Fresh sage leaves and whole dried apricots soaked in a little white wine.
- Diced apple, onion and fresh bread crumbs moistened with cider vinegar.
- Snipped bacon, plump raisins and cooked rice seasoned with black pepper and chopped fresh parsley.

TRICK OF THE TRADE

TUNNEL STUFFING
This simple technique makes a pocket in a boned and rolled loin of pork. It saves having to untie and reroll the meat.

Insert the tip of a small knife into the eye of the loin and work to make a tunnel right through. Spoon stuffing into tunnel.

BONING A LOIN

Although most butchers will bone a loin of pork if asked, you can easily do the job yourself with a boning knife. Remove any skin and trim the excess fat before boning, stuffing, rolling and roasting (see page 148).

1 Holding the loin, cut between the ribs; do not cut the meat deeper than the thickness of the ribs.

2 Cut down behind the ribs using a cleaver, cleaning as much meat off the bones as possible.

3 Work the knife around and under the chine bone, lifting it away from the meat as you cut.

5 Roll up the loin, starting at one of the long sides, and tie securely with kitchen string (see page 121). The meat is now ready for cooking.

4 Open the loin out flat and then cut two lengthwise slits through the meat, taking care not to cut right through. Insert stuffing (see box, above left).

STUFFING PORK CHOPS

By making a single horizontal cut in a pork chop you can create a pocket to contain a stuffing. This adds flavor and helps make the meat go further, as well as basting the meat on the inside during cooking and making it moist. The most suitable chops for this technique are those cut from the loin. They can be panfried or broiled, or braised in the oven (see page 149).

1 Insert a boning knife in the fatty side of the chop and work it horizontally to the bone to make a pocket.

2 Spoon the stuffing (see box, right) into the pocket and press the edges firmly together.

STUFFINGS FOR CHOPS

- Chopped spinach seasoned with freshly grated nutmeg or tossed with chopped Parma ham.
- Shredded arugula and snipped sun-dried tomatoes.
- Roughly chopped prunes and chestnuts with finely grated orange zest.
- Spoonfuls of fruit chutney
- Chopped roasted peppers and crushed garlic.

PREPARING A TENDERLOIN

Boneless lean tenderloin, also called pork fillet, requires very little in the way of preparation. The tendon and sinew are chewy, so they must be cut away before cooking. A whole tenderloin can be roasted or braised, with or without a stuffing (see below) or it can be cut into noisettes for broiling and panfrying, or strips for stir-frying.

1 Carefully pull any fat and membrane away from the tenderloin. Discard the fat and membrane.

2 Cut just underneath the tendon and sinew with a boning knife, pulling it away from the flesh.

MAKING NOISETTES
Cut the tenderloin diagonally into ½– ¾ in. thick slices, using a chef's knife.

STUFFING TENDERLOINS

There are several ways in which pork tenderloins can be stuffed. The first shown here splits a whole tenderloin so that it can be opened out, flattened slightly, stuffed and reshaped; the second goes one step further and ties two split tenderloins together around a stuffing to make a larger, more substantial roast. Both can be roasted or braised as they are, or wrapped in bacon before tying.

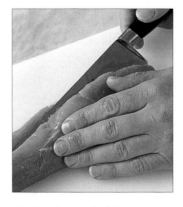

1 Cut the tenderloin lengthwise two-thirds of the way through with a chef's knife. Open out and pound gently to flatten.

2 Spread stuffing of your choice along the center of the tenderloin and roll it up lengthwise to enclose the stuffing. Tie with kitchen string (see page 121).

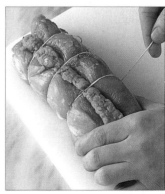

STUFFING TWO TENDERLOINS
Split and flatten two tenderloins, following step 1, left. Sandwich together around a stuffing, then tie to secure.

ROASTING & BRAISING

Using the prepared cuts of pork (see pages 146–147) for roasts and braises can yield splendid results if you follow these simple instructions and timing guidelines. Rubs, stuffings and glazes will boost the flavor of the meat.

(see pages 146–147)

ROASTING PORK

Leg, loin and shoulder of pork are all suitable cuts for roasting, either with the bone in or boned, rolled and tied, with or without stuffing. The technique is the same, but cooking times vary (see box, left). If you like crackling, buy the meat with its skin intact, score it and pat it dry, then rub with oil and salt. Do not baste it during roasting or it will not be crisp. Make deep incisions through the skin and insert slivers of peeled garlic, if you like.

1 If the skin has been removed, as shown here on a leg of pork, score in a diamond pattern with a boning knife. Brush with a little oil and rub with salt and pepper or a dry spice mix such as cinnamon, mustard powder and brown sugar.

2 Place the meat on a rack in a roasting pan and roast until well-done (see chart, left). If there is no crackling, baste the pork with the fat from the pan every 30 minutes.

ROASTING PORK TENDERLOIN

Tying the tenderloin around a contrasting stuffing (see page 147) makes an attractive presentation when sliced. Roast the tenderloin in a roasting pan at 425°F for 30–35 minutes, turning it halfway. For a special French touch, make a jus to accompany the meat by deglazing the cooking juices with wine or port.

1 Tie the rolled tenderloin along its length. Brush with oil, season and roast (see left), basting with the juices.

2 Let rest, loosely covered with foil, for about 5 minutes. Remove string and slice on the diagonal.

ROASTING TIMES

Pork is usually roasted until well-done, to an internal temperature of 180°F. All times are approximate.

- ROAST at 450°F for 10 mins. Reduce to 350°F and follow times below.

- ROASTS ON THE BONE
  30 mins per 1 lb. plus an extra 30 mins

- BONED, ROLLED ROASTS
  35 mins per 1 lb. plus an extra 35 mins
  (For stuffed roasts allow an extra 5–10 mins per 1 lb.)

CRANBERRY SAUCE

Fruits are traditionally served with pork to offset its richness. Apple sauce is the classic; this tangy cranberry sauce is more unusual.

Simmer
8 oz. cranberries in 1¼ cups water until the berries begin to burst, about 10 minutes. Remove from the heat, add 8 oz. sugar and 2 tbsp. port and stir until the sugar dissolves. Chill and serve.

ROASTING SPARERIBS

These ribs are the Chinese fingerfood ribs which need to be roasted so the meat is crisp enough to bite off the bones. If they are sold in a sheet, separate them with a cleaver or chef's knife.

1 Put the ribs in a single layer in a roasting pan, brush with your chosen glaze (see box, right). Let marinate for at least 1 hour.

2 Roast at 425°F for 20 minutes, then reduce to 400°F and roast for 40–45 minutes. Turn often to cook evenly; remove with tongs.

GLAZES FOR RIBS

Glazes flavor the ribs and help to produce a sticky coating during roasting.

- Mix honey, pineapple juice, oil and a little wine vinegar. For extra bite, add a spoonful of chili sauce.
- Mix soy sauce, oil, rice wine and five-spice powder.
- Mix grain mustard and honey and thin with a little oil.

ROASTING PORK CHOPS

The best cooking method for thick pork loin chops is roasting. The technique shown here works well with plain or pocket-stuffed chops (see page 147). The apple rings add flavor and moistness to the pork and pulp down into the juices, but they are not essential.

1 Heat a little oil in a frying pan, add the chops and sear over a moderate heat.

2 Roast in a baking dish with the pan juices at 350°F for 30–40 minutes.

PORK IN MILK

4 lb. boned and rolled loin of pork
2 tbsp. olive oil
1½ quarts milk
5 garlic cloves, crushed
2 tbsp. fresh sage leaves
Grated zest and juice of 2 lemons
Salt and freshly ground pepper

Sear the pork in the oil in a deep casserole. Add the remaining ingredients and bring to the boil. Cover and braise at 350°F for 2–2½ hours. Serve sliced, with the sauce spooned over.

BRAISING PORK IN MILK

This unusual method of cooking pork is traditional in Italy. During long gentle cooking, the milk and the fat in the pork intermingle, making the most delicious sauce and moist succulent meat. Don't be put off by the slightly curdled appearance of the sauce – this is as it should be.

1 Sear the rolled loin in hot olive oil. Keep the heat moderate to high and turn the meat constantly to make sure the fat browns evenly on all sides. Use the fork to steady the meat, not pierce it.

2 Add the seasonings and milk, bring to the boil, cover and braise. Stir the cooking liquid and spoon it over the pork during cooking. This will amalgamate the fats and the flavors.

QUICK COOKING

The simple methods of broiling and frying lend themselves to small cuts of pork, producing tender and flavorful meat in a matter of minutes. Grilling pork in a ridged pan on the stovetop or under the broiler, is perfect for cooking chops or kebabs; stir-frying in a wok over high heat is best for cooking pork strips.

STIR-FRIED PORK

1 lb. pork tenderloin, cut
    into thin strips
1 onion, sliced
1 garlic clove, sliced
1 red chili, finely chopped
½ cup dark soy sauce
½ cup sesame oil
1 tbsp. vegetable oil
2 peppers, sliced
2 tsp. cornstarch

Marinate the pork, onion, garlic and chili with the soy sauce and sesame oil for 30 minutes. Remove the pork and vegetables and stir-fry in batches in the vegetable oil. Add the peppers and stir-fry for 3–4 minutes, then blend the cornstarch with the marinade, add to the wok and stir-fry until thickened. Serves 4.

CHARGRILLING PORK CHOPS

For succulent and tasty meat, chargrilling on a stovetop grill pan is one of the best ways to cook thin or medium cut pork loin chops and it's healthier than panfrying because it uses less fat. You can use the same technique for cooking under a conventional broiler. Allow 6–8 minutes on each side, 2 in. away from the heat.

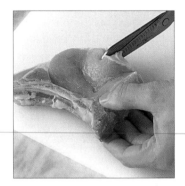

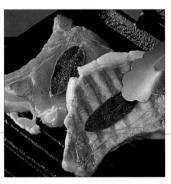

1 Snip fat and membrane at regular intervals. Brush with oil, press sage leaves into the meat and season.

2 Heat a stovetop grill pan until hot but not smoking. Add the chops and cook for 12–16 minutes, turning once.

STIR-FRYING

Pork tenderloin, sliced on the diagonal (see page 147), can be cut into strips and stir-fried. A recipe for stir-fried pork, using the techniques shown here, is given in the box, left.

1 Before stir-frying, marinate the pork strips for at least 30 minutes at room temperature or overnight in the refrigerator. The highly flavored ingredients of the marinade will make the meat more tasty and tender.

2 To stir-fry the pork, first heat a wok over a moderate heat until hot, then add the oil and heat until hot but not smoking. Add about one-third of the drained pork and toss it in the wok for 2–3 minutes, separating the strips with chopsticks. Repeat twice until all the pork is cooked, then return all the pork to the wok. If you follow these directions the meat will cook quickly and evenly and will not stick to the wok.

SAUSAGES, BACON & HAM

However you cook sausages or bacon, it is essential to use the correct techniques to enjoy them at their best. The preparation and presentation of a whole ham is a particularly useful technique when entertaining guests.

COOKING SAUSAGES

As sausages cook the meat expands; to ensure they do not burst, pierce the skins before cooking. Sausages have quite a high fat content, which helps keep them moist. To counteract their richness, they can be glazed with a sweet mixture such as mango chutney or honey.

PRICKING THE SKINS
To prevent sausages bursting during cooking, prick all over with a skewer or fork.

BROILING
Coil Cumberland or Italian Luganeghe sausages and secure with skewers. Broil for about 10 minutes.

POACHING
Add sausages to boiling water, cover and simmer for 3–5 minutes; Frankfurters only need 1–2 minutes.

USING BACON IN COOKING

Rindless center-cut bacon strips are used to line terrines and loaf pans, or rolled around a filling to be served as an hors d'oeuvre. They need to be stretched before use, to prevent shrinkage during cooking. Bacon lardons are used in French cooking as a flavoring ingredient – their strong, often salty, taste is essential in many classic dishes such as boeuf bourguignon.

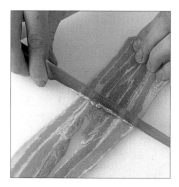

STRETCHING
Hold two strips together and run the back of a chef's knife along their length.

ROLLING
Roll stretched strips around filling; secure with wooden toothpicks.

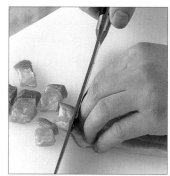

MAKING LARDONS
Cut thick strips lengthwise. Stack the strips and cut crosswise into dice.

TYPES OF SAUSAGES

Most sausages are made of pork, but beef, veal and lamb varieties are becoming more popular. They can be plain or seasoned.

VARIETIES FOR GRILLING:
Choose French varieties such as *andouillette* and *boudin noir*, English ones like chipolatas, Cumberland and Lincolnshire or Italian Luganeghe.

VARIETIES FOR POACHING:
Sausages that are most suitable for poaching are the French *andouille*, *cervelat* and *boudin blanc*, and the German *Frankfurter*, *Bockwurst* and *Knockwurst*.

TYPES OF BACON

The flavor varies according to the curing ingredients (such as sugar for a sweet cure), and the wood that is used in smoking.

- Unsmoked bacon is also referred to as "green" and has a white rind. When smoked, the rind turns brown.
- Center-cut bacon is from the chest of the pig; it is a fatty bacon called *lard* in French.
- *Petit sale* and *pancetta* are similar cuts from the belly of pork. The curing process makes them quite salty, with a strong smoky flavor.

9–11 lb. whole cured ham
4 oz. brown sugar
4 tbsp. English mustard

Soak the ham in cold water overnight. Drain, weigh it and calculate the cooking time, allowing 30 minutes per 1 lb. Put in a pan of cold water, bring to the boil and simmer for half the cooking time. Drain and cool slightly, then remove the skin. Score the fat, warm the sugar and mustard and spread over the fat. Bake, covered loosely with foil, on a rack in a roasting pan at 350°F for the remaining time, removing the foil for the last 30 minutes. Serves about 12.

PREPARING AND PRESENTING A HAM

A boiled ham must have its skin removed before serving or it will be very difficult to carve, but the fat underneath the skin is unappealing. A recipe for glazed ham, using the simple technique for scoring and glazing shown here, is given in the box, left. This is essential for an attractive presentation if you are planning to serve the ham whole at the table.

1 Score the fat of the boiled ham attractively in a diamond pattern with the tip of a small knife. This will allow the glaze to penetrate and flavor the meat.

2 Warm the glaze until melted, then spread it evenly over the fat with a spatula. Take time to work the glaze into the cuts so that it will seep into the meat and flavor it.

USING GROUND MEAT

Use lean meat with a light marbling of fat for best flavor and succulence. Ground meat is extremely versatile: it absorbs seasonings well and can be made into a variety of dishes from *moussaka* to meatballs. Try grinding your own meat (see page 123) and experiment with lamb, veal and pork.

Add texture and flavor by topping or accompanying burgers with tasty extras.

- Top a cooked burger with a slice of mozzarella or crumbled blue cheese and broil to melt.
- Stir chopped roasted peppers into *salsa* – spoon onto melting cheeseburger.
- Panfry sliced red onions until caramelized, adding a few sliced mushrooms towards the end. Season with Worcestershire sauce and grain mustard and spoon over burgers.

MAKING BURGERS

You can make burgers with ground meat, but this food processor method makes a chunkier burger more like chopped steak. For best results, use meat such as chuck steak that has 20 percent fat and take care not to overwork the meat or it will be rubbery.

1 Put chunks of beef in a food processor fitted with the metal blade. Pulse just until roughly ground.

2 Place the chopped meat in a bowl. Add onion, garlic and seasonings of your choice. Mix until combined.

3 Shape the mixture into even-sized balls, then flatten them until they are about 1½ in. thick.

MAKING DIFFERENT SHAPES

When shaping ground meat, use your hands moistened with a little water and keep the shapes fairly loose – if you make the shapes too compact the texture of the cooked meat will be dense and rubbery.

BROCHETTES
Take a small handful of ground meat (lamb is traditional) and shape it around metal skewers, pressing with your fingers.

MEATBALLS
Roll ground meat between the palms of your hands to form a ball, or roll it on a board if you prefer. Size can vary from 1–2 in.

MAKING A MEATLOAF

For this classic American dish, use slightly fatty ground meat from cuts such as shoulder. A combination of beef, veal and pork is best for flavor and moisture, and the addition of milk-soaked breadcrumbs is important to absorb meat juices.

FREEFORM
Moisten your hands with water to prevent sticking, then form meat into a rectangular loaf shape on a lightly greased baking sheet.

MOLDED
Press meat into a lightly greased loaf-shaped dish. Level the surface with a spoon, then turn it out onto a lightly greased baking sheet.

MAKING CREPINETTES

These little French delicacies are a kind of homemade sausage – ground meat with breadcrumbs and seasonings encased in a parcel of caul (see box, right). Traditionally, pork sausage meat is used, but you can use ground lamb, veal or poultry. Crépinettes can be panfried as directed here, or broiled or baked for the same length of time.

Mix ground meat with finely chopped onion, bread crumbs and seasonings. Form into patties with your hands, then place a herb sprig on top of each (this will show through the melted caul and look attractive when serving). Wrap in squares of soaked and drained caul and panfry in hot oil and butter for 3–4 minutes.

CAUL

This is the thin membrane, veined with fat, that encloses an animal's stomach; pig's caul is the most readily available. Called *crépine* in French, it is used to moisten and flavor food and to hold ingredients together during cooking. Depending on thickness, caul either melts completely during cooking, or it will remain and can be discarded before serving. It can be obtained from butchers, but it may have to be specially ordered. Soak for 1–2 hours in cold water before use.

MAKING STEAK TARTARE

A dish of finely chopped raw beef topped with a raw egg yolk, steak tartare is one of the great French classics. In France it is usually served with cornichons *(baby gherkins), capers and Tabasco sauce, with a pot of mustard on the side. Only the freshest and finest quality fillet steak is used, chopped by hand just before serving.*

Allowing 4 oz. per person, trim fillet steak of all fat, membrane and sinew, then chop the meat with two knives (see page 123). Mix with finely chopped onion and fresh flat-leaf parsley and salt and pepper. Shape into rounds, place on individual plates and hollow out the centers slightly with the back of a spoon. Slide egg yolks into the hollows. Serve immediately.

Most butchers sell casings for sausages. Beef and pig intestines provide a natural alternative to manmade casings.

- For an Italian style, mix meat with chopped sun-dried tomatoes, garlic and basil.
- Try Indian flavorings such as curry powder, chopped fresh cilantro and mango chutney to moisten and bind.
- For more traditional flavorings, try mint and onion with lamb, sage and apple with pork, and horseradish or mustard with beef.

MAKING SAUSAGES

The bonus of making your own sausages is that you know exactly what goes into them. Ground pork is the classic meat, but beef, lamb and venison are equally good. Casings can be natural or manmade, and you can vary the flavorings and seasonings to taste (see box, left).

1 Soak the casings in a large bowl of cold water for 1–2 hours. This will remove any excess salt and make the casings more pliable.

2 Fill a piping bag fitted with a large plain nozzle with sausage meat. Hook the casing over the nozzle and squeeze in the filling.

3 When the casing is full, twist sausage at intervals into links. Secure twisted ends with string. Remove string after cooking.

ORGAN MEATS

Organ meats are the innards and extremities of the animals we eat. Ranging from familiar liver and kidneys to more adventurous parts, all are nutritious, and with careful preparation and cooking, as delicious as any meat.

SAFETY FIRST

Organ meats need careful handling, and freshness is crucial. Choose moist and shiny flesh with no dry patches; avoid any with a greenish colour, slimy surface or strong smell. Store fresh organ meats in the refrigerator and use within two days; wash very thoroughly before using.

TYPES OF LIVER

- Calf's liver is very mild and tender. It is best broiled, sautéed or panfried.
- Lamb's liver tends to be drier and less delicate than calf's liver, but it can also be sautéed.
- Pig's liver is strong, and is good for pâtés and terrines.
- Chicken livers are mild and delicate; they are usually panfried and used for pâtés.

PREPARING LIVER

Chicken livers are sold whole; other livers are generally pre-sliced but can be ordered whole. When preparing a whole liver, divide the lobes and cut off any exposed ducts or connective tissue. Cut away any blood vessels, taking care not to damage the flesh. Calf's liver is being prepared here.

1 Peel off the opaque outer membrane with your fingers, holding the liver down to stop the flesh tearing.

2 Cut the liver into slices about ¼ in. thick with a chef's knife, and cut away any internal ducts.

TRICK OF THE
TRADE

SOAKING LIVER

Pig's liver has a strong, pronounced flavor. Soak it in milk to "sweeten" it before cooking.

Prepare the liver (see left). Fill a bowl with enough cold milk to cover it, add the liver and turn to coat. Let soak for about 1 hour.

PREPARING KIDNEYS

Beef, veal and pig's kidneys should be plump, firm, and encased in a shiny membrane. When buying kidneys encased in fat, it should be off-white (see box, right). Avoid kidneys with a strong odor.

1 Trim away any fat and connective tissue, then pull off the outer membrane with your fingers.

2 Cut the kidney in half lengthwise, slicing through the fatty core. Hold the core with your fingertips and cut it away with a boning knife.

3 Thread the prepared kidney halves on to a skewer to keep them flat. They are now ready for broiling or panfrying.

PREPARING HEART FOR PANFRYING

Heart has a firm texture and rich flavor, but it can be tough if not properly handled. To prepare heart, trim away any visible fat. After removing the tubes, cut away any sinew with kitchen shears. Rinse the heart and pat dry with paper towels before slicing.

1 Cut off the tubes from the top of the heart using a chef's knife.

2 Cut the heart in half lengthwise and then cut it into slices or cubes.

STUFFING HEART

The natural cavity in a heart can be filled with a variety of stuffings. All hearts can be stuffed, but large beef hearts should be skewered or tied to retain their shape during cooking. Heart is lean so requires slow cooking, stewing or braising, to keep it moist. Each stuffed heart will serve 2, apart from beef heart, which serves 4.

1 Follow step 1 above. Cup the heart firmly in one hand and spoon stuffing into the cavity; press down firmly.

2 Thread 2–3 wooden skewers through the top edge of the heart to secure the stuffing during cooking.

155

PREPARING AND COOKING TONGUE

Soak tongue in several changes of cold water for 2–3 hours – this will draw out the blood from a fresh tongue, salt from a salted tongue. Put the tongue in a large pan, cover with cold water and bring to the boil. Blanch for 10 minutes, then drain and refresh under cold running water.

Poach the tongue in water to cover with flavoring vegetables, such as a *mirepoix* of onion, carrot and celery, and a bouquet garni until tender, 2–4 hours according to the type of tongue. Let cool in the liquid until tepid, then lift out and cut away bones and gristle from the root end with a sharp knife. Slit the skin lengthwise with the knife, then strip it off with your fingers.

The tongue is now ready to slice and serve hot, or to press and served cold. Espagnole sauce (see page 225) is a classic accompaniment to hot tongue.

PREPARING AND COOKING OXTAIL

Trim away the excess outer fat from the oxtail with a paring knife. Chop off the base of the tail with a meat cleaver and discard. Chop the tail crosswise into 3 in pieces.

To bone oxtail, slit the tail lengthwise to expose the bone and, with a sharp knife, scrape the flesh away from the bone until it is released. Discard the bone. Roll up the oxtail, starting at the wider end. Tie with string.

Pieces of bone-in or boned oxtail are good braised slowly with strong-flavored ingredients, such as beef stock, red wine, bouquet garni and garlic. Cook for at least 2 hours.

SWEETBREADS

Sweetbreads are the thymus glands of young lambs and calves. They are highly perishable and should be soaked and cooked on the day of purchase. Once prepared as shown, they can be coated in egg and bread crumbs and fried; in classic French cuisine, they are served with sauce poulette *(see page 223).*

1 Soak for 2 hours in several changes of cold water. Rinse, put in a pan and cover with cold water. Bring to the boil and blanch 3 minutes.

2 Drain and refresh under cold running water, then remove outer skin and any pieces of membrane.

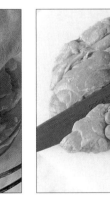

3 Place sweetbreads between two plates, put a weight on top and chill for 2 hours until firm.

4 Slice the sweetbreads at an angle using a sharp knife. The sweetbreads are now ready for cooking.

TRIPE

The muscular lining of an ox's stomach, ivory-coloured tripe is usually sold "dressed," that is cleaned, soaked and scalded, but further blanching is required before cooking to sweeten its smell. It is usually stewed, either with milk and onions, or in an Espagnole sauce (see page 225), with sliced carrots added at the end.

PIG'S TROTTERS

These are usually braised, or served cold in a vinaigrette (see page 230). Before this, first scrape away the hairs between the toes, halve or bone them as shown here, then poach in stock for about 1½ hours.

HALVING
Cut lengthwise right through the middle of the trotter, between the bones.

BONING
Cut through the skin of the trotter down to the bones, then lift and scrape the flesh away from the bones until it is released.

Rinse the whole sheet of tripe thoroughly in cold water to remove any traces of dirt. Drain in a colander, pat dry with a kitchen towel, then cut into strips or squares with a chef's knife. Place the tripe in a pan with a bay leaf, an onion stuck with cloves, and cold water to cover. Bring to the boil, then drain. The tripe is now ready for cooking.

VEGETABLES & SALADS

CHOOSING VEGETABLES

Choose vegetables in season when they are at their freshest and most readily
available; this is when they will taste their best and be at their most nutritious.
Always look for crisp, fresh looking vegetables that have brightly colored leaves.
Avoid any that have brown patches, wilted leaves, bruised or pulpy flesh.

CARROTS should have fresh
looking, healthy leafy tops,
not discolored or wilting

ONIONS should have dry
papery skins; red onions
should have no brown
discoloration

POTATOES should be firm and
well shaped with no "eyes"
or green patches

TOMATO SKIN should be
smooth and firm with no
cuts or blemishes

ROOTS & TUBERS

Carrots, potatoes, beets,
rutabagas, celeriac and
radishes should have firm,
heavy flesh and wrinkle-free
skin. Avoid soft patches or
sprouting.

MUSHROOMS

Choose firm, fresh looking
mushrooms that have a soft
"bloom" and fresh smell. The
stalk end should be moist; if
dry they may be slightly old.

ONIONS

Choose firm bulbs with
even-colored skins and no
signs of sprouting. Avoid any
that look damp or smell musty.
Leeks and scallions should have
dark green leaves and fresh
looking roots.

VEGETABLE FRUITS

Tomatoes, eggplants, peppers
and avocados should have firm,
smooth, shiny skins and a deep,
even color. Avoid any that are
soft, pulpy or wrinkled.

SALAD LEAVES

Choose lettuces that smell fresh and look slightly damp on the surface. Check the heart is well formed. There should be no wilting or brown patches on the leaves.

LEAFY GREENS

Choose endive, Swiss chard and spinach with crisp, fresh looking greens. Leaves should feel springy to the touch; avoid any that appear limp or wilted. There should be no sign of insect damage.

STALKS & SHOOTS

Celery, artichokes, fennel, asparagus and Belgian endive should have tightly packed, firm heads with no visible brown patches on outer layers.

ASPARAGUS should have plump stalks with tight buds, even in size and color

LEAFY GREENS should have full, well formed head, crisp leaves with fresh green tips

PEAS should not have any visible dry or brown patches

SPINACH LEAVES are best when small and moist, with fine stalks

PODS & SEEDS

Select peas and beans with bright green pods that are full and plump. Choose corn with tight green husks and plump, even, shiny kernels. The kernels should be tightly packed on the cob.

BRASSICAS

Look for cauliflower, broccoli, Brussels sprouts and cabbage with undamaged tight compact heads. Outer leaves should be fresh with no signs of wilting or yellowing. Stalks should look moist and freshly cut.

BROCCOLI of the purple "hearting" variety should have dark colored tightly formed florets, firm stalks, no signs of yellowing

BRASSICAS

This large family of vegetables includes cabbages, cauliflower, broccoli and Brussels sprouts, as well as Oriental greens like mustard cabbage and *bok choi*.

SETTING THE COLOR OF RED CABBAGE

Once cut, red cabbage has a tendency to turn blue or purple. This simple technique helps it keep its red color.

1 Pour hot red wine vinegar over shredded cabbage (about 4 tbsp. is enough for ½ small head of cabbage). Mix well and let stand for 5–10 minutes, then drain off excess vinegar.

2 Serve the red cabbage raw, tossed in a vinaigrette dressing (see page 230) and sprinkled with chopped parsley, or use in cooked dishes.

CORING CABBAGE

The hard white core at the center of all cabbage is tough and inedible and should be removed to allow easy shredding and even cooking of the cabbage leaves.

Remove any outer, damaged leaves. Cut the cabbage lengthwise into quarters with a chef's knife. Cut off the base of each quarter at an angle to remove the hard white core. The cabbage is now ready to be shredded.

SHREDDING CABBAGE

After cutting a cabbage into quarters and coring it (see above), it can be shredded for eating raw in salads and coleslaws (see below), or for stir-frying, steaming or simmering in soups such as minestrone. Cabbage can be shredded either by hand or in a food processor.

BY HAND

Lay each cabbage quarter on a cutting board. Cut across to form even strips.

BY MACHINE

With the processor running, feed each cabbage quarter into the machine and shred.

COMBINING COLORS

A colorful mixture of shredded red, white and green cabbage leaves looks very attractive and, with its mix of textures and flavors, makes an excellent winter salad.

Shred the cabbage either by hand or machine (see above) and place in a bowl. Toss in a vinaigrette or cooked dressing (see page 230), or in mayonnaise (see page 228).

PREPARING BROCCOLI AND CAULIFLOWER

The delicate florets and hard stalks of broccoli and cauliflower cook at different rates so you need to separate them before cooking. Broccoli is illustrated here.

1 Holding the vegetable over a colander, cut off the florets leaving only the stalk. Divide the larger florets into smaller ones.

2 Remove the leaves from the stalk. Peel away the tough, outer layer with a vegetable peeler, then cut the stalk lengthwise in half.

3 Put the stalk cut-side down and remove the ends. Cut the stalk lengthwise into slices; cut the slices lengthwise into sticks.

SUPERSTAR VEGETABLE

Brassicas are all good sources of vitamin C and minerals, but broccoli is particularly high in many vital nutrients.

- 4 oz. of broccoli provides over half the recommended daily intake of vitamin C.
- Broccoli is rich in carotene. High intakes may provide protection against cancer and heart disease.
- Broccoli is rich in folate (folic acid) which is needed by the body to form DNA and process proteins.
- The minerals iron, potassium and chromium, are found in significant amounts in broccoli.

PREPARING BRUSSELS SPROUTS

To ensure even cooking of large sprouts, a cross is cut in the base. This is not necessary for small sprouts.

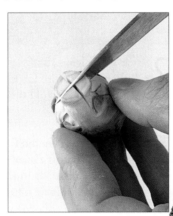

Cut a cross shape in the base of sprout with a chef's knife. Cut only a quarter of the way into the sprout, or it may fall apart during cooking. Trim the base stalks and remove any discolored outer leaves.

TRICK OF THE TRADE

PREVENTING DISCOLORATION

White vegetables, such as the cauliflower shown here, have a tendency to discolor when cut and exposed to the air. To prevent discoloration, put the prepared vegetable in a bowl, cover with cold water and add 1 tbsp. lemon juice or white wine vinegar. This acidulates the water and preserves the color of the vegetable.

From left to right:
Broccoli; Brussels sprouts; Cauliflower

POTATOES

Although potatoes appear in many shapes and colors (see box, opposite page), they fall into two basic categories – waxy and floury. For best results it is crucial to choose the right variety. Waxy potatoes have a high moisture and low starch content, ideal for sautéing, boiling and salads. Floury varieties have more starch, hence a light, fluffy texture. They are the prized "bakers" and offer the creamiest results in purées and gratins.

EXOTIC VEGETABLE

Potatoes are commonplace vegetables today but at one time they were as exotic as taro are now. A staple food of the Peruvian Incas, they were brought to England in the 16th century by Sir Francis Drake. Surprisingly, at first they were thought fit only for animals, and were held responsible for diseases such as leprosy.

Sir Francis Drake (1540-1596)

SCRUBBING

Potato skins are full of nutrients and flavor, so it is best not to remove them before cooking. Scrub or scrape clean rather than peel.

Hold the potato under cold running water and remove "eyes" with a knife tip. Scrub the skins all over with a stiff brush to remove any earth.

PREPARING FOR ROASTING

Potatoes can be roasted unpeeled or peeled. Small potatoes can be left whole, but for even and quick cooking, large potatoes are best prepared hasselback-style, or cut into smaller shapes. Pommes châteaux are the classic French shape. For two different roasting techniques, see pages 188 and 189.

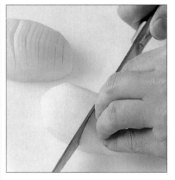

HASSELBACK
Slice off the bottom of the potato to steady it. Make thin parallel cuts from the top almost to the bottom.

POMMES CHATEAUX
Cut potato lengthwise into quarters with a chef's knife. Shave off the flat edge of each quarter to round it.

PRICKING FOR BAKING

Large, floury potatoes are best for baking in the oven in their jackets. To prevent them bursting during cooking, the skin should be pierced by pricking it with a fork. If you like, rub with oil and salt to crisp the skin during cooking, or bake them on a bed of salt. You can also cook them on metal skewers – the heat is conducted through to the center of the potatoes quicker this way.

Scrub potatoes (see above) and prick them all over with a fork, piercing right through to the flesh. Bake at 425°F, 1–1¼ hours.

MAKING POMMES PARISIENNES

This is the classic French way to prepare potatoes for sautéing. The name comes from the melon baller used to cut the potatoes, called cuillère parisienne or Parisian spoon. It produces small balls that cook in butter, or a mixture of butter and oil, to an even brown color. Large floury potatoes are best – they produce a crisper result than waxy potatoes.

Press a melon baller into peeled potato and scoop out as many balls as possible. Drop the balls into a bowl of cold water as you work.

PREPARING POTATOES FOR DEEP-FRYING

There are many ways potatoes can be prepared for deep-frying, from ordinary fries to elaborate latticed potatoes or gaufrettes. They are usually peeled first, and must always be uniform in size and thickness. Drop them into cold water as you cut them to prevent discoloration. This also removes some of the starch and helps to make them crisp. Drain the shapes and dry them thoroughly before immersing in hot oil – see page 191 for the technique of deep-frying potatoes.

BY HAND

A sharp chef's knife can be used to cut thick sticks, such as the pommes pont neuf *shown here. Pommes frites* and allumettes *can also be cut by hand, but they are easier and more regular cut on a mandolin.*

POMMES PONT NEUF
Named after the oldest bridge in Paris, these are always served stacked. Trim the ends and sides of potato to make a rectangular block, then slice ½ in. thick. Stack the slices and cut into sticks ½ in. wide.

BY MACHINE

A mandolin, with its choice of blades and cutters, is the best tool to use for these classic wafer-thin French fries. See the box on page 167 for information on mandolins.

POMMES ALLUMETTES
Work potato against the fine shredding blade set to ¼ in. thickness. *Pommes pailles* (straw potatoes) are made in the same way, with the ramp positioned in line with the straight blade.

POMMES FRITES
Work potato against the coarse shredding blade set to ¼ in. thickness.

POMMES GAUFRETTES
Work potato against the rippled cutter set to ⅛ in. thickness and discard the first slice. Turn the potato 90° and cut the next slice. Repeat along the potato, turning it 90° after each slice.

POMMES SOUFFLES
Slightly thicker than game chips. Work potato against the straight blade set to ¼ in. thickness.

WAXY POTATOES

An all-purpose potato, the firm flesh has a high moisture content, low starch and thin skin.

NEW: Small, thin-skinned, recently harvested potatoes which have not been stored. Excellent for boiling and salads.
ROUND RED: Thin skinned with white, waxy flesh. For boiling, frying.
ROUND WHITE: Thin skinned with white flesh and firm, waxy texture. For boiling, frying.
YELLOW: Sold as Finnish Yellow, Yellow-Rose and Yukon Gold, they are thin-skinned with creamy yellow flesh and mild buttery flavor. For boiling and frying. Some types are also suitable for baking.

FLOURY POTATOES

Also called a baking potato, it is starchier and becomes light and fluffy when cooked.

LONG WHITE: Thin skinned potato with firm, smooth texture. For boiling, frying, baking and roasting.
PURPLE: Purple skinned with purple flesh and a dry, mealy texture. It retains its color when cooked. For baking and frying.
RUSSET (IDAHO): Thick skinned potato with a dry, mealy texture. For baking, frying, mashing and roasting.

ALLUMETTES

FRITES

PONT NEUF

GAUFRETTES

SOUFFLES

169

MUSHROOMS

The term "mushroom" is used loosely to mean the whole family of edible fungi. There are three broad categories: common cultivated white mushrooms, exotic cultivated ones such as shiitake and oyster mushrooms, and wild fungi such as chanterelles, cepes and truffles.

PREPARING CULTIVATED MUSHROOMS

Mushrooms can be eaten raw or cooked. Ordinary white mushrooms are grown in pasteurized compost, so need only wiping. If very dirty, rinse briefly. Do not soak them or they will become soggy. Button mushrooms can be left whole or halved, larger ones may be sliced or chopped.

1 Trim off the woody ends of the stalks with a small knife. Save the trimmings for use in stocks and soups.

2 Wipe the mushrooms gently with damp paper towels, removing any compost still clinging to them.

SLICING
Put the mushrooms stalk-side down on a cutting board. Slice lengthwise with a chef's knife.

PREPARING WILD MUSHROOMS

Fresh wild mushrooms deteriorate quickly, so use them as soon as possible. If storing briefly, keep them in a paper bag in the refrigerator. Most wild mushrooms do not need washing or peeling, but check with your supplier.

1 Gently brush off any earth that is still clinging to the mushrooms with a small brush or a clean cloth. Be careful not to damage the delicate flesh of the caps.

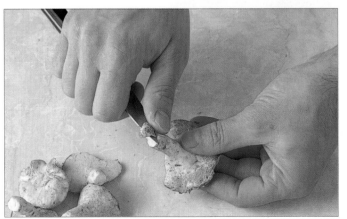

2 Trim off the woody ends of the stalks with a small knife. Leave as much of the flesh as possible. Many wild mushrooms are left whole or simply halved lengthwise, to preserve their attractive shape, but they can also be sliced in the same way as cultivated mushrooms.

PREPARING WOOD EARS

Also known as cloud ears, wood ears are an Asian fungus, commonly sold in dried form. Like dried mushrooms below, they must be reconstituted before use, when they swell into clusters of dark gelatinous lobes up to five times their dried size. They are used in stir-fries, soups and braised dishes.

Soak wood ears as for dried mushrooms below, then rinse thoroughly under cold running water to rid them of sand and grit lodged in the crevices. Dry thoroughly with a kitchen towel before use and trim off and discard the hard central stalks. Slice or chop wood ears according to individual recipe instructions.

RECONSTITUTING DRIED MUSHROOMS

Many different varieties of mushroom can be bought dried. These include Asian varieties such as shiitake and oyster mushrooms, and wild ones such as morels, cepes and chanterelles. Dried wild mushrooms are expensive but their flavor is highly concentrated, so even a very small quantity added to a dish will give a superb richness and depth. Add to dishes such as sauces, soups, omelettes, risottos, pasta sauces and stir-fries.

1 Put mushrooms in a bowl and cover with warm water. Leave to soak for 35–40 minutes or until they have softened.

2 Drain, then squeeze to extract the liquid. Strain the liquid and use with mushrooms.

TRUFFLES

There are two main types – the French black truffle from Périgord and the white truffle from Piedmont, northern Italy. The black truffle is eaten raw, used in stuffings and sauces, and braised or baked in pastry. White truffles are usually eaten raw.

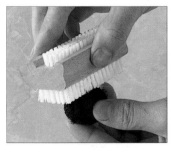

CLEANING A BLACK TRUFFLE
Carefully scrub the truffle with a brush. If you like, peel off the knobby skin with a vegetable peeler, finely chop the peelings and use in cooked dishes.

SLICING A TRUFFLE
Shave black or white truffles as thinly as possible with a vegetable peeler. Use shavings in cooking, or sprinkled raw on dishes like pasta, risotto, polenta and omelettes.

WILD MUSHROOMS

CEPE: *Porcini* "little pig" in Italian, this variety has a chubby shape and bulbous cap.
CHANTERELLE: Golden-hued and concave, tasting of apricots.
MOREL: This type has a slim conical cap and honeycomb exterior, with a sweet intensity to rival truffles.
PIED DE MOUTON : Cream-colored and fleshy with tiny white spines under the gills.

SAFETY FIRST

If you pick wild mushrooms yourself, do not eat anything you cannot positively identify as being edible. Eat wild mushrooms as soon as possible as they quickly deteriorate.

From top to bottom, left to right: shiitake; pied bleu; chanterelle, wood ears; pied de mouton

THE ONION FAMILY

Members of the onion family are essential to so many dishes, either as a subtle flavoring or as the star ingredient. When they are prepared correctly, following the methods shown here, they will release their flavor more readily and be more easily digested.

PEELING AND SLICING ONIONS

All onions must be peeled before use to remove the papery skin. Here the technique of slicing a whole onion into rings is shown. For smaller, half-moon slices, cut the onion in half lengthwise, place cut-side down and cut into vertical slices.

1 Trim away the root end without cutting right through. Peel off the skin with a small knife.

2 Cut off the tough root end with a chef's knife. Reserve for using in stocks.

3 Hold the onion on its side and slice downwards to form rings. Separate into individual rings, if you like.

DICING ONIONS

Many recipes call for onions to be diced or chopped. The size of the dice depends on the thickness of the first cuts. Keep the root end intact to prevent the onion from falling apart during chopping; it may also prevent tears (see box, above).

1 Cut peeled onion lengthwise in half. Place cut-side down and make a series of horizontal cuts without cutting the root.

2 Make a series of vertical cuts down through the onion, again making sure the root is not cut.

3 Hold the onion firmly on the chopping board and cut it crosswise into dice. For fine dice, continue to chop until the dice are the desired size. The tough root end that remains can be reserved for use in stocks.

PREPARING PEARL ONIONS

These small onions, also known as baby or button onions, are ideal for braising whole or pickling. The skins are thin and papery and can be difficult to remove. Steeping them in hot water first helps to loosen the skins before peeling.

1 Place the onions in a bowl and cover with hot water. Let steep for a few minutes until the skins begin to soften.

2 Drain the onions, rinse under cold running water, then peel away the skins with a small knife. Keep as much length to the stem ends as possible to prevent the centers from popping out. Discard skins.

CRUSHING GARLIC

Choose firm, plump garlic heads and separate them into cloves before peeling.

1 Lay the flat side of a chef's knife over a garlic clove and strike it with your fist.

2 Peel the clove and cut it lengthwise in half. Remove the green shoot from center.

3 Finely chop the clove by moving the knife back and forth in a rocking motion.

CUTTING LEEKS

Trimmed leeks are often cooked whole or gently braised in stock or baked au gratin. Sliced leeks are baked in quiches or added to soups and stews. Diced leeks are used as a flavoring in classic French cooking (see mirepoix, page 166). If you are cooking leeks whole, they must be washed thoroughly to dislodge any earth that may be trapped between the tightly furled leaves.

1 Slit the green tops. Rinse under cold running water to remove any trace of dirt.

2 Cut leek lengthwise in half. Lay leek flat and slice, thickly or thinly, across.

CUTTING SCALLIONS ASIAN-STYLE

Scallions are frequently used in Asian cooking, especially in quick stir-fries and soups. Sliced or shredded scallions, using both the white and green parts, are also used as a flavoring ingredient and a garnish on hot dishes of rice or noodles, or sprinkled over steamed or braised fish and meat dishes.

SHREDDING
Cut off the dark green top. Cut the light part lengthwise in half, then into strips.

ANGLE SLICING
Start at the dark green top and slice at an angle, using the line of your knuckles as a guide. Slice right down to the root end; discard the root.

UNUSUAL VEGETABLES

Vegetables from Africa, Asia, South America and the Middle East are becoming more widely available. Sometimes these are exotic varieties of more familiar types like eggplants and radishes, but there are also completely new species which require different methods of preparation and cooking. Sea vegetables, in their dried form, are shown opposite.

1 EGGPLANTS There are many varieties of eggplant apart from the familiar Mediterranean one. They are all prepared in the same way (see page 178).

2 WHITE & YELLOW EGGPLANTS It would seem most likely that the name eggplant derives from this white variety from Africa, because of its egg-like coloring and shape.

3 LOTUS ROOT Used in Chinese cooking, this vegetable cuts into attractive lacy slices. The skin must be peeled before cooking, then the flesh can be sliced and either steamed or stir-fried.

4 PEA EGGPLANTS These are one of the more unusual types of egplant from Thailand. They can be added whole to curries or puréed for use in spicy dipping sauces.

5 DASHEEN The coarse skin of this tropical root must be peeled off before cooking. The flesh can then be cut into chunks and either baked or boiled.

6 CASSAVA This is a starchy potato-like root vegetable from Africa and South America. Peel and cook as for potatoes.

7 THAI EGGPLANT This green eggplant is prepared like white or purple eggplant (see above). The flesh should be sliced and then fried or roasted. It is also often used for pickling.

8 SALSIFY Also known as oyster plant because of its supposed similarity in taste to the seafood, the skin must be scraped off before the flesh is cooked. To cook, cut into short lengths and boil.

DRIED SEAWEEDS

1 WAKAME Mild in flavor. Good in salads, soups and stir-fries. Can also be toasted and crumbled, over rice dishes.

2 ARAME Delicately flavored. Used in Japanese *miso* soup.

3 KOMBU A dried form of kelp used in the making of Japanese *dashi* (see page 18).

4 DULSE Salty and spicy tasting, this is particularly good in stir-fries and in salads.

9 DAIKON This vegetable, also called white radish and mooli, is much used in Asian cooking. It can be either shredded and eaten raw or thinly sliced and stir-fried or steamed.

10 LOOFAH An edible gourd generally used in Asian cooking, this vegetable must be peeled before cooking and can then be steamed or stir-fried.

11 CHINESE BITTER MELON A Far Eastern edible gourd, the flesh must be salted (dégorged) in order to draw out the bitter juices. The flesh is then best either sautéd or stir-fried.

12 EAST INDIAN ARROWROOT A hard root with tough skin, this is used in Southeast Asian stir-fried dishes. Once peeled the flesh can be shredded or diced.

13 EDDO This is a tuber from West Africa and the Caribbean, which can be prepared and cooked like potatoes.

14 ICICLE RADISH Also called green radish, this rather bitter Asian vegetable is used for pickling and preserving but can also be thinly sliced for stir-frying.

15 YARD-LONG BEANS These are an Asian vegetable which can be cooked whole or sliced on the diagonal like green beans.

16 TARO A hard mealy root vegetable from Southeast Asia and India. Peel before cooking and cut into chunks or slices and boil.

17 KOHLRABI This is a slightly unusual European vegetable that should be prepared and cooked like turnip (see page 167).

Chiles Rellenos

A popular classic from Mexico, chiles rellenos is literally translated as "stuffed peppers." Traditionally for festive occasions, the chilies are dipped in batter and deep-fried, and served as finger food at casual buffets. Here a lighter grilled version, without batter, is also given, so you can mix and match according to personal preference.

SERVES 6–8

*26 assorted chilies
(jalapeños, poblanos,
red and yellow Anaheims,
Scotch bonnets)*

Vegetable oil, for frying

*½ lb. Monterey Jack or
Cheddar cheese, grated*

*½ lb. white crabmeat (fresh,
defrosted or canned)*

2 tbsp. chopped fresh cilantro

Juice of ½ lime

Prepare the chilies (see box, below). Heat 3 tbsp. oil in a frying pan and fry the chilies for 3–5 minutes, turning them so they cook evenly on all sides. Work in batches to prevent the chilies from overcrowding the pan. Let drain on paper towels.

For cheese-stuffed chilies, press grated cheese into jalapeños and poblanos with your fingers, allowing about 1 tbsp. cheese for jalapeños and 3 tbsp. for poblanos.

For crab-stuffed chilies, pick over the crabmeat to remove any bits of shell or cartilage (if using frozen or canned crabmeat, drain it thoroughly first). Flake the crabmeat with a fork and mix in the chopped cilantro and lime juice. Spoon the mixture into yellow Anaheim and Scotch bonnet chilies.

To broil (for all chilies): place chilies on a baking sheet and put under a hot broiler for about 2 minutes, just until the cheese is melted.

To deep-fry (for stuffed jalapeños and poblanos and whole red Anaheims): make batter (see box, right). Heat about ½ in. oil in a large frying pan until it is very hot. Holding chilies by their stalks, dip them into the batter to coat, then deep-fry in batches in the hot oil until golden, 2–3 minutes for each batch. Drain on paper towels before serving.

BATTER FOR DEEP-FRIED CHILIES

1 cup all-purpose flour
Pinch of salt
1 egg
½ cup milk

Sift the flour and salt into a bowl and make a well in the center. Lightly beat the egg and pour into the well. Gradually begin to draw the flour from the sides into the egg, beating with a wooden spoon. When almost all incorporated, beat in the milk to make a smooth batter. If necessary, sieve the batter to remove any lumps (see page 39).

Preparing Chilies

The technique shown here is suitable for jalapeños and poblanos, and red Anaheims if you like. It retains the shape of the chilies so they can be stuffed whole. For round-topped chilies such as yellow Anaheims and Scotch bonnets, cut off the tops and scoop out the cores and seeds. Keep the tops for presentation.

Make a lengthwise slit in the side of each chili, from the shoulder down, using a small paring knife. With your fingers, carefully open out the slit to expose the seeds in the center of the chili.

Run your finger down the inside of the chili to remove the seeds, starting from the shoulder. Take care to wash your hands thoroughly afterwards or the juice from the chilies may sting.

VEGETABLE PUREES, MASHES AND MOLDS

Softened, cooked vegetables are popular accompaniments to meat, poultry and fish, offering contrast in color and texture. They can be pressed into a smooth or coarse purée or taken one stage further by being shaped in timbale molds and baked.

MASHED POTATOES

For the best mashed potatoes you need to select the right type of floury potato (see page 169). Once it is made, choose from the following – all variations on a similar theme – to create a smooth, creamy dish. Season to taste with salt and freshly ground pepper before serving.

- Hot milk and a generous amount of unsalted butter; cream can also be added.
- Crème fraîche and olive oil.
- Olive oil and crushed garlic.
- Hot creamy milk or cream and roasted garlic flesh (see page 188).
- Cream or creamy milk, unsalted butter and grated Gruyère cheese.

COOKING SPINACH

Wash spinach thoroughly, remove and discard the tough stalks and tear the leaves. Although spinach can be cooked in lots of boiling water, to retain its vitamins, minerals and color, it is far better to steam it (see page 187). Other good methods are to cook it in only the water that clings to the leaves after washing, or to sauté it in olive oil – both methods will take just 2 minutes.

MAKING PUREES AND MASH

A food processor or blender can be used for puréeing leafy vegetables (see below). For cooked root vegetables, such as carrots, you can use a machine, but sieving after mashing gives a finer texture. For the smoothest, fluffiest mashed potatoes, use a drum sieve, which has a very fine mesh, or a food mill, which sieves the potatoes at the same time as puréeing them. Never purée potatoes in a food processor or blender – they may turn gluey.

DRUM SIEVE
Hold sieve secure over a bowl and firmly press cooked vegetables through the mesh with a plastic scraper.

FOOD MILL
Place cooked potatoes in the mill set over a bowl; turn the crank to force potatoes through into bowl.

MAKING TIMBALES

Puréed vegetables make attractive single servings when cooked in small molds and turned out upside-down. Spinach is used here, but you can use carrots, broccoli or peas, all of which should be boiled before puréeing (you will need ¾ cup cooked purée). If you like, you can line the molds with blanched spinach leaves, as for the fish terrine on page 77.

1 Cook ¾ lb. spinach (see left). Purée in a blender with 3 eggs, 1 cup heavy cream, nutmeg and seasoning. Pour into four buttered 1 cup timbale molds.

2 Put the timbale molds in a *bain marie* and bake at 375°F for 20–25 minutes or until firm. Insert a skewer in the center of a timbale – it should come out clean.

3 Remove the molds from the *bain marie* and run a knife around the insides to loosen the timbales. Invert onto serving plates and gently lift off the molds.

LEGUMES, GRAINS & NUTS

LEGUMES

Dried beans, peas and lentils, the edible seeds of pod-bearing plants, are known as legumes. Rich in minerals, vitamins and fiber, yet low in fat, they are invaluable in the kitchen. Here's how to prepare and cook them.

SAFETY FIRST

Many legumes contain harmful toxins, so it is important to boil all beans vigorously for 10 minutes at the beginning of cooking. This destroys toxins and renders the beans harmless.

SOAKING AND COOKING

Dried beans and peas need to be soaked to soften them before cooking; lentils do not. The quick-soak method is an alternative to the one shown here: boil in plenty of water 2 minutes, cover and let soak 2 hours. Always season legumes after cooking or the skins will be tough.

 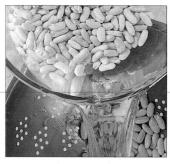 

1 Put the beans in a large bowl. Add cold water to cover. Soak for 8–12 hours.

2 Drain the beans into a colander; rinse thoroughly under cold running water.

3 Boil beans in unsalted water, 10 minutes. Simmer for time in chart (see left).

MAKING REFRIED BEANS

These are fried twice, hence their name. Soften chopped onions in oil, then add cooked pinto beans and a little of the bean cooking liquid and fry together, mashing the beans to a paste with a potato masher. Chill the paste overnight, then fry in oil again until crispy.

FIRST FRYING
Add cooked beans to onion and oil and mash to a paste.

SECOND FRYING
Stir bean paste over a high heat just until crisp.

Outer circle from bottom left: soy beans; black-eye beans; black beans; lima beans; red kidney beans; yellow split peas; mung beans. **Inner circle, from bottom left:** adzuki beans; chick peas; cannellini beans; navy beans

MAKING PATTIES

Legumes make perfect patties – they purée easily, marry well with flavorings such as garlic, onion, herbs and spices, and hold their shape. Falafel (see box, right) from Israel are the traditional ones, but you can make them with other legumes. Here chick peas and dried lima beans are used together.

1 Soak and boil legumes of your choice, then drain and reserve the cooking liquid. Work to a purée in a food processor, with a little of the reserved liquid. Turn into a bowl and mix with flavorings until well combined.

2 Shape the mixture into even-sized balls with wet hands (this helps prevent sticking), then flatten them into ovals, each one about 1 in. thick.

FALAFEL

1 cup chick peas, soaked, cooked and puréed
5 garlic cloves, finely chopped
1 onion, finely chopped
4 tbsp. chopped fresh cilantro
1 tbsp. all-purpose flour
1 tsp. ground cumin
1 tsp. ground allspice
Salt, pepper and cayenne
Vegetable oil, for frying

Mix ingredients; shape into balls. Shallow-fry in hot oil until golden on each side, 3–4 minutes. Drain on paper towels. Serves 4.

MAKING LEGUME PUREES

Puréed with olive oil and garlic, cooked legumes make aromatic dips, spreads and creamy side dishes. Here chick peas are used to make the Middle Eastern hummus; other good choices are cannellini beans, black or red kidney beans, or lentils. For a pungent flavor, add a few crushed dried chilies.

1 Purée cooked chick peas in a food processor with a little cooking liquid, and salt and crushed garlic to taste.

2 With machine running, add olive oil through tube. Add lemon juice to taste, and 1–2 tbsp. hot water.

MAKING DHAL

Confusingly, dhal is the name for both this spicy Indian lentil dish and the legume, of which there are hundreds of different varieties. Here yellow lentils (channa dhal) are used, but any other type can be substituted. For a special touch, top with the traditional tadka: sliced garlic and cayenne fried in ghee.

1 Fry onions and garlic in ghee with curry powder and chili powder. Add lentils and stir-fry for 1–2 minutes.

2 Cover with stock or water and simmer until lentils are tender. Stir often and add more liquid, as necessary.

COOKING TIMES

All timings are approximate. There is no need to soak lentils before cooking.

• BROWN/YELLOW/GREEN (PUY) LENTILS 30–45 mins
• RED LENTILS 20 mins

Top row, from left to right: Puy lentils; green lentils; brown lentils
Bottom row: red lentils; yellow lentils

COOKING RICE

From fragrant pilafs to creamy risottos, rice is the foundation of countless dishes. Because not all grains cook the same, it is essential to select the right rice – and cooking technique – for the dish you are making.

TYPES OF RICE

LONG-GRAIN: All-purpose rice; cook by hot water method. White rice takes 15 minutes; brown, 30–35 minutes.

ARBORIO: Italian short-grain; has creamy texture and nutty bite. Cook by risotto method (see page 198), 15–20 minutes.

BASMATI: Aromatic, for use in pilafs and Indian dishes; soak (see step 1, opposite page) before cooking by absorption method, 15 minutes.

CONVERTED: Processed so the grains stay separate; follow packet instructions, 10–12 minutes.

JAPANESE: Short-grain white rice that is plump, glossy and sticky; see opposite page for cooking.

PUDDING: Short-grain that is very soft when cooked; white rice takes 15–20 minutes, brown, 30–40 minutes. Can also be oven-baked, 1–1½ hours. See page 278 for methods.

THAI: Jasmine fragranced; cook by absorption method, 15 minutes.

WILD: Not a true rice, but an aquatic grass with a nutty flavor; cook by hot water method, 35–40 minutes.

HOT WATER METHOD

White or brown long-grain rice can be cooked in a large, unmeasured amount of boiling water. After cooking, drain the water off and rinse the rice. Rinsing removes excess starch, leaving the grains separate and dry, and the rice can be left to cool and be reheated without sticking.

1 Bring a pan of water to the boil. Add salt, then the rice. Simmer, uncovered, until tender (see box, left).

2 Turn the rice into a colander or sieve; rinse with boiling water. Toss in butter or oil to reheat.

ABSORPTION METHOD

This method, best for basmati and Thai rice, cooks rice in a measured amount of water that becomes completely absorbed when the rice is cooked. Use 2½ parts water to 1 part rice and cook over a low heat, keeping the pan tightly covered so the rice cooks in its own steam.

1 Put water, rice and salt in a pan; bring to the boil. Stir, lower the heat and cover.

2 Simmer for 15 minutes, then let stand 15 minutes. Fluff up grains with a fork.

Top row, from left to right: wild rice; brown basmati rice; white basmati rice; Thai (jasmine) rice.
Bottom row, from left to right: Long-grain and converted rice; Arborio (or risotto) rice; Japanese rice; pudding rice

MAKING A PILAF

Pilafs are popular in the Middle East and India, and cooks in both areas make them in much the same way – usually by the absorption method. For a main dish, fold in chopped cooked meat, poultry, or seafood and vegetables at the end. Seasonings can be as varied as you like.

1 Cover rice with cold water and let stand for 1 hour, changing the water several times until clear. Rinse well.

2 Soften chopped onion in oil in a frying pan. Add rice; stir over a moderate heat until grains start to burst.

3 Stir in hot stock (twice the volume of the rice). Add salt, lower the heat and cover. Simmer for 15 minutes.

JAPANESE VINEGARED RICE

The Japanese have a special kind of sticky, short-grain white rice. It is served at the end of every meal, and is also used to make vinegared rice for sushi. To cook Japanese sticky rice, rinse it until the water is clear, then soak it in a pan of water 30 minutes, allowing 2½ cups water for 2 cups rice. Bring to the boil, cover and simmer over a very low heat 15 minutes, then let stand 15 minutes. For the vinegared rice shown here, let cool to room temperature.

1 Boil 4 tbsp. each rice vinegar and sugar with a pinch of salt, stirring until the sugar has melted. Remove from the heat and let cool.

2 Put the cooled, cooked Japanese rice (see left) in a wooden bowl and drizzle the sweetened vinegar syrup evenly over it.

3 Mix the rice and vinegar syrup together with a rice paddle (see box, right) or a wooden spoon. Cool the rice slightly by fanning it with cardboard while fluffing it up with the rice paddle. Use the vinegared rice immediately, or cover with a damp kitchen towel to retain moisture and use within a few hours.

A special recipe for sushi, using this quantity of vinegared rice, is given on page 64.

A special recipe for sushi, using this quantity of vinegared rice, is given on page 64.

RICE ON THE MENU

A staple food in many countries, rice has long been revered for its nutritional qualities – the Chinese word for cooked rice is fan, meaning meal. Vegetarians the world over know that rice, eaten together with legumes, forms a complete protein, equivalent to that in meat.

BIRIANI: Indian favorite pairs fragrant basmati rice with aromatic spices, herbs and meat or vegetables.

DIRTY RICE: Robust Cajun pilaf combines rice with lightly sautéed chicken livers, onions, garlic and green pepper.

KEDGEREE: British classic with curried long-grain rice, smoked haddock and hard-boiled eggs.

PAELLA: Colorful Spanish mix of saffron-stained rice, chicken, seafood, ham, chorizo sausage and tomatoes.

RISI BISI: Rustic Italian dish featuring Arborio rice, ham, peas and Parmesan cheese.

STIR-FRIED RICE: A Chinese rice dish flavored with pork, seafood, vegetables and egg.

RICE PADDLE

In Japan, this small, flat utensil, made out of wood or bamboo, is used to turn cooked sticky rice, a technique that fluffs it up and enhances its appearance.

The paddle is also used to serve rice to guests. It is the custom for each person to get two paddlefuls from a wooden tub, regardless of the quantity of rice that has been cooked.

When fluffing up rice, use a sideways cutting motion.

Seafood Risotto

Here the popular Italian rice dish, risotto, is given an elegant finish with saltwater crayfish (also known as langoustines), scallops, squid and shrimp in a creamy sauce. For the creamiest consistency, be sure to use a short-grain risotto rice such as Arborio.

SERVES 4

12 *raw saltwater crayfish, in their shells*

Court bouillon (see page 66)

½ *lb. prepared squid (see page 86), pouch cut into rings*

8 *shelled scallops*

1 *cup heavy cream*

¼ *lb. peeled cooked shrimp*

Parmesan curls (see page 236), to garnish

FOR THE SEAFOOD STOCK

1 *tbsp. olive oil*

1½ *tbsp. butter*

¼ *cup* mirepoix *(see page 166) of onion, carrot and celery*

¼ *cup cognac*

1 *tbsp. tomato paste*

1 *ripe tomato, chopped*

1 *garlic clove, crushed*

1½ *quarts fish stock*

1 *bouquet garni*

Salt and freshly ground pepper

FOR THE RISOTTO

2 *tbsp. olive oil*

½ *onion, finely chopped*

1 *cup risotto rice*

¼ *cup dry white wine*

¼ *cup crème fraîche*

2 *tbsp. freshly grated Parmesan cheese*

Poach the crayfish in court bouillon, 7–8 minutes; let cool in the liquid, then remove them and pull off the heads and shells. Coarsely crush the heads and shells.

Make the seafood stock: heat the oil and butter in a saucepan over a high heat and sauté the crushed heads and shells with the *mirepoix*. Deglaze the pan with some of the crayfish stock and the cognac. Add the tomato purée, stir for 1–2 minutes, then add the chopped tomato and crushed garlic and cook for a few minutes more. Add the fish stock and bouquet garni and bring to the boil. Lower the heat and simmer until the liquid has reduced to about 1¼ quarts. Strain the stock and season lightly.

Pour 1 quart of the stock back into the saucepan and keep it at a low simmer. Pour the remaining stock into another pan and set aside.

Make the risotto: heat the oil in a wide heavy pan and sweat the onion until soft. Add the rice and stir for 1–2 minutes to coat the grains with oil, then start adding the simmering stock, about ⅔ cup at a time (see box, below). When all the stock has been added, add the wine. The total cooking time will be 20–25 minutes.

While the risotto is cooking, bring the second pan of stock to the boil, then lower the heat. Add the squid and scallops and gently poach

them for 3–5 minutes; remove with a slotted spoon.

Reduce the stock by about half, then stir in the heavy cream. Add the crayfish, squid, scallops and shrimp and heat through gently. Check the seasoning.

Stir the crème fraîche and grated Parmesan into the risotto, then check the seasoning. Mound the risotto in the center of warmed serving bowls, doming it neatly, or press it into oiled timbale molds and turn it out. Surround with the seafood and sauce, garnish with Parmesan curls and serve immediately.

Making Risotto

For a successful risotto, the stock must be added gradually so that the rice, although always kept moist, is not drowned in liquid. Italian cooks literally stand over the pot all the time a risotto is cooking, stirring constantly at first, and then, as the rice cooks, stirring less frequently. This stirring technique ensures a creamy texture and a perfectly cooked risotto.

Add the first ⅔ cup of stock, regulating the heat so the risotto is bubbling gently. Wait until the stock is almost all absorbed before adding the next ⅔ cup.

When ready, the rice grains should be separate and firm but tender (*al dente*, like pasta). The starch released from the rice will give the risotto a creamy consistency.

COOKING OTHER GRAINS

Seeds of the grass family, grains are available in a variety of forms, and offer endless preparation possibilities. Choosing the right cooking technique is vital because different cooking processes affect both taste and texture.

POLENTA

Also called cornmeal, it can be served moist, enriched with butter and grated Parmesan cheese as a side dish, or in firm, crisp-crusted pieces that have been panfried or chargrilled. These are usually topped with chargrilled vegetables or a fresh tomato sauce.

1 Bring 2 quarts salted water to the boil. Reduce heat to very low and simmer. Slowly add 2 cups polenta, stirring constantly.

2 Cook, stirring, until it pulls away from the pan, 20 minutes. You can now serve the polenta, with butter and Parmesan stirred in.

3 For fried or chargrilled polenta, omit butter and Parmesan and spread polenta ¾ in. thick on a work surface. Leave until cold.

4 Trim the rough edges to form a rectangle. Cut lengthwise down the center of the rectangle, then cut into wedges, as shown here, using a chef's knife.

5 Separate the wedges. Brush the tops with olive oil. Panfry or chargrill, turning halfway through and brushing with more oil, until golden brown, about 6 minutes.

COUSCOUS

Most couscous is precooked, and only needs moistening and steaming according to packet instructions. The method shown here gives a richer result. Serve it as a side dish, mixed with finely chopped nuts, dried fruits or fresh herbs.

1 Put 1½ cups couscous in a lightly buttered pan. Add 2 cups hot water; stir with a fork until well blended.

2 Cook couscous over a medium-high heat for 5–10 minutes. Lower the heat and stir in 3 tbsp. butter.

3 Stir with a fork to fluff up and separate the grains, and coat them with the melted butter.

BULGAR

Also known as bulghur wheat, pourgouri and burghul, these are grains of wheat that are boiled until cracked, then dried. The grain is simplicity itself to prepare, but care must be taken to squeeze out as much water as possible after soaking. Bulgar is most often used in Middle Eastern pilafs, and in tabbouleh *and* kibbeh, *all of which will taste insipid if the grain is watery.*

1 Place the bulgar in a bowl. Add enough cold water to completely cover. Let stand for 15 minutes.

2 Tip bulgar into a fine sieve set over a bowl. Squeeze handfuls to remove excess water and place in a bowl.

POPPING CORN

There is nothing quite like the taste of freshly popped corn, tossed in salt, as here, or in sugar or spice, or left just as it is. Only pop a very small quantity at a time – just enough to cover the bottom of the pan to one kernel deep. As it pops, the corn swells up to make a larger amount than you imagine. First measure the volume of the corn, then use oil equal to half that measure.

1 Heat oil in a large pan over a moderate heat until very hot, but not smoking. Add the corn and cover with a tight-fitting lid.

2 Shake the pan over the heat just until the popping stops. Remove from the heat and pour popped corn into a bowl. Sprinkle with salt.

In North Africa, the couscous grain gives its name to a spicy dish of meat and vegetables cooked in a special bulbous pot. Called a *couscousière*, this pot comes in two parts. The stew cooks in the bottom part of the pot, while the grain steams in a perforated pot on top, gaining flavor from the heady aromas of the stew beneath. The stew and grain are then served together.

DIFFERENT GRAINS AND THEIR USES

BARLEY: A nutty grain that is most commonly used as a thickener in soups and stews.

BUCKWHEAT (GROATS/KASHA): This fruit used as a grain is most popular in Eastern and Central European cooking. Use as part of a stuffing, as a hot breakfast cereal or a side dish; buckwheat flour is used to make blinis and Breton crêpes.

HOMINY: Served as grits in the American South, hominy is made from yellow or white corn bathed in a lye solution. It must be soaked overnight in water before cooking.

MILLET: Favored for its crunchy texture and nutty flavor, millet flakes and grains are used in stews, stuffings and curries.

OATS: Rolled and flaked oats are used as the basis for both muesli and porridge.

QUINOA: This has a grassy flavor. Use in soups, salads and breads, and as a substitute for rice.

RYE: Available as grains, flakes and flour, rye is used to make breads and whisky.

WHEATBERRY: This is the unprocessed kernel of wheat. Use in pilafs instead of rice, and in breads and stuffings.

NUTS

Seeds or fruits with an edible kernel enclosed in a hard shell, nuts add a crunchy texture, flavor and rich color to a wide range of sweet and savory dishes. The techniques for shelling, skinning and preparing a selection of nuts are described on these pages.

SHELLING PISTACHIOS

Buy pistachios with partially open shells. If closed, the nut is underripe and the shell will be very difficult to remove.

Pry the shell open with your fingernails to reveal the green-skinned nut. Once the hinge of the shell snaps, the nut will pop out. The pistachios are now ready for blanching and skinning (see right).

Top row, from left to right: peanuts; pistachios; walnuts; pine nuts (*pignoli*).
Bottom row: hazelnuts; pecan; almonds; Brazil nuts

BLANCHING AND SKINNING

Almond and pistachio skin is bitter, and will spoil the delicate flavor of the nuts if it is left on. Here almonds are blanched to ease skinning; the technique is the same for shelled pistachios (see left). The nut skins are easiest to remove when still warm after blanching, so do not leave them too long after draining.

1 Cover nuts with boiling water. Let stand, 10–15 minutes. Drain; let cool.

2 Pinch the softened skin between your thumb and index finger and slip it off.

TOASTING AND SKINNING

Hazelnuts and Brazil nuts are best toasted rather than blanched before skinning. Here, hazelnuts are toasted in the oven, but if you like you can toast them by dry-frying them on top of the stove. Put them in a non-stick, heavy frying pan and stir over a low heat until lightly toasted on all sides, 2–4 minutes.

1 Spread the nuts evenly on a baking sheet and toast at 350°F for 10 minutes, shaking the sheet occasionally.

2 Wrap the toasted nuts in a kitchen towel to steam for a few minutes, then rub to remove the skins.

SHREDDING AND CHOPPING NUTS

Although most nuts can be bought ready chopped, flaked and shredded, you may not always find what you need. Nuts that are cut just before use will taste fresher and be more moist.

SHREDDING
Place nut, flat-side down, on a chopping board and cut lengthwise into shreds.

FLAKING
Place nut, thin-side down, on a cutting board. Steady one side; cut into long, thin flakes.

CHOPPING
Put shredded nuts on a board. Steady knife and work blade backwards and forwards.

PEELING CHESTNUTS

These sweet, starchy nuts have a hard, brittle shell and papery skin, both of which should be removed whether the chestnuts are to be used raw or cooked. Allow plenty of time because the skins tend to stick to the nuts and are difficult to remove. There are three different techniques.

CUTTING
Hold nut between your fingers and cut away shell and skin with a sharp knife.

TOASTING
Pierce shell with the point of a knife. Broil until the shells split. Cool, then peel.

BLANCHING
Put nuts in water and bring to the boil. Drain and skin while hot.

MAKING A NUT BUTTER

Chilled nut butters make tasty toppings for hot food, and are quick and easy to make in the food processor. Almond butter is good with fish, hazelnut or pistachio with poultry and meat. If sugar and spice are added, nut butters taste good on hot barbecued fruits.

Grind toasted nuts in a food processor fitted with the metal blade. Add twice as much butter as nuts and blend together using the pulse button. Turn out the nut butter and shape into a log on baking parchment, then wrap and refrigerate. Slice as required.

COCONUT

Exotic in appearance and tropical in taste, coconuts are a staple ingredient in Asian, Caribbean and Latin American kitchens. They have three layers – a hard hairy husk, creamy white meat beneath, and thin milky liquid in the center. Select coconuts that are heavy for their size and sound full of liquid.

USING COCONUT AND COCONUT MILK

- Use the juice from the middle of the coconut as a drink or a light stock.
- Serve chunks of coconut flesh with fresh fruits in a warm chocolate fondue.
- Top curries, cakes and desserts with toasted coconut shreds.
- Use coconut milk to enrich Thai and Indian curries.
- When making crème anglaise for homemade ice cream (see page 286), use coconut milk instead of cow's milk.
- Use coconut milk to flavor cream sauce (see page 268) and rice (see page 130).

OTHER TYPES OF COCONUT MILK

- Desiccated coconut can be used instead of freshly grated, following the same technique.
- Blocks of creamed coconut work equally well. Chop with a chef's knife, then dissolve in boiling water. This type does not need straining before use.
- Coconut milk powder is very convenient to use. Either mix it to a paste with boiling water, or sprinkle the powder directly into sauces and curries.
- Canned coconut milk has a thick layer of "cream" on the top that can be scooped off and used separately.

PREPARING A WHOLE COCONUT

Before dealing with the flesh of a coconut, you need to crack open the hard shell with a hammer. The technique shown here is the easiest way. After removing the thin brown skin that surrounds the flesh, shred or grate the flesh according to individual recipes.

1 Pierce a metal skewer through the indentations or "eyes" in the stalk end of the husk. Drain off the juice through the holes.

2 Crack the coconut by tapping it with a hammer all around its girth. Keep turning it around until it splits in half.

3 Pry the flesh out of the shell by working a small knife between them. Pare away the dark outer skin with a vegetable peeler.

MAKING COCONUT MILK

The juice in the center of a coconut is not the coconut "milk" used in cooking. This is made by steeping the flesh in water, then squeezing it to extract coconut-flavored "milk." You can steep and squeeze it more than once if you like, each time getting a thinner milk.

1 Rub the coconut flesh against the coarsest grid of a box grater, or grate it in a food processor fitted with the metal blade.

2 Put the grated coconut flesh in a bowl and pour over boiling water to cover. Stir well to mix, then leave to soak for 30 minutes until the water is absorbed.

3 Turn into a muslin-lined sieve set over a bowl and let the "milk" drain through. Draw up the muslin and squeeze hard to extract as much milk as possible.

PASTA

•

HOMEMADE PASTA

Although there are hundreds of types of commercially made pasta, it is still a uniquely satisfying experience to make your own. Here the techniques are shown for making pasta dough by hand and machine, together with flavoring ideas. To roll and cut the dough, see pages 208–209.

To roll and cut the dough, see pages 208–209.

WHO WAS FIRST?

It is quite widely believed that the 13th-century traveler Marco Polo discovered pasta in China, and brought it back to Italy. What excited his interest was that the Chinese were eating something like macaroni from his homeland.

Pasta was certainly common in Italy by the time the Roman Apicius wrote his famous book *The Art of Cooking* in the first century A.D., but it appears that noodles were being eaten in China much earlier than that.

Marco Polo (1254–1324)

FLOUR FOR MAKING PASTA

The very best flour to use for making pasta is durum wheat or semolina flour, but unfortunately this is not always easy to obtain and it is also very hard to work with. The next best choice is unbleached all-purpose flour, either white or wholemeal. Unbleached all-purpose flour often has a protein count which is as high as bread flour – 12–13 grams per cup. Other bleached varieties have 10–12 grams of protein per cup.

BY HAND

Making pasta by hand is a simple technique that requires only a little time and yet produces quite excellent results. The technique of gentle kneading and the warmth from your hands both help to create a very elastic dough that can be stretched and shaped with ease. Here 1 lb. egg pasta – pasta all'uovo – is made, enough for 6–8 for a first course, 4 for a main course.

1 Sift 2½ cups unbleached all-purpose flour onto a work surface. Make a large well in the center with your hand. Add 3 lightly beaten eggs, 1 tsp. salt and 1 tbsp. olive oil to the well.

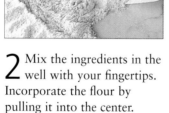

2 Mix the ingredients in the well with your fingertips. Incorporate the flour by pulling it into the center.

3 Continue incorporating the flour, drawing it in from the sides of the well and using a pastry scraper to mix the dough.

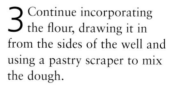

4 Work the ingredients until the egg is absorbed by the flour. The dough should be moist; if sticky, sprinkle over a little more flour.

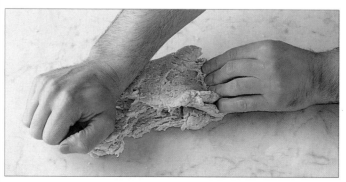

5 Begin kneading the dough by holding one end and pushing the other away from you with the palm of your hand. Continue kneading until smooth and elastic, 10–15 minutes.

6 Let the dough rest, covered, for up to 1 hour before rolling and cutting.

BY MACHINE

If you have a food processor, you can use it, fitted with the metal blade, to make pasta dough. This will save time and effort at the mixing stage, but it is still very important to knead the dough by hand after mixing. Overloading the machine will prevent it from mixing evenly – use a maximum of 1 lb. flour for any one batch.

1 Sift 2½ cups unbleached all-purpose flour and put into the food processor with 1 tbsp salt. Add 1 tbsp. olive oil and 1 egg. Work until the egg is incorporated.

2 With the motor running, add two more eggs, one at a time through the funnel, and work until a dough begins to form.

3 Turn the dough out, then knead the dough until it is smooth and elastic (see step 5, opposite page). Cover and let rest for up to 1 hour before rolling and cutting.

ADDING FLAVORS

To give interest to homemade pasta, you can add different flavorings. Whatever your choice, the only rule is that the flavoring should always be evenly incorporated.

Dry ingredients, such as crushed peppercorns or dried herbs, should be mixed with the sifted flour, while wet ingredients or those that contain more moisture, such as chopped spinach, fresh herbs and squid ink, should be added with the last egg.

BY HAND

SPINACH
Add 2 tbsp. finely chopped, well-drained cooked spinach to the wet ingredients in the well and mix thoroughly.

BY MACHINE

TOMATO
Add 1 tbsp. sun-dried tomato paste to the dry ingredients at the same time as the oil and the first of the eggs.

SAFFRON STRANDS

FRESH HERBS

CRUSHED PEPPER

WHAT'S IN A NAME?

PAGLIA E FIENO: "Straw and hay" – spinach and egg.

PASTA ALL'UOVO: The most popular pasta in northern Italy, made with eggs.

PASTA NERA: Black pasta that gets its color, and a unique flavor, from squid ink.

PASTA ROSSA: Usually a tomato pasta with an orange tint. Can also be made with a deeper red color using beets.

PASTA VERDE: A green pasta made with spinach, but can also include Swiss chard or basil.

TRICOLORE: "Three colors" – spinach, tomato and egg.

ROLLING & CUTTING

Pasta can be rolled into sheets by hand or, more quickly and thinly, with a pasta machine. After a brief drying time the pasta sheet can then be cut, by hand or using the attachments on the pasta machine, into a wide variety of shapes and sizes, depending on your chosen recipe.

ROLLING PASTA BY HAND

Hand-rolled pasta is thicker than pasta rolled by machine. You will need a spacious work surface: each ball of pasta dough will roll out into a very large sheet. To make handling easier, cut the dough in half, then roll out each half separately, keeping an even thickness.

 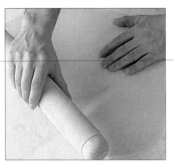 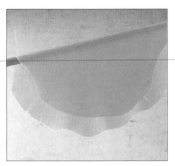

1 Cut rested dough (see pages 206 and 207) in half. Keep one half covered and flatten the other into a round. Roll the dough into a thin round sheet.

2 Bring the edge of the sheet furthest from you up over the pin and use it to help stretch the sheet, as shown. Turn the sheet 45° and repeat seven times.

3 When paper thin, hang the sheet of dough over a suspended floured broom handle. Repeat with the remaining piece of dough. Let dry, about 15 minutes.

ROLLING PASTA BY MACHINE

A pasta machine rolls sheets of pasta until smooth and elastic, and of uniform thickness. Turn the handle and feed the pasta dough through different roller width settings by progressing one notch at a time. Before and between rollings, flour the pasta sheets and the machine rollers.

1 Cut rested dough (see pages 206 and 207) into four pieces. Flatten the pieces with your hands to form rectangles, roughly the same width as the machine.

2 Feed one piece of dough through the pasta machine, with the rollers set at their widest setting. Repeat with the remaining pieces.

3 Fold each piece of dough into thirds and roll again. Repeat three or four times without folding, reducing the notch width each time. Let dry as in step 3 above.

CUTTING PASTA BY HAND

Handmade pasta must be cut by hand. After drying the rolled out pasta for about 15 minutes, the pasta sheets should feel leathery but supple enough to cut without sticking together. If the pasta is too dry it will be brittle and difficult to cut. Before you start cutting, you can cut the sheets into more manageable-sized pieces, if you like. Use a chef's knife to do this, and try to avoid dragging the dough as you cut it.

1 Take one sheet of the dried pasta dough and roll it into a loose but even cylinder. Transfer the cylinder to a board.

2 Cut the cylinder crosswise on the diagonal into strips about ½ in. wide. Unroll the strips and dry as in step 3 below, or as bundles (see tagliatelle, right).

DRYING PASTA

Fresh egg pasta must be dried thoroughly before storing. Dust it with a little flour and place it in an airtight container in the refrigerator for two days.

TAGLIATELLE
Take a few strands and curl them loosely around your hand to make bundles. Place side by side on a floured dish. Let dry 1–2 hours.

LASAGNE
Put lasagne rectangles or squares side by side on a floured kitchen towel. Cover with another floured kitchen towel. Let dry 1–2 hours.

CUTTING PASTA BY MACHINE

The great advantage of the pasta machine is that it cuts flat noodles (tagliatelle) cleanly, evenly and quickly. By adjusting the roller settings, the noodles can be cut to varying widths. Keep the dough and rollers lightly floured to prevent sticking.

1 Cut the pasta sheet into 12 in. lengths as it passes through the rollers on the thinnest setting. Place the sheets on a floured kitchen towel until all the dough has been rolled.

2 Feed each length of dough through the machine set on the desired cut.

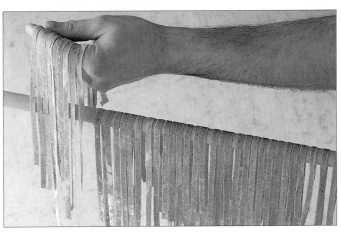

3 Hang the cut pasta over a floured suspended broom handle or over the back of a chair, or lay them flat on floured kitchen towels. Let dry 1–2 hours.

MAKING FRESH STUFFED PASTA

The dough used in stuffed pasta should not be too dry – it must be moist enough to shape easily and seal well. Shapes vary from squares to half moons. Stuffings vary too, but many contain cheese, with egg to bind. Stuffed pasta is usually cooked in water or broth, or baked with a sauce.

MAKING RAVIOLI

Stuffed pillows of pasta can be made by sandwiching the filling between two sheets of pasta (see recipe, page 216) or by folding one large sheet in half, as shown here. Alternatively a special pre-formed mold can be used (see box, left). Cover any pasta that is not being used with a damp kitchen towel, to keep it moist. Do not overfill. The technique shown here uses rolled-out handmade dough (see rolling pasta by hand, page 208).

RAVIOLI-MAKING EQUIPMENT

Most specialist cookware shops sell equipment specifically designed for making uniformly shaped ravioli. Make sure pasta is not too dry and to prevent it sticking, flour the tools before use.

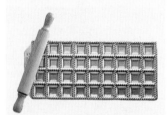

Ravioli molds come in a variety of sizes and are good for making even-sized ravioli. The metal tray has a series of small indentations with ridged edges – often 40 to a tray. The molds are usually sold together with a small wooden rolling pin, which is used to flatten the dough on the mold and to seal the ravioli. Use this mold once the dough is cut to size (see step 1, right).

Ravioli cutters have wooden handles with metal cutters attached. They are available in various sizes and cut only one ravioli at a time (see page 216).

1 Trim one pasta sheet to a 12 x 24 in. rectangle, using a chef's knife. Use the trimmings to make tagliatelle (see page 209).

2 Put 16 rounded teaspoons of filling (see box, opposite page) over half the sheet, making sure that they are evenly spaced.

3 Brush a border around each mound with a little water. This will help the pasta stick together.

4 Fold over the plain half of the pasta sheet to cover the filling, making sure the edges meet. Press between the mounds of filling using the side of your hand to seal the two layers of pasta and exclude any air.

5 Dust a fluted metal pastry wheel lightly with flour. Cut around the edges of the pasta to neaten them and make them square, then cut around the mounds of filling to make the ravioli shapes.

6 Place the ravioli between two floured kitchen towels. Leave them to dry about 1 hour, turning them halfway through. Meanwhile make another batch of ravioli with the second sheet of pasta and more filling.

MAKING TORTELLINI

A specialty of Bologna, tortellini are supposedly modelled on Venus's navel. Shaping them takes some time and practice, but they can be made a day ahead and stored in the refrigerator.

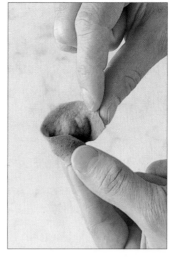

1 Make and roll out pasta dough (see pages 206–208). Cut out rounds from the pasta sheets with a floured 3 in. plain ravioli cutter or pastry cutter. Keep rounds covered to prevent them drying out. Put a small spoonful of filling (see box, right) in the center of each.

2 Using a small brush, dampen the edges of the rounds with a little water. Then pick up each round in your hands and fold it in half, carefully pressing the edges of the dough together to form a sealed crescent around the filling.

3 Wrap the crescent around one index finger, turning the sealed edge upward at the same time. Pinch the pointed ends firmly together. As you make each one, put the tortellini between two floured kitchen towels while you make the others. Let them dry for about 1 hour.

CHICKEN AND SAGE FILLING

¼ lb. skinless boneless chicken
  breast
1 small onion
2 garlic cloves
Leaves of 1 flat-leaf parsley sprig
  and 1 sage sprig
Salt and freshly ground pepper
1 egg, lightly beaten

Cut the chicken into pieces. Peel the onion and garlic; cut the onion into quarters. Place in a food processor fitted with the metal blade. Process until roughly chopped, then add the remaining ingredients and process again until finely chopped. Transfer to a bowl, cover and refrigerate until required. Makes about 5 oz. filling, sufficient for 32 ravioli or tortellini or 4 cannelloni.

MAKING CANNELLONI

Ready-made cannelloni tubes are available but this recipe follows the Neapolitan tradition in which sheets of pasta are boiled, then rolled around a filling.

1 Make and roll out pasta dough (see pages 206–208), then cut the pasta sheets into 4 x 3 in. rectangles. Bring a large pan of water to the boil and half fill a large bowl with cold water. Add 1 tbsp. oil and 1 tsp. salt to the boiling water, then add a few pieces of the pasta. Cook, just until wilted, about 1 minute.

2 Remove the pasta very carefully with a spatula and immerse immediately in the bowl of cold water. When cool enough to handle, remove the pasta from the cold water and place in a single layer on a kitchen towel to drain. Repeat with the remaining pieces of pasta.

3 Using a piping bag and a large plain tube, add a line of filling (see box, above) down one long side of each rectangle. Alternatively, use carefully placed spoonfuls. Roll the pasta around the filling, keeping the cylinder as even as possible. Put the cylinders seam-side down in a well-buttered baking dish and coat with the sauce of your choice. Fresh tomato sauce (see page 331) is a classic with cannelloni, so too is béchamel sauce (see page 222). Sprinkle with grated Parmesan cheese and bake at 400°F for 20–30 minutes.

MAKING GNOCCHI

Italian for "little dumplings," these can be made with a variety of ingredients. The two most common are "alla Romana" made with semolina, and the plumper version using potato. Both are a challenge – they must be light in texture but firm enough to shape and not break up when cooked.

SEMOLINA GNOCCHI

The semolina is added in a constant stream, stirring all the time, to incorporate air and prevent lumps forming. Infuse the milk first, if you like. Bring it to the boil with seasonings such as onion, cloves and bay leaves, cover and let stand 1 hour. Strain the milk before using.

1 Bring 1 quart milk to the boil in a large pan. Lower the heat and pour in 1½ cups semolina in a steady stream, stirring constantly with a wooden spoon to prevent lumps forming.

2 Bring the semolina mixture to the boil and cook, stirring constantly, until thick and smooth, about 5 minutes.

3 Whisk together 3 egg yolks. Remove the pan from the heat and beat the eggs, a little at a time, into the semolina mixture until evenly incorporated.

4 Spread the mixture in a lightly oiled shallow dish. Rub the surface with some butter, to prevent a crust forming. Let cool, preferably overnight.

5 Lightly oil a plain pastry cutter and cut the mixture into rounds or use a chef's knife to create shapes of your choice (see left). Arrange the gnocchi shapes, overlapping them slightly, in an oiled baking dish, brush with melted butter and sprinkle with freshly grated Parmesan cheese. Bake at 450°F for 15–20 minutes until golden brown. Serve hot.

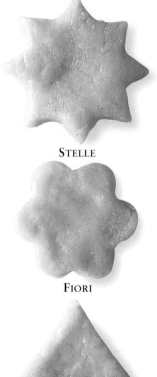

ROMBI

STELLE

FIORI

TRIANGOLI

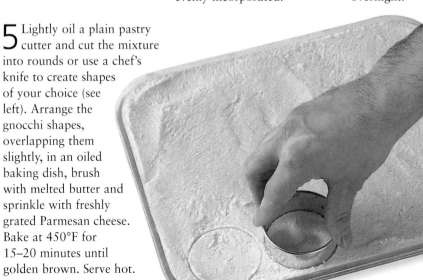

POTATO GNOCCHI

It is not easy to make potato gnocchi – Italians say that you need to "feel" the right consistency of the dough rather than measure out the exact quantities of ingredients. The type of potato is very important: floury varieties like Russet need the addition of flour and egg to moisten them; waxy types, like the round white shown here, only require flour. Keep the amount of flour to a minimum, just enough to hold the potato together – too much will make the gnocchi heavy. Cook the potatoes in their skins to reduce the amount of moisture they absorb.

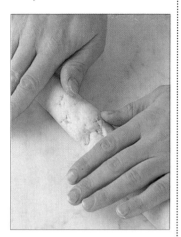

1 Cook 1½ lbs. potatoes, in their skins, in boiling salted water for 20 minutes or until tender. Drain, leave until cool enough to handle but still warm, then peel off their skins.

2 Mash the potatoes in a large bowl, then add 1½ cups all-purpose flour, salt and freshly ground pepper to taste. Mix with a spatula, combining the ingredients evenly to make a dough.

3 Turn the dough onto the work surface and knead with your hands until smooth. Cut the dough in half. Roll each piece into a long sausage shape, about 1 in. in diameter.

4 Cut the lengths of dough crosswise into small pieces. Shape the pieces into ovals by rolling them between your fingers. If the dough feels moist and sticky, lightly flour your fingers, but take care not to use too much flour or the gnocchi will become heavy. Mark the shapes with a fork (see box, right), if you like.

5 Working in batches, drop the gnocchi into a pan of boiling unsalted water and cook them until they rise to the surface, 1–3 minutes. Cook for a further 20 seconds, then remove with a slotted spoon. Serve hot, with melted butter and Parmesan.

WHAT'S IN A NAME?

Gnocchi differ in fillings and names depending on the region they come from.

- *Canederli*, from Trentino, are large gnocchi, each containing a prune.
- *Gnocchi di riso*, a speciality of Reggio Emilia, are made from cooked rice mixed with eggs and bread crumbs.
- *Gnocchi di zucca*, from Lombardy, are made with cooked pumpkin.
- *Gnocchi verdi* from Emilia-Romagna are made with spinach, ricotta, Parmesan and eggs added to potato.

TRICK OF THE TRADE

MARKING WITH A FORK
The technique of making ridges in gnocchi is not just decorative: it helps compress the gnocchi so that they keep their shape, and the grooves help hold the sauce when the gnocchi are served.

Take a piece of gnocchi and press one side of it against the tines of a large fork, rolling it off the fork onto a board. Repeat with the remaining pieces.

213

COOKING PASTA

It is important to know how to cook pasta properly: undercooked pasta is chewy and tastes raw; overcooked pasta has a mushy texture. For perfect results, test frequently toward the end of the cooking time.

COOKING SHORT PASTA

Use a large pan so the pasta shapes can move freely in the boiling water. As an approximate guide, allow 5 quarts water and 1 tbsp. salt for 1 lb. pasta. Adding a little oil to the water helps prevent the shapes sticking together during cooking.

1 Bring a large pan of water to the boil. Add salt and 1 tbsp. olive oil.

2 Add the pasta all at once, bring the water back to the boil, then start timing (see opposite page).

3 Cook, uncovered, at a rolling boil until the pasta is *al dente* (see box, opposite page), stirring occasionally.

4 Drain the pasta thoroughly in a colander, shaking it vigorously to release all the water. Return it to the pan and reheat with 1–2 tbsp. of butter or olive oil. Or turn it into a warmed serving bowl and toss with a sauce.

PASTA EQUIPMENT

A pasta cooker is a worthwhile investment for cooking large quantities, especially as it can be used for other cooking purposes too, such as jam-making and preserving. Made of stainless steel, it consists of a perforated pan which fits inside a solid pan. When the pasta has finished cooking, the inner perforated pan containing the pasta can be lifted out, allowing the water to drain into the outer pan. The pasta can then be transferred safely and easily to a serving dish.

A simple way to lift long strands of spaghetti or tagliatelle out of the cooking water is to use metal tongs. These grasp the pasta without cutting it and are ideal for lifting out one or two strands when testing for doneness.

Left from top to bottom: wholewheat spaghetti; plain spaghetti; lasagne sheets. **Middle from top to bottom:** conchiglie; ditalini; orecchiette. **Right from top to bottom:** wholewheat penne; rigatoni; cannelloni

COOKING LONG PASTA

The technique for long dried pasta, such as spaghetti, linguine and tagliatelle (unless it has been curled into nests before drying) is to gently ease it into the water. As the pasta becomes submerged in the boiling water it softens and bends so that it can be coiled round in the pan without being broken. The special Italian pasta pot (see box, opposite page) is ideal for cooking long pasta. Calculate the cooking time from the moment the water returns to the boil after all the pasta is submerged.

1 Bring a large pan of water to the boil. Add salt and oil as for short pasta (see opposite page), then take a handful of pasta and dip one end in the water. As the pasta softens, coil until submerged. Cook until *al dente* (see right).

2 Drain the pasta thoroughly. Rinse out the pan then return to the heat and add 1–2 tbsp. butter or olive oil. Return the cooked pasta to the pan and toss over a high heat until the pasta is glistening.

COOKING TIMES

Calculate cooking times of all pasta types from the moment the water returns to the boil after the pasta has been added and always test before draining (see box below). If the pasta is to be cooked further (baked in lasagne, for example), reduce the boiling time slightly.

- FRESH PASTA
  1–3 mins

- FRESH STUFFED PASTA
  3–7 mins

- DRIED PASTA NOODLES
  8–15 mins

- DRIED PASTA SHAPES
  10–12 mins

COOKING ASIAN NOODLES

Most Chinese and Japanese noodles need to be cooked before they are stir-fried. Exceptions are cellophane and rice noodles, which only require soaking (see page 218). Cook noodles in boiling salted water until just tender, then drain and rinse under cold water to prevent them cooking any further. Drain the noodles again, ensuring all the excess water is removed. They are now ready for stir-frying with flavorings of your choice.

Heat a wok until hot but not smoking. Add 1–2 tbsp. vegetable oil and heat until hot. Add the noodles and flavorings and stir-fry over a high heat for 2–3 minutes, tossing noodles until they are glistening with oil and warmed through.

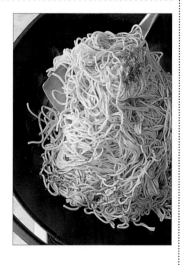

TESTING PASTA FOR DONENESS

Whether it is boiled or baked, pasta should be cooked until it is what Italians call al dente, *which means "firm to bite." If it is overcooked, it will be mushy.*

Just before the end of the recommended cooking time, lift a piece of pasta out of the water with tongs and test it by biting into it. When it is perfectly cooked, the pasta should feel tender, without any hint of rawness, but there should be just a touch of resistance to the bite. If the pasta is done, take it off the heat and drain immediately. If not, continue testing every 30–60 seconds until it is.

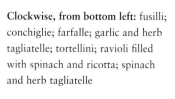

Clockwise, from bottom left: fusilli; conchiglie; farfalle; garlic and herb tagliatelle; tortellini; ravioli filled with spinach and ricotta; spinach and herb tagliatelle

Ravioles d'escargots au beurre d'herbes

Tender and tasty snails are often stuffed back in their shells with a herb and garlic butter, then baked or broiled. Here, instead, they are stuffed into pasta pillows with a flavoring of pastis and served with a warm buttery herb and shallot sauce.

SERVES 4 AS A FIRST COURSE

FOR THE PASTA DOUGH

3⅓ cups unbleached all-purpose flour

1 tsp. salt

4 eggs

1 tbsp. olive oil

FOR THE FILLING

4 tbsp. olive oil

¼ cup shallots, finely chopped

¼ cup pastis, such as Pernod or Ricard

12 canned snails, well drained

FOR THE HERB BUTTER SAUCE

½ cup shallots, finely chopped

½ cup dry white wine

2 tbsp. white wine vinegar

1¼ cups butter, cut into small pieces

1 bunch of fresh basil, shredded

1 bunch of fresh chervil, shredded

2 tbsp. chopped fresh parsley

Salt and freshly ground pepper

TO GARNISH

Carrot and zucchini julienne (see page 166), blanched

Make the pasta dough: put the flour and salt in a food processor. Break the eggs into a bowl and whisk them lightly with the olive oil. With the machine running, gradually add the eggs and oil to the flour through the feed tube until a slightly wet, crumb-like dough forms. Turn out the dough and knead and stretch it with the palm of your hand (see step 5, page 206) until it is smooth and elastic. Leave the dough to rest at room temperature, covered with an upturned bowl, for about 1 hour.

Make the filling: heat the oil in a small pan and sweat the shallots. Add the pastis, stir well and bring to the boil. Remove from the heat, add the snails and let cool.

Cut the pasta dough into two equal pieces. Using a pasta machine if available, roll out each piece as thinly as possible to a rectangle measuring 6 x 20 in.

Put one sheet on a work surface, and cut it in half. Evenly space six spoonfuls of the snail mixture on one half of the dough, allowing one snail per spoonful. Brush the dough around the mounds very lightly with water just to moisten. Lay the second half of the dough on top. Press firmly, then cut out fluted rounds (see box, below). Repeat with the remaining dough and snails. Cover the ravioli and set aside.

Bring a large pan of water to the boil. Meanwhile, make the sauce by combining the shallots, wine and vinegar in a pan and reducing until almost all the liquid has evaporated. Whisk in the butter, a few pieces at a time, to form an emulsified sauce. Add the herbs and season with salt and pepper. Keep the sauce warm.

Add 1 tbsp. salt and a splash of olive oil to the boiling water, then add the ravioli. Cook for 3–4 minutes or until *al dente*. Remove with a slotted spoon and drain in a colander.

Arrange three ravioli in each of four warmed bowls and spoon over the herb butter sauce. Garnish with carrot and zucchini julienne and serve immediately.

Cutting Ravioli

A ravioli cutter or stamp (see page 210) is the traditional tool for cutting out these stuffed pasta shapes, but you can also use a fluted or plain biscuit cutter.

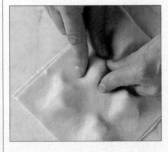

With your fingers, press down firmly around each mound of filling to eliminate any air pockets in the pasta.

Stamp out the ravioli shapes with the cutter, taking care to keep the mound of filling in the center.

Bruschetta & Crostini

These Italian toasts make excellent first courses and delicious snacks. Prepare the bruschetta or the slightly thinner crostini following the instructions on page 246, using slices of baguette or halved slices of ciabatta. Each topping below is enough for six. Serve a selection, allowing two or three for each person.

Shrimp and Cherry Tomato

3 red cherry tomatoes, sliced

3 yellow cherry tomatoes, sliced

Olive oil

Salt and freshly ground pepper

6 cooked shrimp, peeled and deveined

Fresh cilantro leaves, to garnish

Arrange the tomato slices on the bruschetta or crostini, drizzle with a little olive oil and sprinkle with salt and pepper to taste. Top with the shrimp and garnish with cilantro leaves.

Walnut, Pear and Goat's Cheese

2 oz. soft goat's cheese

1 small bunch of arugula

1 pear, cored and thinly sliced lengthwise

A little fresh lemon juice

Freshly ground pepper

Walnut halves

Spread a little goat's cheese on each bruschetta or crostini. Cover the cheese with a few arugula leaves and arrange pear slices on top. Sprinkle with lemon juice and pepper and add a walnut half to each.

Prosciutto and Fig

6 slices of Prosciutto

2 ripe but firm figs, cut lengthwise into thin wedges

Freshly ground pepper

Fresh chives, to garnish

Place a slice of Prosciutto on each bruschetta or crostini, folding it slightly. Arrange fig wedges on top and sprinkle with pepper. Garnish with long stems of fresh chive.

Chargrilled Vegetable and Pine Nuts

1 red pepper

1 yellow pepper

1 small red onion, quartered

Olive oil

Pitted black olives

2 tbsp. pine nuts, toasted

TO GARNISH

Fresh basil leaves

Parmesan curls (see box, left)

Roast the peppers and onion (see page 189). Cut the peppers into thin strips, discarding the cores and seeds. Arrange on the bruschetta or crostini, fanning the onion wedges slightly. Drizzle with a little olive oil. Finish with olives, pine nuts, basil and Parmesan curls.

Making Parmesan Curls

Thin shavings of fresh Parmesan cheese make an attractive and tasty garnish for bruschetta and crostini as well as for salads, pasta dishes and risottos. For best results, use fresh Parmesan at room temperature. The dry, crumbly type of Parmesan will not curl. Pecorino romano can also be used.

Cut a curved triangular shape out of one of the long sides of a piece of Parmesan, using a small sharp knife.

Shave curls out of the indentation with a vegetable peeler. For larger curls, simply increase the size of the triangle.

CHOOSING FRUIT

Where possible choose fruit from a loose display, this will allow you to check the produce and, in the case of some fruits like grapes and cherries, to sample them first. There should be no bruising or mold and avoid any fruit that looks damp and smells musty. Ripe fruit spoils quickly so handle it as little as possible and only buy what you can use within a few days.

MELON smooth skin free of blemishes and bruising, it should feel heavy for its size

MELONS

Galias, honeydews, cantaloupes, crenshaw and watermelons are best bought in season to ensure their freshness. Select those that feel heavy, give slightly when gently pressed at the ends and smell aromatic and fragrant

APPLES should be sweet smelling with firm flesh and smooth shiny skin

LEMONS should have smooth glossy skins, even in color, and feel heavy for their size

HARD FRUITS

Apples and pears should have smooth shiny skins, be free of blemishes and have a good depth of color, although the evenness of the color will depend on the variety. The flesh should be firm with no sign of bruising. When buying pears choose those that are underripe, then wrap loosely in a paper bag and allow to ripen at room temperature.

FRUITS WITH PITS

Check the flesh of peaches, nectarines, plums, cherries and apricots is firm but not hard. When fully ripe, the flesh will give slightly to gentle pressure. Select plump well-rounded fruit with an obvious seam, that feel heavy. The velvety skin should not be bruised or cut.

NECTARINES' skin should be smooth gold/red with a slight sheen; avoid any that are very hard and green. They should have a strong fragrance. To check ripeness, press gently along the seam

KUMQUATS should be plump and firm with a shiny deep orange skin. Avoid any that are shrivelled or dull

BLUEBERRIES should be plump with a blue/grey "bloom"; check they are firm not soft

CHERRIES should exhibit smooth glossy skins and be well rounded and plump. Stems should be green

STRAWBERRIES of choice should be well shaped, glossy and deep red throughout. Hull should be green and fresh looking

CITRUS FRUITS

Choose plump citrus fruits – lemons, limes, oranges, kumquats, grapefruit, tangerines and clementines – and make sure they feel firm and juicy. The skin should have an even color and look glossy, almost moist. The fruit should be free of blemishes and not shriveled, and the skin should be unbroken. In general, the smoother the skin, the thinner it will be.

BERRIES

Choose bright colored black-, blue-, straw-, rasp-, and loganberries that are plump and fragrant. Check for soft or moldy berries before buying and ensure the basket is clean and not stained or wet, an indication that the fruit may be damaged underneath. Handle the fruit as little as possible; only wash them if absolutely necessary as this speeds mold.

PREPARING A MANGOSTEEN

Use a paring knife to slice the fruit in half, cutting through the thick skin just to the firm flesh. Gently scoop out the white segments of fruit with a small spoon. These segments contain pits which are not edible.

PREPARING A POMEGRANATE

Slice fruit in half. Pressing on the rounded base, invert one half over a sieve set over a bowl. Use fingers to separate the seeds from the pith and membranes. To extract the juice, use the back of a spoon to crush the seeds against the sieve.

1 MANGOSTEEN This hard, round tropical fruit is, surprisingly, not related to the mango. It contains sweet, delicately flavored succulent white segments that offer a pleasing bite of acidity. They are best eaten raw.

2 POMEGRANATE Mediterranean in origin, this tough, leathery, shiny red-skinned fruit contains tightly packed seeds surrounded by deep pink, intensely sweet flesh. Use the seeds in fruit salads or press through a sieve and then use the juice to flavor ice creams and mousses. Discard the very bitter skin, pith and membranes.

3 PRICKLY PEAR The fruit of a Mediterranean cactus, this can be eaten raw or cooked. It has a yellow or pinkish flesh speckled with crunchy but edible seeds. The fruit has a subtly sweet, mild flavor that benefits from a squeeze of fresh lemon juice. Discard the spiny skin, using gloves to peel it off.

4 GRENADILLO This is a type of passion fruit (see page 262). It has a shell-like, hard inedible skin. The flesh can be spooned out and eaten as it is or added to fruit salads, or it can be sieved and used to flavor sorbets and ice creams.

5 STAR FRUIT Of Asian origin, this waxy fruit looks beautiful sliced crosswise in fruit salads or as a decoration. The flavor is refreshing but insipid.

PREPARING A STAR FRUIT

Cut unpeeled fruit crosswise into slices with a small knife. Remove the central seeds. Because the sweetness of the fruit varies (some varieties are quite acidic), taste before adding to salads and adjust dressings accordingly.

PREPARING A LYCHEE

Starting at the stalk end, carefully cut through the rough, brittle skin with a small knife; it will peel off cleanly. The pearly white flesh of the fruit contains a long, brown inedible seed. Ripe fruit has a pink or red blush on its skin.

6 & 7 MANGO There are thousands of mango varieties – hundreds in Thailand alone. The skin colors vary greatly (here we show a blushing-red variety on the left and an elongated yellow on the right). A ripe mango will have an intense fragrance and should also give slightly when pressed. Unripe mangoes are used as a cooked vegetable in chutneys and curries. Luscious scented ripe mangoes are best eaten raw with a little lime or lemon juice or in fruit salads or *salsas*. They also make delicious sorbets and mousses. See page 255 for two different preparation techniques.

8 LYCHEE The fragrant juicy flesh is encased in a brittle inedible shell which is deep blushing pink when ripe. Eat raw or poached in syrup.

9 KIWANO This striking fruit has a spiky inedible orange rind and a green watery interior which is eaten with a spoon.

10 RAMBUTAN This Asian fruit looks like a hairy lychee and tastes very similar.

11 PITAHAYA The fruit of a South American cactus, this can be yellow, ivory or deep pink. Cut in half and spoon out the green or shocking-pink flesh.

12 DURIAN This Indonesian fruit is famed for its unpleasant smell when fully ripe. The flesh is creamy and intensely sweet. It is eaten raw, or used in cakes. Discard the seeds.

POACHING & PRESERVING

Choose firm fruits for poaching that are not too ripe so they hold their shape. Preserving fruits in alcohol is an ideal way of storing fruits to be eaten later in the year when your favorite fresh fruits are out of season.

FLAVORS FOR POACHING FRUITS

Serve poached fruits for a simple dessert, or purée and use as the basis of desserts, such as mousses, soufflés and fools. Different flavorings, some subtle, others strong, can be added at the beginning of cooking to infuse the sugar syrup.

- Strips of pared orange, lemon or lime zest.
- Whole spices such as cloves, star anise and cinnamon sticks.
- A split vanilla pod (see page 331).
- Fresh lavender sprigs.
- A slice of fresh ginger.
- A bruised stalk of lemongrass.

POACHING IN SUGAR SYRUP

Infuse the natural sweetness of fruits with a flavorful poaching liquid. The amount of sugar in the syrup is determined by the fruits to be cooked. A light sugar syrup is suitable for hard fruits and fruits with pits, which hold their shape well, while soft berries are best in a heavy syrup, which will help them hold their shape. Sugar syrup quantities are given on page 281. For flavorings, see box, left.

1 Add pitted fruits (here plums are shown) to simmering sugar syrup, making sure the fruits are completely submerged.

2 Poach fruits until tender, 10–15 minutes. Remove with a slotted spoon. Boil the syrup to reduce it, strain and serve poured over the fruits.

POACHING IN WINE

Fruits that are poached in wine take on the flavor of the alcohol and, in the case of red wine, the color. This is the classic French technique for poaching whole pears, as shown here. Before poaching, peel and core pears (see page 250), leaving their stalks intact. This will help to make slicing easy and will give an attractive presentation.

1 Heat wine with flavorings (see box, above left) and sugar until sugar dissolves. Add prepared pears and bring slowly to a simmer. Poach for 15–25 minutes.

2 Remove from the heat, cover and let cool in the liquid. Remove pears with a slotted spoon, reduce liquid and cool. Serve the fruit sliced, on a pool of syrup.

MAKING A DRIED FRUIT COMPOTE

A compote is a mixture of fruits poached together to make a delicious blend of colors and flavors. Here, dried fruits are soaked overnight in liquid and flavorings (see box, right). Sugar inhibits the cooking of the fruits, so it is added at the end.

1 Place fruits and soaking liquid in a pan. Add water to just cover fruits. Bring to a gentle simmer, stirring.

2 Poach the fruits gently, just until tender, 15–25 minutes. Remove fruits with a slotted spoon.

3 Sweeten the cooking juices, then reduce by about one-third. Serve fruits with the juices ladled over.

COMPOTE COMBINATIONS

Soaking overnight plumps up dried fruits and allows them to absorb as much flavor as possible. Try the following ideas:

- Make a classic combination of dried apricots, figs, peaches and dates with white wine and honey.
- Mix a tropical blend of dried mango, pineapple and papaya, with rum, coconut milk and cinnamon sticks.
- Soak dried apples, pears, apricots and prunes in tea, then cook in orange juice flavored with cloves.

PRESERVING AND STORING WHOLE FRUITS IN ALCOHOL

Alcohol is used to preserve fruits so they can be kept for an indefinite period of time, although it is advisable to use them within a year in case of fermentation.

Choose fruits that are just ripe and in good condition. For a selection of fruit and alcohol combinations, plus some recommended serving suggestions, see box, right.

Place the prepared fruits in sterilized jars, and add whole spices, if you like. Pour alcohol into a pan and bring to the boil. Add sugar and stir to dissolve, then remove from the heat and leave to cool. Pour enough of the cooled alcohol into the jars to cover the fruit completely. Seal the jars. Store in a cool dark place for at least 2–3 weeks so that the flavors have time to develop before using.

TRICK OF THE TRADE

MAKING RUMTOPF

A rumtopf ("rum pot") is a traditional German method of preserving fruit in alcohol. From summer to autumn, ripened fruits are layered with sugar in stone or glass jars, covered with rum and sealed.

Sprinkle fruits with sugar and let marinate overnight. Layer fruits (here blueberries and sliced strawberries are shown) in a sterilized jar, covering each layer with rum. Fill to about 1 in. from the top. Seal and leave to mature for at least 1 month.

FRUITS IN ALCOHOL

Fruits preserved in alcohol make delicious instant desserts all year round. Here are some suggestions for fruit and alcohol partnerships, with ideas for serving them. Citrus fruits need to be peeled first, hard fruits like pears need to be peeled and sometimes poached.

- Cherries with brandy or kirsch. Spoon over vanilla ice cream.
- Grapes with whisky. Fold into whipped cream with crushed meringues.
- Clementines with rum, star anise, cinnamon sticks and cloves. Serve with crème fraîche or warm chocolate sauce.
- Plums with port. Spoon over hazelnut ice cream.
- Mangoes with white rum. Serve with rum and raisin ice cream.
- Pears with vodka. Top with soured cream.
- Summer berries with kirsch. Top with whipped fresh cream.

BROILING & FRYING

Broiled or chargrilled fruit makes a simple and speedy hot fruit dessert. Fruits can also be deep-fried in batter to make fritters, or sautéed and flambéed. Choose ripe but firm fruits that hold their shape well.

BARBECUING

Cut fruits into slices or wedges, like the pineapple, papaya and mango shown here, or cut into chunks and thread onto oiled skewers to make kebabs. Some fruits, such as bananas, can be barbecued whole. Brush the barbecue grid with oil before putting on the fruit. You can also brush the fruit with flavorings such as lemon juice and honey, but use spices sparingly as they can easily scorch.

UNWRAPPED
For a chargrilled effect, cook fruits directly on an oiled grid of the barbecue, turning once, 3–5 minutes.

WRAPPED
For whole fruits to be served *en papillote*, wrap in foil and cook on the barbecue grid for 5–10 minutes.

GRILLING EN SABAYON

Fresh soft fruits, such as the strawberries and blueberries used here, are covered with a sabayon sauce (see page 292) and placed under a hot broiler until browned. The sabayon sauce produces a caramelized topping, protecting the sweet juicy fruit below. Choose heatproof bowls that will withstand the intense heat.

1 Arrange prepared fruits decoratively in an even layer in heatproof bowls.

2 Spoon sabayon sauce over fruits – it will melt and spread over the fruits during cooking. Place under a hot broiler until lightly browned, 1–2 minutes.

COATING IN A SUGAR GLAZE

This technique gives fruits a caramelized coating, and is best suited to fruits that are firm enough to hold their shape, such as the orange segments shown here, grapes, cherries, underripe peach or pear slices and wedges or chunks of apple.

Take care when cooking the syrup before the fruits are added. It should be light golden, not brown, or the fruits will taste bitter. Keep the pieces of fruit in a single layer, and do not overcrowd the pan or the fruits will stew and become soggy.

For about ½ lb. prepared fruits, dissolve 3 tbsp. sugar in ⅓ cup water over a low heat. Add 1 tbsp butter and then heat gently until melted and light golden. Increase the heat and simmer until the syrup bubbles and becomes a glaze, then add fruits. Shake the pan until the fruits are evenly coated with the glaze.

FLAMBEEING

Flambéed fruits make a spectacular dessert, and have a special intensity of flavor. Grapes or cherries are best suited to this technique, and any high-proof alcohol such as brandy, rum, a fortified wine like Madeira, or a fruit-based liqueur.

1 Melt butter in a frying pan. Add sugar and prepared fruits; sauté for 1–2 minutes. Warm alcohol in a separate pan and ignite it off the heat, then pour the flaming alcohol over fruits.

2 Baste the fruits constantly with the flaming sauce until the flames have died down, using a long-handled large metal spoon for safety. Serve immediately.

MAKING ASIAN FRITTERS

Fruits deep-fried in Asian-style tempura batter are crisp and light on the outside, sweet and juicy within. The batter is so light that the color of the fruit shows through. Firm fruits, such as apples and pears, are suitable and tropical fruits like the pineapple, mango, papaya and kiwi fruit shown here. Dry the fruit well before coating it or the batter will not adhere.

1 Peel and slice or segment the fruits or cut them into chunks, keeping the shapes as equal in size as possible. Pat the fruits thoroughly dry with paper towels.

TEMPURA BATTER

5 tbsp. all-purpose flour

5 tbsp. cornstarch

1½ tsp. baking powder

1 egg, beaten

¾ cup iced water

Mix the dry ingredients in a bowl. Whisk the egg with the water, then stir into the dry ingredients to form a smooth batter.

2 Prepare tempura batter (see box, right). Dip the fruit pieces in the batter until coated, using a pair of chopsticks or a two-pronged fork. Allow the excess batter to drain back into the bowl. Deep-fry in 375°F oil until the fritters are crisp and golden, 2–3 minutes. Drain before serving.

SORBETS & GRANITAS

Icy textures, dazzling colors and clean, lively flavors make sorbets and granitas a refreshing finale to any meal. Techniques for making simple sorbets and granitas are given here, plus clever ways to present them.

BLUEBERRY SORBET

¾ cup superfine sugar
¾ cup water
2 cups sieved blueberry purée
Pinch of black pepper
¼ cup egg white

Make a sugar syrup (see page 280) with ⅔ cup of the sugar and ⅔ cup of the water. Remove from the heat and stir in the blueberry purée and pepper. Let cool, then chill in the refrigerator, 2 hours. Put the mixture in a sorbetière and work until partially frozen, 40 minutes. Meanwhile, make an Italian meringue (see page 272) with the egg white and a hot sugar syrup made from the remaining sugar and water. Add to the sorbet and continue working the machine until sorbet is completely frozen, 45 minutes. Makes about 1 quart.

FLAVORINGS FOR SORBETS

Choose from the following strongly flavored ingredients that will stand up well to freezing.

• Fresh blackberry, black currant, raspberry, or strawberry purée.
• Poached fresh peach or apricot purée.
• Freshly squeezed orange, lemon or lime juice, or a mixture of these.
• Melon pulp (watermelon, gallia and crenshaw are especially good).

MAKING A SORBET BY MACHINE

Using an electric sorbetière speeds up the freezing process and so helps produce an ice that is both fine-textured and smooth, but the real secret of making an ultra-smooth sorbet lies in the addition of Italian meringue.

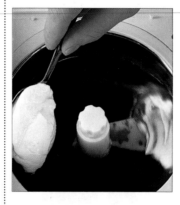

AS FREEZING BEGINS
Add Italian meringue when sorbet is partially frozen, then continue freezing.

AT THE END
After 1½ hours in sorbetière, check consistency of sorbet. It should be firm and smooth, with no ice crystals. Decant into a bowl and serve, or store in a rigid container in the freezer.

MAKING A SORBET BY HAND

A sorbet is ideally made in a sorbetière, but quite good results can be obtained without a machine if you are prepared to spend some time whisking the mixture during freezing. This is the only way to break down ice crystals and produce a fairly smooth result – the more you whisk the smoother the sorbet will be. Generally speaking, you will get a better result by hand with a fruit purée than with a fruit juice. This is because the high water content of fruit juice produces more ice crystals than a purée.

1 Mix together sugar syrup and fruit purée of your choice and freeze until semi-frozen, about 2 hours.

2 Whisk semi-frozen sorbet with a balloon whisk. Return to freezer. Whisk regularly until frozen, 2 hours.

MAKING FROZEN FRUIT CUPS

Called fruits givrés or frosted fruits, these are made by hollowing out fruits and filling them with a sorbet of the same flavor. Lemon is shown here, but lime or orange can also be used. Use the flesh to make the sorbet for the filling – each fruit will take up to 3–4 tbsp. sorbet. If not serving the cups the same day, pack them in freezer bags once they have hardened.

1 Cut off the top of each fruit and a thin slice off the bottom so it will sit level. Remove the flesh. Put the fruit shells in the freezer.

2 Spoon sorbet into center of each fruit, mounding it 1–2 in. above the rim. Replace tops and place in the freezer until serving time.

PIPING SORBET

Slightly softened sorbet is easy to pipe. For a dramatic effect, use long-stemmed glasses that have been frozen or well chilled. Top with decorations, such as the candied zest used here, to echo the flavor of the sorbet.

Fit a piping bag with a star nozzle, fill with sorbet and pipe into glasses. Place in the freezer until serving time.

GRANITA

Granita's signature is its crystalline texture – the name comes from the Italian for granite. Here coffee granita is made, following the recipe in the box, right.

ADDING SUGAR SYRUP
For sparkling ice crystals, strain the sugar syrup into the cooled coffee mixture, then stir the two together until evenly combined.

FORKING THROUGH
Break up the ice crystals with a fork several times during freezing so the granita acquires its characteristic slushy texture. To serve, remove the granita from the bowl by scraping it with a spoon.

COFFEE GRANITA

1 cup sugar
2 cups cold water
1 cup instant espresso coffee powder
2 cups boiling water

Make a sugar syrup (see page 280) with the sugar and cold water; let cool. Dissolve coffee powder in boiling water; let cool. Strain cold syrup into coffee and stir to mix thoroughly. Freeze for at least 4 hours until firm, breaking the mixture up with a fork as often as possible during this time. Serves 6–8.

WHAT'S IN A NAME?

SORBET: A sorbet is a soft-textured water ice made of a sugar syrup combined with a flavoring such as fruit juice or fruit purée, then mixed with Italian meringue or whisked egg whites. Sometimes alcohol is added for extra flavor. Sorbets are most commonly eaten as desserts, but they are also sometimes served as a "refresher" between courses to cleanse the palate.
SHERBET: This is the Western version of *sharbat*, an iced drink that originated in Persia. It is made by pouring fruit syrup over crushed iced, then adding fizzy water. Modern sherbets are often light fruit ices, made with milk, which gives them a creamy texture but without the richness of ice cream.
SPOOM: Here, meringue is incorporated into a frozen wine- or champagne-based sherbet to make a spoom – the result is very frothy and sweet. Spooms take longer to freeze than sherbets, because of their alcohol content. An old-fashioned variation is called a shrub.

Croquembouche

Traditionally prepared for weddings in France, this spectacular confection consists of tiers of choux buns filled with an enriched crème pâtissière and embellished with caramel. Croquembouche is straightforward to make; each element is prepared individually before the final assembly.

SERVES 20

4 lbs. nougatine (see page 281)

Crystalized sugar, to decorate

FOR THE ROYAL ICING

2½ cups confectioners' sugar

1 egg white

1 tbsp. lemon juice

FOR THE CHOUX BUNS

2 cups water

1 cup unsalted butter

1 tsp. salt

1 tbsp. sugar

2 cups all-purpose flour

8–9 eggs

FOR THE EGG WASH

1 egg

1 egg yolk

Pinch of salt

FOR THE CREME MOUSSELINE

12 egg yolks

1⅔ cups sugar

¾ cup all-purpose flour

¾ cup cornstarch

1½ quarts milk infused with
1 vanilla pod (see page 331)

1 cup unsalted butter,
softened

6 tbsp. liqueur of your choice

FOR THE CARAMEL

5 cups sugar

¾ cup water

¾ cup glucose

Make the nougatine and roll it out thinly (see step 1, page 281). Using a 12-in. cake board as a guide, cut out a large disk of nougatine – this will be the base of the croquembouche; set the disk aside on the board. Using a 4-in. metal cutter, cut out 2 disks of nougatine and 3 quarter moons for the top.

Make royal icing (see page 318) using the ingredients listed left; pipe around the edge of the large disk (see box, below), and around the edges of the 2 small disks.

Make 100 choux buns (see page 298), using the ingredients listed left and brushing with egg wash before baking. Let cool.

Make the *crème mousseline* as for *crème pâtissière* (see page 276), whisking in the butter and liqueur a little at a time at the end; let cool. Using a small plain nozzle, pipe the crème through the hole in each choux bun.

For the caramel, dissolve the sugar in the water and bring to the boil. Skim off any scum, then stir in the glucose. Lower the heat and cook, swirling the pan occasionally, until turned to a blond caramel. Plunge base of pan into iced water to cool slightly, then dip tops of buns in the caramel and place them caramel-side down on a tray

to set. Dip a few of the buns into crystalized sugar.

Cover a large cone-shaped mold with foil and oil it well. Wrap a roll of foil around the base to support the bottom tier of buns.

Arrange buns for the bottom tier: dip the sides of the buns in caramel and stick them to each other not the foil. Add the next tier of buns (see box, below). Continue building tiers; place the buns with crystalized sugar at random. Leave to harden.

Unmold croquembouche (see box, below); set it on the nougatine base and decorate the top, sticking the shapes on with caramel.

Assembling the Croquembouche

The key to success is to take your time and work with care. The assembled croquembouche should be kept in a cool place for no longer than 4–6 hours until serving time. It should not be stored in the refrigerator because the caramel will become sticky.

Using a small star nozzle, pipe a border of royal icing shells around the edge of the large nougatine base.

Arrange tiers of choux buns around the cone, sticking them side by side and to the previous tier, not to the foil.

Gently lift the croquembouche off the mold, then carefully remove the roll of foil followed by the foil lining.

WHISKED CAKES

A whisked sponge boasts the lightest texture of all cakes. Its volume relies on the amount of air incorporated when eggs are whisked with sugar over a gentle heat. Butter can be included for richness.

BASIC WHISKED SPONGE CAKE

4 eggs
1½ cups superfine sugar
1¼ cups all-purpose flour, sifted with a pinch of salt

Grease, flour and line an 8-in. round cake pan (see page 308). Whisk the eggs and sugar in a heatproof bowl over a pan of hot water until the mixture is thick. Remove the bowl from the pan of hot water and continue whisking off the heat until the mixture is cool. Sift and fold in the flour. Pour into the prepared pan and bake at 350°F for about 25 minutes. Turn out, remove paper and let cool on a wire rack. Serves 6–8.

SERVING A WHISKED SPONGE

A plain whisked sponge can be simply layered with whipped cream and jam and sprinkled with confectioners' sugar, or it can be elaborately decorated. Try one of the following ideas.

• Fill with raspberry mousse and whole raspberries (as shown in the Swiss roll, opposite page).
• Imbibe with sugar syrup and liqueur, then layer and coat with whipped cream and fruit purée (see page 315).
• Fill and decorate with crème Chantilly and fresh fruits (see page 321).

MAKING A WHISKED SPONGE

Pastry chefs use a very large balloon whisk to incorporate as much air as possible, but you can use a hand-held electric mixer if you prefer. To speed up the thickening process, the bowl is set over hot water – take care not to let it touch the water or the mixture will start to cook.

1 Put the eggs and sugar in large heatproof bowl and whisk vigorously for a few seconds to break up the eggs and start mixing them with the sugar.

2 Put the bowl over a pan of hot water and whisk until the mixture is thick enough to leave a figure-eight ribbon trail on the surface when the whisk is lifted.

3 Remove the bowl from the heat and continue whisking until the mixture has cooled and is very thick, 3–5 minutes.

4 Fold in flour in batches with a rubber spatula. Cut cleanly through, to avoid knocking out the air.

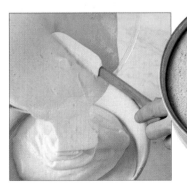

5 Pour finished batter slowly into the prepared pan, gently guiding it in with the spatula.

6 When fully cooked, the sponge will be golden, well risen and firm but springy to the touch.

ENRICHING A WHISKED SPONGE

Add melted butter to the basic whisked sponge mixture to enrich the batter and make it more moist. Take care that the butter is thoroughly cooled after melting and add it to the whisked mixture slowly, after the flour has been folded in. Bake the cake as soon as possible after mixing or batter may deflate.

1 Melt 1½ tbsp. unsalted butter and let cool. Pour slowly over the surface of the whisked mixture.

2 Gently fold in the butter, cutting through the mixture with a spatula so as not to knock air out of it, until evenly incorporated.

WHAT'S IN A NAME?

A whisked sponge is often called a Genoese sponge cake or *génoise* in French. Considered one of the great French classics in cake making, it actually originated in Genoa, northern Italy, hence its name. Recipes vary — some are fatless, others enriched with melted butter. For layered cakes, the fatless sponge is lighter — butter gives a denser texture.

MAKING A SWISS ROLL

The sponge for a Swiss roll is baked in a shallow rectangular pan, then turned out, cooled and rolled around a filling. Follow the whisked sponge technique on the opposite page, using 4 eggs, ⅔ cups sugar and ½ cup all-purpose flour. Bake in a 9 x 13 in. jelly roll pan at 375–400°F, 4–5 minutes. For fillings, see box, opposite page.

1 Lift sponge out of pan on lining paper and place on wire rack. Let cool.

2 Place crust-side down on parchment dusted with sugar. Peel off lining paper.

4 Carefully roll up the sponge, using the baking parchment to help. For a tighter roll, see box, right. Place finished Swiss roll, seam-side down, and dust with confectioners' sugar just before serving.

TRICK OF THE TRADE

Use this chef's technique to tighten a Swiss roll for a neat presentation.

Push a spatula under the sponge in the parchment. Pull the parchment away from the knife.

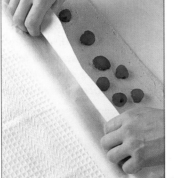

3 Transfer sponge, still on the baking parchment, to a towel. Spread over your chosen filling. Fold over 1 in. of sponge along one long edge, using the parchment to guide you. This will make rolling easier.

GLOSSARY OF TERMS

AL DENTE: Italian for "to the tooth"; describes just-cooked vegetables or pasta that offer slight resistance when bitten.

ALBUMEN: The protein-rich white of an egg; contains the chalazae, the stringy cord which anchors the yolk to the shell.

AROMAT: Any spice or herb (basil, cumin, rosemary) which gives flavor and fragrance to food.

ASPIC: A clear fish, poultry or meat jelly made of clarified stock or consommé and gelatin; used as a base for molded dishes or as a glaze for cold food.

ATA/ATTA FLOUR: An extremely fine whole-wheat flour used in making flat breads; found in Asian shops.

BAIN MARIE: A "water bath" made by placing a pan or bowl of food in or above a larger pan of boiling water. Used in the oven or on top of the stove.

BAKE: To cook food in an oven. For best results, use an oven thermometer – most ovens heat to temperatures other than their gauges read.

BAKE BLIND: To bake a pastry crust before it is filled. To keep its shape, the shell is often pricked and lined with parchment or foil and baking beans.

BALLOTINE: Meat, poultry or fish that has been boned, stuffed, rolled and tied in a bundle; usually poached or braised.

BARD: To wrap pieces of fat (typically back fat or bacon) around lean cuts of meat to keep them moist.

BASTE: To spoon or brush a liquid stock (pan juices or fat) over foods during cooking; adds flavor and moisture.

BATTER: The uncooked mixture of crêpes, pancakes and cakes. Can be thick or thin. Also used to describe a coating for foods to be fried, such as fish.

BEURRE MANIE: French for "kneaded butter." A paste made from equal parts flour and butter, used as a thickener for sauces, soups and stews.

BLANC: A stock containing water, flour and lemon juice that is used to cook and preserve the color of vegetables; most often used for artichokes.

BLANCH: To plunge vegetables or fruits into boiling – then iced – water to stop them cooking, loosen skins, set color and remove bitterness. Also reduces salt content in bacon or other cured meats.

BLEND: To use a spoon, beater or electric blender to evenly combine two or more ingredients.

BOIL: "Bring to the boil" refers to heating a liquid until bubbles break the surface (212°F). The term also means to cook food in a boiling liquid.

BRAISE: To brown foods in fat, then cook them, tightly covered, in a small amount of flavorful liquid, at low heat, for a lengthy period of time.

BROCHETTE: French for "skewer"; food threaded or molded onto a metal or wooden skewer and broiled or barbecued.

BRUNOISE: Finely diced carrot, celery, leek or zucchini, used singly or together as the classic garnish for consommé.

BUTTERFLY: To split a food (leg of lamb, chicken breast, shrimp) down the center, cutting almost – but

not completely – through. The two halves are then opened out to resemble a butterfly.

CANELLE (CANELLER): A decorative effect for the skins of fruits or vegetables made with a canelle knife. When sliced, these have grooved borders.

CARAMELIZE: The process of heating sugar until it liquefies and becomes a syrup, ranging in color from golden to dark brown. Sugar can also be caramelized by being sprinkled on food and broiled until it melts (as for crème brûlée). This term also often applies to onions and leeks that are sautéed in fat.

CAUL: A thin membrane taken from an animal's stomach, normally a pig. Used to encase and moisten lean meats and ground meat mixtures during cooking.

CHARGRILL: To prepare foods on a metal grid that is set over hot coals, or by using a stovetop grill pan.

CHIFFONADE: Leafy vegetables or herbs that have been rolled together and then sliced crosswise into thin strips.

CHINOIS: A fine-meshed conical sieve that requires the food to be pushed through with a ladle or spoon. Most often used to strain sauces.

CHOP: To cut food, more coarsely than mincing, using a knife. The knife tip is held stationary with one hand, while the other moves the handle up and down.

CLARIFY: To rid a liquid of impurities. The process usually involves simmering egg whites (and shells) with stock; the whites attract foreign particles. Also applies to the process of slowly heating butter and removing the milk solids.

COAT: To cover food with an outer coating, such as flour, beaten eggs, bread crumbs, mayonnaise or icing.

COMPOTE: A mixture of fruits that is slowly cooked, often in a sugar syrup infused with spices or liqueur.

CONCASSEE: A coarsely chopped mixture, usually tomatoes that have been peeled, deseeded and chopped.

CONFIT: A method of cooking meat (usually duck, goose or pork) very slowly in its own fat, then storing it in the fat. Vegetables, such as baby onions, can also be cooked in the fat.

COULIS: A sieved purée or sauce, often made with tomatoes, or fruits combined with a sweetener and a small amount of lemon juice.

CREAM: To beat ingredients together until light, fluffy and smooth. Typically involves creaming a fat, such as butter, with sugar.

CRIMP: To create ridges around the edge of pies by pressing with your fingers and tapping with the back of a knife blade.

CROSS-HATCH: To score criss-crossing diagonal lines on the surface of food to create a diamond pattern. This allows food to absorb marinades, drain excess fat, or be more easily removed from their skins (as with mangoes).

CURE: To preserve a food by treating it with salt, smoke, acid-based brines or bacteria.

CUTLET: A cut of meat, such as lamb, pork or veal, that is taken from the leg or rib sections.

DARNE: A thick cross-section slice of a large round fish, such as salmon or tuna.

DEGLAZE: After sautéing, the food and any excess fat are removed from the pan and a small amount of liquid stirred into the pan juices to dilute them and form a sauce.

DEGORGE: To soak meats, poultry and fish in cold water with salt or vinegar to expel impurities and blood. Also the process of sprinkling some vegetables (especially eggplants) with salt to draw out the juices.

DEMI-GLACE: A thick, intensely flavored sauce, or base for a sauce, made from concentrated stock, wine and sometimes meat glaze.

DETREMPE: A French term for the paste made from flour, salt, melted butter and water in the first stage of puff pastry.

DICE: To cut food into small, equal-sized cubes.

DOUGH: A flour and water mixture, often with other ingredients, worked until it is firm enough to hold its shape but malleable enough to mold by hand.

DRESS: To pluck, clean and truss poultry or game for cooking. The term also applies to adding a dressing such as vinaigrette to a salad, preparing a whole crab or lobster, or putting food on a plate and decorating it before serving.

DROPPING CONSISTENCY: Describes a mixture, usually cake batter, that is soft enough to be dropped by spoonfuls, yet firm enough to hold its shape.

DRY-FRY: Frying without the use of fats or oils. This method is often used for Indian spices and flatbreads, and for Mexican tortillas.

DUXELLES: Classically, a mixture of finely chopped mushrooms and shallots or onions cooked in butter until quite dry.

EMULSION: To combine liquids by the dispersion of one in another. In cooking, to emulsify is to add one liquid to another in a slow, steady stream while stirring vigorously.

ENRICH: Adding cream or egg yolks to a sauce or soup, or butter to a dough to create a rich texture or flavor. Also used to describe flour that has had nutrients returned to it after being lost in the milling process.

ENTRECOTE: French for "between the ribs," this tender cut of beef is usually grilled or sautéed.

FEUILLETE: A puff pastry case that is cut into the shape of a diamond, triangle, square or round.

FLAKE: Using a fork to separate food into small pieces; also used to test fish for doneness.

FLAMBE: French for "flamed." Liqueur is set alight, usually for a spectacular table presentation. Also used to burn off the alcohol content of a dish.

FOLD: To mix together a light, airy mixture with a heavier one. The lighter is placed on the heavier, then a large metal spoon or a rubber spatula is used in a gentle figure-eight motion, which combines the mixtures without losing air.

FONDANT ICING: A soft-textured mixture of water, sugar and glucose, cooked to the soft ball stage then worked until flexible and smooth and used to decorate éclairs. Not to be confused with the decorative icing commonly used for novelty cakes, which is made from sugar, water and cream of tartar.

FONDUE: French for "melted," this term refers to food cooked in a single vessel (a fondue pot) at the table. Traditionally, it involves dipping cubes of bread into melted cheese; variations include dipping meat in hot oil (fondue bourguignonne) and cubes of cake into melted chocolate.

FORCEMEAT: Old-fashioned term for stuffing, from the French word "farce," meaning stuff; a mixture of finely ground meat mixed with bread crumbs.

FRITTER: A small piece of fruit or meat that is coated in batter and deep-fried. A fritter can also refer to a julienne of vegetables that is fried.

FRY: Cooking food in hot fat. Deep-fried foods are submerged in fat. Sautéed or panfried foods are cooked in just enough fat to coat the bottom of the pan and prevent food from sticking. Stir-frying describes small pieces of food that are tossed over a very high heat, traditionally in a wok.

FUMET: A well-flavored stock, that is usually made from fish bones, usually white, or occasionally game, that is used for flavoring mild-tasting liquids. Used frequently in classic French cuisine.

GLAZE: To coat food with a thin liquid (either sweet or savory) that will be smooth and shiny after setting. Coatings include reduced meat stock (aspic), melted jam, egg wash or chocolate. The term also refers to well-reduced meat or fish stocks.

GLUTEN: A protein found in flour that provides elasticity. High-gluten flour is best suited for the kneading process required in bread making. Low gluten flour, such as cake flour, has a softer and less elastic quality.

GLYCERIN: A syrup form of alcohol added to food to maintain moisture. It is often added to royal icing to prevent crystallization.

GOLD/SILVER LEAF (ALSO CALLED VARAK): Ultra-thin, edible sheets of gold or silver used as a decoration for desserts. Sold in specialty baking shops and Indian stores, gold or silver leaf comes in fragile sheets.

GRATIN: A dish topped with grated cheese and dotted with butter, and sometimes bread crumbs, grilled or baked in a shallow dish until crisp and golden brown.

GREASE: Coating a pan with fat (usually butter or oil in the case of cake pan) to prevent sticking.

GRIND: To reduce pieces of meat into small pieces. Knives or grinding machines can be used. Also, to reduce food to powder or to tiny pieces, using a pestle or mortar or a food processor. Special grinders can be used for spices or coffee beans.

ICE-BATH: A bowl containing ice cubes and water; used to cool mixtures and stop the cooking process.

IMBIBE: To soak a cake with a flavored sugar syrup or liqueur; usually applied with a pastry brush.

INFUSE: To flavor a liquid by steeping it with aromatic ingredients, such as spices, citrus zest or vanilla.

JULIENNE: To cut food into fine strips, most commonly used with vegetables to ensure quick, even cooking and provide an attractive presentation.

KNEAD: A pressing and folding technique used to make dough firm and smooth. Kneading stretches the gluten in flour, providing elasticity.

LARD: Inserting strips of fat (usually pork) into lean cuts of meat, creating a more succulent, flavorful dish.

LARDON: Pork fat or bacon cut into small cubes and used to flavor soups, stews or salads.

LEAVENER: A substance used to raise doughs and increase the volume of baked goods. For bread, the most common leavener is yeast. For cakes, baking powder and baking soda are used.

LIAISON: A mixture of egg yolk and cream that is used to thicken sauces, soups and stews. It should always be added off the heat just before serving to prevent curdling.

LINE: To coat a pan with butter or oil and/or flour or baking parchment to prevent sticking. Foods, such as bacon strips, spinach leaves and sponge fingers, can also be used as linings.

MACERATE: To soak foods in a liquid, usually a spirit or liqueur, to soften the texture and infuse them with flavor.

MARBLING: Used to describe the mixing of two different batters in a cake, usually of different colors. Also the flecks or lines of fat found in meat.

MARINATE: To steep foods in a highly-flavored liquid. Marinades add flavor and moisture and often tenderize.

MEDALLION: A small, round nugget of meat. Typically tender and lean, it calls for a short cooking time.

MELANGE: French for a mixture, this term usually refers to a combination of two or more fruits or vegetables that are prepared together.

MEUNIERE: The French term to describe a dish cooked in butter, seasoned with salt, pepper and lemon juice, and then garnished with parsley.

MIREPOIX: Rough dice of mixed vegetables (traditionally carrot, onion, celery and leek) that is used to flavor sauces, soups and stews.

MOUSSE: A light, airy dish of whisked sweet or savory ingredients, folded together until evenly blended. Often set in a decorative mold and usually served turned out, either hot or cold.

MOUSSELINE: A term used to describe a very rich mousse-like mixture, usually with whipped cream added to it. Crème mousseline is crème pâtissière enriched with butter.

NOISETTE: A small tender slice of lamb taken from the "eye" of the rack, encased in a thin strip of fat and often tied with string. The name comes from the French for "hazelnut," and is also used to describe nut-brown butter – as in beurre noisette.

OPEN FREEZE: To freeze foods, such as peas or beans, uncovered in a single layer. When frozen solid, the items can be packed together and will remain free flowing. This term can also refer to liquids frozen in ice-cube trays.

PASTE: Food that is ground to an extremely fine texture. Commonly used for almonds, as in almond paste.

PATE (pâte): Used to describe a pastry mixture, for instance pâte brisée (shortcrust pastry); pâte sucrée is the sweetened version.

PATE (pâté): A smooth or coarse textured mixture, traditionally made of meat and/or liver, but can be vegetable or fish, seasoned or spiced and set in a mold.

PAYSANNE: The French word for "peasant" describes a mixture of vegetables (usually potatoes, carrots, turnips, and cabbage) cut into small squares, triangles, diamonds or rounds. Traditionally used to garnish soups, meat, fish or omelettes.

POACH: To cook food by submerging it in liquid (water, sugar syrup, alcohol) that is just below boiling point.

POT ROAST: To cook meat slowly in a covered container in the oven with little or no liquid.

PRICK: To pierce foods (fruit and vegetable skins) to allow them to release air or moisture during baking. Duck skin is pricked before cooking to release fat.

PROVE: To create a non-stick surface on a pan. To prove, heat pan then rub with salt. Wipe clean and repeat with oil. Also, to prove whether yeast is alive by allowing it to grow, usually in a dough

PUNCH DOWN: To push back yeast doughs after they have risen.

PUREE: Food that is blended or sieved to form a smooth pulp. An electric blender is normally used, but a food mill or sieve achieves the same results.

QUENELLES: Ovals of a soft mixture such as fish mousse or ice cream shaped using two spoons. The term also refers to dumplings of the same shape.

REDUCE: To rapidly boil down liquids in an uncovered pan. This evaporates the liquid and concentrates the flavor.

REFRESH: To plunge an item (typically green vegetables) into iced water after blanching to prevent further cooking and retain a vibrant color.

RENDER: To refine the fat in meat by cooking it over a low heat until it runs free from the connective tissue. The rendered fat can be used for frying.

RIBBON: A term used to describe the consistency of an egg-sugar mixture, beaten until extremely thick. When the whisk is lifted the batter runs down in smooth, thick ribbons. Also the term for the shavings of vegetables, such as carrots and zucchini, made with a vegetable peeler.

ROAST: To cook food in an oven either in its own juices or with added fat. It is usually uncovered so it browns.

ROUX: A flour and fat mixture cooked slowly and stirred constantly over a low heat. Used as a base for, and a thickening agent in, many sauces and soups. There are three classic roux: white, blond and brown; color and flavor are determined by cooking time.

RUBS: A name for finely ground or minced mixtures of flavorful ingredients that are "rubbed" into the surface of foods before cooking.

SADDLE: A tender cut (usually of lamb, mutton or veal), of unseparated loin (from rib to leg). The cut is expensive, and prized for its appearance.

SCALLOP: Thin slice of meat, such as veal or chicken, or fish.

SCORE: To make incisions in the skin, flesh or fat of foods, such as meat, fish or vegetables, before cooking.

SEAR: To brown meat, poultry or fish quickly over a high heat while keeping the center of the cut slightly rare.

SHRED: To separate food by cutting or pulling into thin lengths using a chef's knife, cleaver or grater. You can use a food processor fitted with the shredding disk. Poached chicken and Oriental roast duck are shredded with two forks.

SHUCK: The removal of oysters and clams from their shells; also removing the husk from corn, and peas and beans from their shells.

SIFT: To work dry ingredients through a sieve so that larger pieces are retained in the sieve and separated from the fine powder. Used frequently in baking to aerate ingredients.

SIMMER: To cook food in a liquid that is kept just below boiling point – where the surface of the liquid quivers.

SNIP: This term refers to cutting herbs (most typically chives) or leafy greens into small-sized pieces.

SKIM: To use a spoon or ladle to remove scum, fat or other impurities from the top of simmering liquids.

SOUR: To add an acidic liquid, usually lemon juice, to make the flavor tart.

STEEP: To soak dried ingredients in hot liquid to rehydrate the food and/or infuse the liquid with its flavor.

STOCK: The aromatic liquid created when foods are simmered in water.

SWEAT: To gently cook vegetables in fat or water until soft but not brown.

TENDERIZE: To break down the tough fibers of meat by either pounding it with a mallet or using acid-based marinades.

TEPID: Used to describe the temperature of a liquid when it is luke warm or blood heat (98.6°F).

TERRINE: A mold or the food contained within it. Often a pâté-like mixture of blended ingredients.

TIAN: A French word describing a shallow earthenware dish, as well as the food that is cooked in one.

TIMBALE: A small mold commonly used to shape custards and rice mixtures.

TRANCHE: French for slice, this term usually refers to a slim, rectangular-shaped piece of puff pastry.

TRONCON: French term used to describe a steak cut from a large flat fish.

TURN: A classic French technique for cutting vegetables, such as carrots or turnips, into neat barrel shapes.

WHISK: To incorporate air into ingredients, such as eggs, as a result of beating them with a wire whisk.

ZEST: The outermost, colored skin of citrus fruits (the bitter white portion of the peel is called pith).

INDEX

Q

RECIPE INDEX